The McAllister Contingency

Alex Auburn

eBook ISBN: 978-1-965161-10-4

Paperback ISBN: 978-1-965161-11-1

Hardback ISBN: 978-1-965161-12-8

Dedication

For Mike,

Ali and Terri,

Simon and Dave

With grateful thanks for all of the inspiration, feedback and encouragement provided during the writing of this book.

Much love always.

Per Ardua, Ad Astra

Contents

Prologue

He stood on the rocky outcrop on Edinburgh Peak, catching his breath. The climb had been quite steep (*or I am getting older and less fit than I was in my prime,* he reflected ruefully), but the view was worth it.

He looked out over the South Atlantic Ocean with all its violent majesty and slowly took in the small islands and rocky crags that appeared dotted in the never-ceasing waves. He had an interest in geology through his family's mining interests, but his real love was flora and fauna and he had found that here in abundance, where it was if Man's influence was at its least destructive. It was almost untouched.

And he revelled in that innocence of being. He also rejoiced in the restless movement of the sea, which always calmed him – even when it was at it's most storm-laden and angry.

He looked down towards the South West, seeing the billowing clouds which seemed to be growing in size and darkness, sensed that the next cold front from the general direction of South Africa was on its way and it was likely going to be a "good blow" as one of his colleagues was fond of saying. He was reluctant to relinquish this moment of peace and exhilaration.

He was elated not only from the efforts of his climb but, more importantly, with his recent discovery. He was cradling that closely to himself in a warm sense of intimate and solitary knowledge. Despite the natural instincts of most scientists to work in a collegiate way, sharing ideas and discoveries and working collectively to further "Science" in the broadest sense, he knew he had never sat comfortably within that stereotype. He enjoyed his own company and considered that the results of his own work were just that: his. They were not for sharing any more than his private thoughts, plans, and dreams were. Whilst he engaged with his colleagues on a polite level, he was never as open as might be expected in such a closed and tight-knit working community such as the weather station. After all, living and working with the same small team for up to a year necessitated a little politeness and willingness to "get along."

He grimaced, thinking that it probably wouldn't be so bad if it weren't for the fact that, even though he considered it a blessing that most of the scientists here were South Africans working for their home country's Weather Service, they were only here because the British had given their permission to operate the Station.

"*Permission.*" He almost spat the word out loud in disgust. This is all because Gough Island happened to fall within the British Administrative area, encompassing Tristan da Cunha and Ascension Island, among other small outposts. *Another example of the unrelenting grip of British colonialism*, he thought darkly.

He would now be counting down the days until the supply ship from Cape Town would arrive, and he could leave this place and put the next stage of his plans into action. Then, he would see who was giving the "permission."

He smiled, but it was without warmth or humour, his mouth almost grimacing into place.

He closed his eyes and raised his face skyward,

absentmindedly fingering the rough cast wooden bracelet he wore on his right wrist. He sent up a silent message:

"I have not forgotten my promise to you, father, made to you on your deathbed: the means of our ultimate victory is now very close. It may take a little while for my plans to materialise, but I promise you, we will succeed in our valiant struggle."

A bright ray of sunshine suddenly peeped from behind a cloud, unexpectedly bathing the remote peak with a glorious, almost Biblical light.

He took this to be a sign that his message had been favourably received.

Stealing one last look at the churning sea, he turned from the outcrop and slowly made his way back down the mountainsides, reaching the weather station encampment just before the first large plump rain droplets started to fall.

PART I

Once a jolly swagman camped by a billabong

Under the shade of a coolibah tree

And he sang as he watched and waited 'til his billy boiled

"You'll come a-Waltzing Matilda, with me"

Waltzing Matilda, Waltzing Matilda

"You'll come a-Waltzing Matilda, with me"

He sang as he watched and waited 'till his billy boiled

"You'll come a-Waltzing Matilda, with me"

Traditional/A B Banjo Paterson/Mary C Smith

Chapter 1

Mike McAllister lay on the warm sand in glorious sunshine on what can only be described in English terms as a hot day and listened to the music burbling out of his transistor radio. He sighed to himself: this really was the life, and what a summer it had been! He was sure that the Summer of '76 was going to go down in history as one of *those* summers that stays in the mind forever as being wall-to-wall sunshine, beer and women.

He grimaced as he thought about the work bits in between, but even then, it was only half a grimace. Being stationed at RAF St.Mawgan in Cornwall had been a blessing. Placed right on Watergate Bay, he could finish his shift, quickly change and then either run down to the Bay itself using the steep footpaths leading down to the beach or cadge a lift with some of his mates from the Base either down to the surfing beach or into Newquay.

If he was honest, he enjoyed his life here. It could have been so different, of course, he thought: always in trouble during his youth, restless with unbounded energy and invariably up for a laugh, he could have turned a different corner and been lounging at Her Majesty's pleasure by now. Instead, he was the other side of the wire, as it were. Another smirk.

Shattering his reveries, a shadow loomed above him and a voice cut through the latest tune on the radio:

"I thought I might find you here, McAllister. Don't you have anything better to do?"

Laconically opening one eye, he looked up at the

immaculately dressed Warrant Officer, complete with bristling stereotypical RAF moustache, standing above him, looking faintly ridiculous amongst the scantily clad beach goers who were by now looking on with interest.

"I'm off duty', he replied casually. "What do you want?"

"It's not what *I* want," came the terse answer: "the Station Commander wants you in his office now. So you had better shift yourself."

With that, Warrant Officer Mitchell turned unsteadily on his heel in the sand and strode off back towards the RAF Police driver in the waiting Land Rover, which immediately roared back up the hill towards the Base.

Blast, what now?

Packing up his few things, he started moving quickly towards the road, broke into a jog and was back at the Base within 10 minutes. Showered and changed, it was 30 minutes later that he arrived appropriately attired at the door of the Commander's Office and was met by the Chief of Staff.

Flight Lieutenant Douglas was a small, thin man who wore wire-rimmed spectacles. Today, he had a particularly nasty zit right where the bridge of the glasses rested on his nose, and McAllister couldn't take his eyes off it. He thought that, somehow, it made Douglas look younger and more pathetic than ever. Douglas wilted under the scrutiny – he found McAllister intimidating – and he jumped up from behind the desk and immediately moved over towards the glass door leading to the adjoining office. Douglas threw over his shoulder in his reedy voice: "Thank goodness you are here, McAllister."

Knocking on the door almost before he had finished speaking, Douglas announced McAllister and ushered him in, rapidly closing the door behind him.

McAllister stood in the cool of the rather dark room and took in his surroundings. He hated coming in here – it had the air of a mausoleum. Everything seemed to be grubby, dog-eared, and tired, and unfortunately, that included the very overweight, dishevelled-looking man of indeterminate age who sat behind the large, heavy desk directly in front of him. McAllister thought that, at best, his Commanding Officer was 45 years old – probably more - and time had definitely not been kind to him. Through the fug of cigarette smoke, McAllister could see what looked suspiciously like his personnel file open on the desk. His heart sank.

Without looking up from the desk and with an abstract wave of the hand, Group Captain Symonds directed him to sit down.

"Now then, McAllister," he rumbled. "I have just been looking at your file, and I see that you joined the RAF Police a few years ago after completing an apprenticeship as an electrician. Is that correct?"

"Yes, sir," replied McAllister, wondering just where this was leading.

"And," continued the officer, "that you were promoted to Sergeant whilst in Germany last year and transferred into SIB (Special Investigations): how are you finding that then?"

Careful of his answer, McAllister responded with a non-committal, "Very interesting, Sir, thank you." The fact was he had got bored guarding nuclear warheads and had decided to go for something that he hoped would be a bit more challenging. Even then, the most interesting investigation he had been involved in so far was an attempted fraud on a local man back in Germany: not what he would call stretching.

"Good, good," said Symonds, not really listening to the answer. "Well, I am sorry to say that we shall be losing you for a while." Symonds was privately glad to be rid of this clever, opinionated Welshman. He reflected that although very popular with both the RAF and US Air Force contingents at RAF St.Mawgan, Mike McAllister was always on the edge of trouble, and if he could find a way to wangle things to his advantage, then he would.

Even the Paras liked him – which said everything in Symonds's book. Like today: down at the beach. And it wasn't the first day down there either; looking at him: standing just over 6 feet tall, with ice blue eyes and hair bleached blond by the sun, McAllister just oozed physical fitness, a love of the outdoor life and was absolutely a poster boy for a life in the forces.

Almost as an afterthought, he grudgingly acknowledged to himself that McAllister was definitely a useful bloke to have on your side in a fight if the various reports of brawls and tussles were true. The latest episode with the visiting Royal Marines and their fracas in the Mess a few nights ago was a case in point: apparently, he stood back, let them all fight it out, and then waded in to clear up the hard nuts, including one particularly tough individual who thought he could punch everyone into submission. Apparently, it didn't last long against McAllister. The Guardhouse was full for nearly a week by the time all the paperwork was sorted. A rueful smile touched his lips. And, of course, there was also the rumour that McAllister had a job on the side as a nightclub bouncer down in Newquay. That would fit as well, thought Symonds bitterly.

"Yes," he continued, shoving his thoughts to one side, "this is your last night at RAF St Mawgan for a while. You will meet the 0500 flight in the morning; take all of your kit. You will be given your sealed orders once you are onboard. All I know and can tell you is that you will be away from the UK for quite some time, so if you have phone calls to make, etc, then I suggest you make them. Any questions?"

McAllister thought it was pointless asking any of the questions that were buzzing around in his head, so he simply said no, was formally dismissed, wished good luck with a handshake and ushered out of the room.

Well, that's a turnup for the books. Could life be about to get interesting?

****

The noisy throb of the Rolls-Royce Spey turbofan engines was continuous and provided an unending backdrop to the journey. Although capable of carrying up to 25 crew, this flight had only a small contingent – McAllister counted approximately 12. The inside of the fuselage of the Nimrod MR1 was sparse – this was, after all, the RAF's workhorse aircraft that had come into service in the late 1960s to replace the old Avro Shackleton fleet, he reminded himself.

Since joining the flight as ordered at 0500 that morning, he had been left largely to his own devices and had slept for quite a while. Looking out of the window next to him (one of the few on the aircraft), he could see that they were not flying at low altitude, and his watch confirmed they had been flying for over 4 hours.

He heard a cough at his shoulder and turned to see a neat but non-descript man standing next to him.

"Mike McAllister" (statement not a question, McAllister noted) "good to see you. Sorry about all the cloak-and-dagger stuff. Hope you had a chance to sort out your affairs before leaving Cornwall." McAllister did not say anything and waited.

"My name is Henshaw." Handing over an A4-sized envelope, he continued, "Our first stop will be RAF Masirah, where I shall leave you, and after refuelling, you will continue on to Kai Tak in Hong Kong, where you will have a change of aircraft. You will be met there – details are in the envelope – and you will continue your journey straight away."

"Masirah?" queried McAllister. "Isn't that in Oman? I thought we were closing that station as it is no longer required."

"Yes, we are," replied Henshaw. "But it hasn't closed yet – not until the spring of next year when it looks as though the Yanks will take it over, although that has yet to be confirmed. Likely to be on the ground for about an hour or so, that's all, so please don't wander off."

"And the onward journey?" asked McAllister.

"Australia," replied Henshaw.

McAllister was genuinely taken aback at first but then

thought of the endless opportunities that such a posting could easily offer and smiled to himself.

"As I say," continued Henshaw, "all the details are in there. Good luck. We will be landing shortly."

And with that, Henshaw disappeared back towards the cockpit.

The short stop in Oman was unremarkable, and they were soon airborne again, heading for Hong Kong. At that point, McAllister opened the envelope and read his orders for the first time. It appeared that he was to investigate a suspected national security breach at the Defence Science & Technology Organisation (DSTO) based in Salisbury, South Australia. He was to operate under cover, the concern being that sensitive information relating to the latest developments around a new rocket system called Sea Wolf was being stolen and sold to "enemies" – unidentified, noted McAllister. His heart was starting to pump as his excitement grew.

This was more like it.

Only the Chief Scientist at the DSTO would know his true background, and he would be taking up a position in the electronics section.

So that's why Symonds mentioned my electrical training back in Cornwall.

Not given to self-doubt, he nevertheless did think that completing his apprenticeship may not really equip him to deal with rocket development level physics and electronics (a different discipline entirely to domestic and commercial electricals, but hopefully the basic principles would be the same?): clearly, he may well have to blag his way out of any difficult spots. *It wouldn't be the first time*, he observed to himself with a chuckle. All other communication would be with/through his contact stationed at RAAF Edinburgh, the local support base for the joint UK-Australian Weapons Research Establishment sites at Woomera and Maralinga. The contact would meet him in Hong Kong, and they would travel to Australia together.

Bring it on.

****

By the time the aircraft landed at Kai Tak, the journey was starting to take its toll. McAllister alighted from the aircraft feeling crumpled, tired, and sweaty – not helped as he came down the steps into the sultry, still in the night air. Nevertheless, he was glad to have the opportunity to get off the aircraft and stretch his legs. He glanced to his left and saw another Nimrod, with the RAF roundels clearly warming up.

I wonder if that is my next horse.

He moved quickly over the tarmac towards the office area set to one side of the main passenger lounge. As he walked through the swing doors, two men in plain clothes turned towards him. As they did so, he caught sight of a third man seated on the plastic bench seats. Nothing remarkable in that, he thought immediately – until he spotted that the third man was wearing handcuffs and shackles on his feet.

Mmmmm, definitely interesting.

The man standing on the left was tall. McAllister estimated he was about 6'4:" dark-haired, dark-eyed, with a strong torso and in good shape.

Bit of a boxer, perhaps?

His companion was about 6' tall, slim, and with fairer hair, sharp features and quick, intelligent eyes.

"Hi," said the taller of the two men. "Your carriage awaits."

No pre-amble, no introductions, nothing.

Even more interesting.

Pointing to the shackled guy on the seat, McAllister asked: "Who's your friend?"

The taller man answered again. "No-one you need worry about; he is just along for the ride."

The shorter of the two men looked at him intently and then, shifting his gaze away, looked down at his own shoes.

Ok, so it's going to be like that then.

Suddenly, Australia seemed a *very* long way away.

****

If anything, the internal arrangements on the new aircraft were even more spartan than on the way out from Cornwall. Such seating as was available was fixed along the sides of the fuselage, thus leaving maximum load space in the middle.

Comfort was clearly not a pre-requisite for the designers.

He gave a grim inward smile.

In the centre was a large cage – into which the shackled, handcuffed third man was placed as soon as he was brought on board. He had no seating at all and was left to make himself comfortable on the aircraft floor.

The navigator from the cockpit stuck his head through the interconnecting door to check on progress and confirmed that the pilot was keen to take off as soon as possible – "so get a shifty on."

The two RAAF guys had settled the prisoner and then sat down.

McAllister decided to call the tall one "Lurch"; he grinned to himself. That seemed to fit perfectly. As far as the other one was concerned, time would tell.

The aircraft took off quickly.

Clearly not keen to hang around.

As he was sat several seats down from the RAAF guys who were not going to be the most talkative companions, he thought he would try and get some shut-eye. It was obviously going to be a boring flight.

After a prolonged attempt to find that release, he gave up as sleep eluded him. The time change seemed to already be getting to him. He dug around in his bergen for his book, but after a few pages, he found it difficult to concentrate on that either, and he started staring around the fuselage.

Seeing his restlessness, the second RAAF man stood up and made his way over to where McAllister was sitting.

"Sorry about that, mate," said the man with a clear Australian twang, nodding his head in the direction of the unedifying spectre of Lurch further up the seating line, who by this time was lolling asleep with his mouth open, "Chummie isn't terribly friendly or welcoming to Poms."

"And yet you are all on an RAF aircraft," pointed out McAllister, somewhat bitingly.

A sharp but amused look from his companion.

"Indeed we are, but don't tar us all with the same brush. I'm Dave, by the way, Dave Paterson. I will be your contact at the other end. Careful what you say within earshot of the prisoner – especially as we have to shout over the din. I'll fill you in over a beer later, but he's not one of our most salubrious customers," and he looked over at the prisoner, apparently asleep on the floor of the cage.

McAllister had a barb on the tip of his tongue about prisoner transportation remaining a key business line for Australia, but he thought better of it. He had to work with this guy and cheap remarks could pay bad dividends later on. Besides, McAllister had a distinct sense of relief that his contact wasn't going to be Lurch after all, especially as it appeared that this guy was happy to have a chat and a beer. He decided to reserve judgment.

Just at that moment, Lurch snored so loudly that he woke himself up. He looked dazedly around, and his gaze alighted on the two men sitting and obviously chatting. He was very clearly not amused, and his already thin lips disappeared into a tiny line in his face and his dark eyes became almost unfathomable. McAllister waved cheerily. Lurch's gaze became openly hostile.

This was a bad start but what the hell. Hopefully, our paths will not cross much when we get to the other end, and if they do, I will sort it out then – one way or another.

Dave got to his feet to make his way back to his colleague,

and McAllister nodded to him, then turned his attention to the slumbering prisoner. He noted that the man was quite unkempt, with shoulder-length dark hair falling around his face. He had a thick beard and was dressed in what appeared to be some sort of jumpsuit, with trainers (without laces) on his feet. McAllister put him at about 5'10 or so tall and medium build.

Nothing unusual there, then.

The only personal item that McAllister could see was a two-strand bracelet peeking out from under the handcuff on his left wrist, comprised of what appeared to be rosary beads with a small rustic-looking cross hanging from it.

As if feeling his scrutiny, the prisoner opened his eyes and turned his head slightly towards McAllister. Their gaze locked, and the hatred held in the man's eyes was clear and unbridled. For the first time in a very long time, McAllister felt the hairs on the back of his neck stand up, and an uncomfortable feeling form in the pit of his stomach. The last time he had that reaction, he recalled, had been during the worst of times in Northern Ireland. That was not a good recollection to have – especially here at the start of an assignment, but he held the gaze until the prisoner looked away.

Finally leaning his head back against the wall of the aircraft and closing his eyes, McAllister tried to clear his head of the unwelcome memories from the past that were now trying to fight their way to the front of his mind. To divert himself, he decided that he must remember to ask Dave about the prisoner and why he had been allowed to keep the bracelet on him – and the reference to a Pom: what the hell was that all about? The thought fleetingly crossed his tired mind that this could be similar to the United States and the UK – where both countries were famously said to be separated by a common language. He had the distinct feeling he was going to be on a steep learning curve. His musings exhausted for the time being, he finally fell asleep to mental pictures of sun-kissed palm-fringed beaches, turquoise seas, and even more lovely sun-kissed beauties playing beach volleyball in not a lot of clothing: hopefully, Australia wouldn't be so bad after all.

Chapter 2

The aircraft finally touched down at RAAF Edinburgh in the late afternoon, two days after he had left the UK. McAllister was relieved to be exiting the aircraft and looked forward to stepping out into the Australian sunshine.

His disappointment was palpable when he reached the top of the aircraft steps and found that not only was it raining cats and dogs, with the runway and aircraft stand awash with rainwater, but that there was also a stiff South-Westerly wind blowing across the ground to boot. With a shock, he realised it was actually cold.

Coming to stand beside him, Dave spotted his disappointment and laughed. "It does rain in Australia, mate, especially in the winter." Belatedly, McAllister realised that it was not only the time zones that would be challenging for a while but also the seasons of the Southern Hemisphere. It may have been a glorious June in Cornwall – here it was, in fact, the middle of the South Australian winter.

So much for the beach, then.

Dave said he would meet him in the main reception building on the concourse as soon as the prisoner had been "deposited," and so McAllister made his way through the downpour as directed. He was soaked by the time he reached the terminal, but at least it had freshened him up a bit. He looked out of the large panoramic glass windows and saw a prisoner transport van already in position at the side gate, with the rear doors open and two heavily armed RAAF Provost Officers standing guard. Lurch, Dave, and the shackled prisoner emerged from the aircraft and moved slowly towards the van. Pushing the prisoner forward – who stumbled at the steps due to the shackles – Lurch appeared keen to get him on board, and McAllister watched him physically lift (or, more accurately, throw) the man into the van. Lurch then quickly got in the van himself, followed by the two uniformed Officers.

Dave secured the van doors from the outside and banged on the side of the van to indicate that everything was secure and that it was a go. Almost immediately, the van pulled away, and after watching it depart, Dave turned and walked towards the terminal. McAllister observed that there was an almost tangible sense of relief about his new colleague. Whether that was because the prisoner had been safely handed off or whether it was because he had actually got rid of Lurch for the time being, McAllister couldn't say, but it was certainly an interesting insight.

McAllister turned as a polite female cough came from behind him and was met with the first really friendly smile he had seen since leaving the UK. A small, trim female WRAAF officer stood in front of him with the almost obligatory clipboard and a riot of red/auburn hair escaping from under the front of her cap.

"Sergeant McAllister?" she enquired. He nodded.

Things are already looking up.

"Welcome to South Australia. Here are your accommodation details and the keys to your car." With an almost conspiratorial whisper and wink, she added, "I nabbed you what I think is the best one. It has lovely leather seats, and it's ready for you at the house. I have also left you a folder with some information about South Australia, and Salisbury in particular so that you can start to find your way around a bit."

"Er, thanks very much: ummm - what did you say your name was?"

She laughed.

"I didn't, but it's Lucy Andrews. If you need anything, let me know." Again, that cheeky laugh.

At this point, Dave came in through the terminal doors and walked over to them.

"Hello gorgeous," he said to Lucy. Smiling and turning towards McAllister, he said. You have met one of our greatest treasures, then?" McAllister smiled in return. "Hope you have fixed him up, ok?" said Dave, turning back to Lucy.

"I was just telling him that I have given him the best car in the fleet, Banjo," she said.

"Good girl," said Dave. "That's how we like to treat our visitors. Catch you later, sweet cheeks."

With that, Lucy turned on her heel and sashayed away from the two men who watched her go with tired but admiring eyes.

Did she really say 'Banjo'? Something else to add to the mental list, then.

With that, the two men turned, collected their kit and walked out through the main doors towards the car park. Thankfully, it had stopped raining, but it was still a dark, dismal and windy afternoon. They approached a pale green Holden estate (which Dave informed him was called a station wagon here), threw their kit bags in the back and Dave slid behind the wheel. McAllister was relieved to see that this was a right-hand drive. Although he had driven extensively in Germany in left-hand drive, he preferred the "correct" side of the road and car.

Another tick in the box, then.

As they left the car park and emerged on to the approach road, then onto the main Highway, the conversation finally started.

"You won't be living on Base as you have obviously gathered," said Dave by way of opening.

"Hopefully, you will like the digs. It is in an area of the City called Salisbury East – about a 10-minute drive from the DSTO and about the same distance from here. There should be a welcome pack at the house for you, with stuff in the fridge, which, knowing Lucy, will include the essentials such as some tinnies, so if you want to take it easy tonight, get a good kip in, then I will pick you up in the morning and we can take a drive round and start getting you familiarised with the area."

That sounded like an excellent idea to McAllister, and he said so.

After driving up a long straight road called Smith Road, which had a new and very large Teacher Training College and High School complex on the left-hand side, they passed bungalows of all types. Dave explained that most homes in Australia are single-storey, usually with a sizeable garden as land isn't a problem. Salisbury East, it seemed, was an up-

and-coming suburb of Adelaide, which lay some 12 miles to the South.

The road took a sharp right-hand bend (Dave informing him that this was Bridge Road, which would take him right into the City if he wanted to go there), and about 250 yards further on, they turned off and drew up outside one of the most beautiful bungalows McAllister had ever seen.

18 Weemala Road was cream brick, with a white and fawn tiled roof (to reflect the heat, informed Dave) and had a fairly steep concrete driveway leading up to a garage. It was virtually brand new.

Walking up the path, he climbed a couple of steps up to a small covered porch area. He turned to look out over the homes on the opposite side of the road and realised that there was only one line of them backing on to acres of almond trees rolling down towards a group of buildings, which Dave informed him was a new primary school. He walked through a beautifully carved wooden front door into what proved to be a fairly large home with three double bedrooms, a large bathroom with a walk-in shower and a separate bath, a kitchen/diner, separate laundry and a large lounge. He whistled quietly to himself in appreciation.

"So, who am I sharing this with, then?" McAllister asked.

"No one," said Dave with a smile, walking over to the large two-door fridge in the kitchen. "We thought you would like as much space and freedom as possible whilst you are here."

As predicted, Lucy had arranged "essentials" in the welcome pack, and Dave reached into the fridge and passed back a tin of beer. McAllister looked at it and grinned. "Now that's what I call a welcome," he said.

After a quick tour of the house, they went out to the garage with an air of anticipation to look at the car. McAllister was a bit of a car nut, and he was quite handy with a tool set. It turned out his new found chum was of a similar mind, and so it was with no little enthusiasm that they lifted the roller door.

They both stood there open-mouthed.

"Fucking hell: she's given you Englebert," Dave eventually stammered, and they both burst out laughing.

Standing before them was a gleaming 1964 Austin Freeway saloon with a two-tone colourway and chrome wheel hubs. It was a column shift gear change, and Lucy was right about one thing at least, McAllister reflected: it certainly had fantastic leather seats. In fairness, it looked immaculate – and the boot was cavernous.

That could come in handy. As for speed and agility, well, that will come out in the wash. This is certainly something quite special.

"Dare I ask why it's called "Englebert"? queried McAllister.

Scratching his head and looking bemused, Dave answered: "It was given to us by an older couple, together with the bungalow, to look after as they had to go back to the UK for a while for the family business. The old man was in the British Army during the War apparently and wanted to be sure the place was looked after, so he asked us to caretake it and, as the nearest military unit, put it to good use. For some weird reason, their daughter called the car Englebert – after the singer Englebert Humperdinck, presumably."

"Not the thing to say to a Welshman," said McAllister, laughing: "May have to re-Christen it Tom: after the one and only Tom Jones," at which point he launched into an excellent rendition of "The Green Green Grass of Home," much to Dave's amusement.

McAllister got into the driving seat, turned the key and the car turned over and fired straight away. It had a soothing, relaxing hum to the engine, which sounded as sweet as a nut.

Perhaps this isn't such a bad deal after all and it certainly has character.

"And on that happy note," said Dave," I will leave you to get settled in; we will have a barbe tomorrow night, so when we have finished our tour of acquaintance, I will take you back to my place just five minutes from here and you can meet some of the others and let your hair down a bit."

McAllister thought that sounded ideal, and they arranged to meet at 0930 the following morning.

Life has certainly become more interesting.

When he opened the curtains the following morning, McAllister was relieved to see that it was a different day entirely. No longer dulled by thick, heavy rain clouds, the garden was swathed in glorious sunshine. When he stepped out the back door onto the patio, it was even starting to feel warm.

This is going to be fantastic.

Sitting at the breakfast bar in the kitchen eating some cornflakes (he was pleased to see that they had those here, too), he started flicking through the folder that Lucy had left for him. He had been too tired the night before to even start looking at it. It seemed that the City of Adelaide was about half an hour away, as Dave had basically said yesterday. He noted that the nearest beach was a place called Semaphore; he would really have to explore that, regardless of the weather. He also learned that the small hills that he could see from the back of the weemala house were, in fact, part of Tea Tree Gully and extended out to the other growing suburbs of Modbury and Golden Grove.

This really is an up-and-coming place.

After a quick shower and shave, he was ready when Dave knocked on the door almost exactly at 0930. They decided to take Dave's Holden and set off down to Salisbury to give McAllister his first look at his new work place. Dave informed him he was due to report the following morning to Dr Schuster, who was the Chief Scientific Officer at the DSTO.

Salisbury itself was a fairly small town that had grown from agricultural and farming origins in the mid-1800s. It had really started to extend, however, in WW2 when an explosives factory had been purpose-built and which, at its height, had employed thousands of people and had basically taken over all of the construction trades and outputs from most of Adelaide and the surrounding regions. It also had a direct rail link to the main city and, accordingly, had been perfectly placed to play a leading role in the war effort.

Salisbury had wide roads lined by small shops with walkways covered with verandahs in front. There was something of an American tinge to things: adverts were big and brash, and a new US-style Woolworths superstore had just opened in the arcade in the centre of the town. This was a novelty to McAllister, as large supermarkets were only just starting to make their presence felt back in the UK.

He considered that this new life was a strange mix of the familiar and the wildly different.

So far, the omens are good.

The pair drove into Adelaide itself, and McAllister was surprised at the beauty of a City laid out with no little foresight by Col.William Light in the 1830s and which nestled against the River Torrens. It had swathes of parkland and recreational areas, and it had a gentle, ordered overall appearance. The city had been laid out in a convenient grid system, and a central business district was right in the middle. McAllister was surprised at the number of banks, gold houses, diamond and opal shops that he saw.

Dave informed him that the mining of gold, gems, and precious metals, plus sheep and cattle ranching, was generally big in South Australia and that Adelaide is only a small part of a very large and mainly uninhabited state. As the Capital, Adelaide naturally attracted the big business interests that made the State work and the Houses of Parliament for the State, together with the Premier and his Cabinet, were also based here. It was, therefore, the commercial and political hub.

Even so, there is still something of an old-world air about it; some of the women wear hats and gloves to do their shopping and general business, something long gone back home.

The main shopping precinct was Rundle Mall, which was a

wide, pedestrianised area where all of the major departmental stores were located.

Having completed a quick tour, Dave drove them back towards RAAF Edinburgh, giving a running commentary (which included an outline of the work being undertaken at the Long Range Weapon sites at Woomera and Maralinga) and giving McAllister a quick tour of the Base before finally heading back out to Salisbury East.

Back on Smith Road, instead of driving up the hill towards the Weemala house, Dave turned right almost opposite the High School and then two further right turns in quick succession, announcing as he did so their arrival in Jacaranda Drive and Dave's home at no. 26.

McAllister noted that Jacaranda Drive had homes that were of similar large, open style. No. 26 had a large willow tree in the front, and McAllister was pleased to see a large above-ground swimming pool in the backyard as they walked through the side gate. Hearing them arrive, a woman in her late 20s opened the back flyscreen door and met them with a smile for McAllister and a hug and a kiss for Dave, who introduced her as his wife, Trixi.

Trixi was quite tall and very slender, with long, very curly hair. She had one of those very open, direct type faces and McAllister immediately took to her. She was warm and welcoming, and the two men moved into the house where they were quickly given a beer and Dave was given the tongs, apron and meat for the barbe in addition before being ushered outside again.

Other guests started arriving, and it soon became clear that – even in the winter months – socialising with friends, good food, beer and lots of laughter – was a key ingredient to enjoying your life here. That suited McAllister perfectly.

As the party got into full swing, he finally remembered to ask Dave why Lucy had called him Banjo. He smiled and said that McAllister needed to become better acquainted with his Australian literary history. It was later on in the evening that Lucy herself, the little red-headed WRAAF officer who had met him at the airport and who was a guest at the party, explained that Banjo Paterson is one of Australia's best-known and loved poets, famous for penning the lyrics to "Waltzing Matilda" and writing "The Man from Snowy River" amongst other works.

McAllister had nodded politely (although he had heard Waltzing Matilda) but thought he would give the rest of the cultural exchange lesson a bit of a miss – although he did at least now get the joke about "Paterson."

Seems the RAAF isn't that different from home either – they like nicknames, too.

Taking his leave before it got too late and thanking Trixi and Dave for such a great evening, McAllister made his way out to the front garden just in time to see a red Datsun Cherry drive away from the kerbside and head off towards the end of the street. He couldn't put his finger on it, but something about that seemed odd.

Perhaps I am just tired, and reading things that just aren't there.

He put it out of his mind as he started to walk back to Weemala Road. It was, after all, only 10 minutes away on foot and he felt like he needed the exercise.

Chapter 3

Dr. Stephen Schuster was middle-aged, round in stature, not particularly tall at about 5'6," with a comb-over of grey hair, which appeared to be losing the battle with the onset of total baldness. He wore thick black-rimmed spectacles and a white lab coat.

That is exactly what I would have expected to see.

During the course of the initial conversation, it emerged that although originally from the UK, Schuster had moved out to Australia ten years before and had been heavily engaged in the joint UK-Australian Weapons Research project that had been ongoing throughout that time. He split his workstations between Salisbury and principally Woomera, in the north of the State, with occasional visits to the other main test site of Maralinga. He explained that his family was now settled here in Australia, and barring accidents, as he put it, he would retire here – he loved the place.

It occurred to McAllister that Schuster appeared somewhat – and unexpectedly – nervous. He noted that the scientist fiddled incessantly: pens, paperclips, pieces of paper on the desk, his necktie, etc and his gaze constantly swept the room, rarely resting on his guest but frequently landing on the photograph that was placed on his desk. Having listened to the pleasantries, McAllister decided to cut to the chase.

"I understand that you deal with some very sensitive projects here, Dr. Schuster," he said, and the scientist stilled for a moment to look at him, perhaps for the first time. "Why do *you* think the information has gone missing?" he continued.

There was a long silence, almost as if the scientist realised that there could be no further beating around the proverbial bush, and he would have to face what was about to come head-on. He gave a huge sigh, and his shoulders slumped down as he stared at the desk for a couple of moments before finally looking up and staring at McAllister right in the eyes.

"I had some telemetry and payload calculations, together with some blueprint drawings concerning a new naval defensive missile system that we are developing, called Sea Wolf, in my safe. It is an automated point defence system intended as a final line of defence against sea-skimming missiles. It should also be able to identify and destroy high-angle anti-ship missiles and aircraft. With a speed of Mach 3, and a flight ceiling of 3000 metres (or 9800 feet in old money), it is far ahead of anything else available or, as far as we know, currently under development elsewhere.

We have undertaken significant development and testing, largely at Woomera, over the last ten years or so. We are very near completion, and we have the final trials and test firings pencilled in for early October, with a final display for some senior people – both from the UK and Australia – in the late Spring.

Our projected delivery date of the first batch to the Royal Navy is early next year. We had a burglary here approximately three weeks ago when all of the offices were ransacked. I didn't think to check the safe at the time, as everything was such a mess and nothing seemed to have been taken. However, I went to the safe two weeks ago to get the blueprints out to do some work on them and discovered that they have disappeared."

The obvious questions from McAllister followed: who has access to the safe? Has the access code to the safe been changed? Are there duplicates and if so, where and who has access? Why not check the safe at the time if the blueprints were so important? Etc. Etc.

The discussion, in the end, took several hours, by which time McAllister had formed the view that even if not an "inside job" in the commonly accepted sense of that phrase, someone in the factory had probably done some talking somewhere along the line even though the DSTO itself was widely known in South Australia, and in Salisbury in particular. The burglary could have been a smokescreen for something else, of course, but it just didn't seem to make sense to McAllister.

Surely, the first thing Dr. Schuster checked was the safe? Whatever the answer, one thing is clear: the prints are definitely gone.

Despite close questioning, Dr. Schuster was unable to say who exactly he thought may be wanting to obtain the prints – although when pushed, he nervously added that "it was believed" the French were in the very early stages of developing something similar and the Chinese were improving their capability options all the time; the Russians were also in the mix, as were the South Africans who of course were currently the subject of an arms embargo.

So, all of the usual suspects – and none.

The discussion had gone on for so long that McAllister was reluctant to arrive at his new workstation late on what was apparently his first day and he therefore agreed with Dr Schuster that he would start work the following morning when the rest of the teams clocked on. He was told who to ask for, and it would then be up to him to take the investigation forward as he saw fit.

As he was getting up to leave, McAllister indicated the photograph on the desk and picked it up quickly. It was of a girl, aged in her early teens.

McAllister asked, "Your daughter, Doctor?" The scientist looked at him with wide, almost scared eyes, McAllister thought, and said it was; her name was Zoe, aged 21 now, and she was his only child. But that was it. He added nothing further, which McAllister found rather odd.

Handing the photograph back to his agitated host, McAllister took his leave, let himself out of the office, and made his way down to the car park outside. He was relieved to be outside for some reason, and that also worried him. His personal warning antennae were starting to ping, and he realised that he had not taken to Dr. Schuster particularly – largely because he thought he was lying to him.

Never a good start that, Mikey, my boy, never a good start.

As the day was much more pleasant weatherwise than the one had been for his arrival in South Australia, McAllister decided to utilise his newly freed-up afternoon by going down to the beach and having a look at the coast. He drove down to Semaphore and then along to the old village of Glenelg, where the lace-wrought iron and glass verandahs were still in place on so many of the original buildings. It was great. He took a walk along the foreshore and started to relax as he mulled over in his mind what a mix of events and emotions the past 48 hours had actually provided and the enormity of the task that it seemed he now faced.

He drove back to Salisbury East, and as he turned into Weemala Road, he saw Dave's pale green Holden parked outside the house.

His immediate reaction of pleasure to seeing Dave soon changed as his new friend raced down the drive and waited for McAllister to come to a halt by the kerb. Clearly, something was very wrong.

"Where the hell have you been?" demanded Dave.

"Looking around down at the beach," replied McAllister. "Why? What's the problem?"

"Did Lucy come home with you last night?"

Getting out of the car, McAllister stopped.

"No," he said.

"We chatted at your place at the barbe, but that was it. I walked home afterwards and didn't see anyone. Why?"

"It seems she has gone missing. The SA Police and our lads are out looking for her now, but she seems to have just disappeared – no traces so far. I had hoped that she had hooked up with you and that it would all be a false alarm," said Dave.

"Sorry," said McAllister, "but I haven't seen her at all since then. Do you want to come in for a beer? Is there anything I can do to help?"

Dave said no to both questions as he got quickly into the Holden and said he had to get back to the Base, but he would keep McAllister updated. With that, he drove off, leaving McAllister standing on the roadside.

Mmm. This is not going to plan either.

He fervently hoped that, despite possibly having had too much to drink at the party, Lucy Andrews was safe and well somewhere and had spent the day sobering up. But the noise of his little warning antennae notched up a gear.

Chapter 4

McAllister arrived for his first day at work at the DSTO the following morning with a sense of trepidation. No news about Lucy overnight, and that worried him.

He reported to reception as Schuster had asked him to, and he was taken through a labyrinth of offices and corridors to the rear part of the building, which was closed off with security doors. An electronic pass was required to get in, and the lady showing him down to the section swiped her card and the doors opened towards him.

A man in a white coat with plastic eye protectors looked up from his nearby bench and walked over.

"This is Mr McAllister," said the receptionist to the man, and she promptly turned on her heel and left. McAllister stuck out his hand in greeting.

"Mike McAllister," he said by way of introduction.

"Ron Broad," came the response, and they shook hands.

The man was of medium height and build, with greying hair and wild super-fuzz eyebrows. As with Flight Lt Douglas's zit back in Cornwall, McAllister had trouble concentrating on something other than the eyebrows. He mentally christened him as Ron "the Brows" Broad.

Tuning back in, Ron Broad was explaining that this was the electronics section, it was high security due to the sensitivity of the work being conducted there, and it operated on a "need to know only" basis – "no loose chatting in the canteen, Mike" accompanied by a semi-playful wag of the finger.

He showed him over to a bench next to his own and said that would be McAllister's workstation. Setting off at a quick trot, he then shepherded McAllister through the section, with brief introductions to the five others who were working in there, and then it was into the testing section. It was clear to McAllister that Brows was definitely a man who loved his work: he was very enthusiastic, and he was obviously enjoying showing off the fruits of his labours.

"Yes," carried on Brows, oblivious to the fact that McAllister appeared to be only half listening, "Pretty excited that we have managed to reach Mach 3 with the Sea Wolf – *and* that we can get her up to a flight ceiling of 3000 metres. Really setting the pace," he added. His face was alight with excitement.

"We are due to go up to Woomera next week," he continued.

"I really think you should come along and have a look at that end of the project; we are getting ready for the test trials in October, so it will be a great opportunity for you to get a feel for things before it all really gets going."

He was nodding enthusiastically. McAllister smiled and said that sounded ideal.

Back at his workstation, Brows passed over a white coat, some eye protectors, a board with an electrical system attached, and a diagram. He asked him to get acquainted with it, and they would talk further later. An array of tools hung from the wall behind the workstation, and McAllister looked through the diagrams and looked at the plate in his hands. He reflected that this might be more akin to creating an explosive device than electrical work and that perhaps Group Captain Symonds had simply seized on the electrical training part of his history as an excuse to get rid of him. He let out an involuntary laugh, at which Brows came over and asked if everything was alright. Having satisfied him that it was, McAllister said that he was going to have a bit of a look around – store rooms, that sort of thing so that he was fully familiar with the site. Brows reluctantly agreed, saying words like "Don't be too long," and McAllister set off at a quick pace.

He found the security office at the back of the building. The one security guard there was clearly absorbed in something much more interesting than maintaining a vigilant watch. From what McAllister could see over the guard's shoulder, the subject of his deep attention appeared to have blond hair, long legs and sizeable breasts and was this month's centrefold in Playboy. Hiding a rueful smirk, McAllister knocked on the door, causing the security guard to look extremely embarrassed, and hurriedly put down the magazine.

"Hi," said McAllister. "I have just joined DSTO; I wanted to introduce myself."

"Right-o mate," said the guard. "I'm Toby, but my friends call me "Jugs" – he grinned wickedly "and not because of the size of my ears!" McAllister laughed.

That's more like it.

The two men fell into conversation, and it appeared that, during the day, there were always two officers on duty based in the office and one guard at the entrance to the site where McAllister had come in that morning. The three officers did a shift rotation of 10 hours (0700 – 1700), switching between the security office, undertaking patrols around the inside of

34

the buildings and the entrance security duties. There were no night security guards, the night-time arrangements being left to electronic means and the good offices of the South Australian Police, who carried out regular but random drive-by patrols throughout the night. They had a large base in Salisbury and could be on-site in minutes in the event that any of the alarms went off.

At that point, another security guard walked into the office – an older man – early 50s, McAllister guessed, and with a round open face. Round of belly also, McAllister noted. Running and physical exercise were not particularly high on this chap's priority list. He noted that the new guy was carrying a pistol secured in a holster around his waist. He was introduced as "Bonza" – real name Sid – but as his stock response to most statements and questions was "Bonza" or "Bonza mate," the name had stuck. Introductions were made, and McAllister made his excuses to leave before he outstayed his welcome or raised any suspicions. He made a mental note to revisit the office and have a bit of a look around later on.

With that, he turned back towards what he guessed was the administrative area of the building. Roaming along a corridor upstairs on the second floor and having heard the thud of a typewriter, he opened a partially glazed door into an office where a very attractive young woman was sitting at a desk behind the aforesaid typewriter. She looked at him enquiringly as McAllister half entered the room. She was small-framed, ash blonde, and as she shuffled some papers together on the desk, McAllister noted that she had the most beautifully manicured and lacquered fingernails. Nothing brassy or trashy: just beautifully done.

35

How on earth did she keep them like that, having to use that heavy old typewriter every day?

Giving him a genuine smile, she introduced herself as "Caryle – with a y" and said that she was the Secretary and Personal Assistant to the Chief Executive of the site, Norman Reynolds. McAllister went through the routine of introducing himself, and they fell into conversation.

It transpired that Norman Reynolds had been jointly appointed by the UK and Australian governments to run the site; Dr Schuster may have been the chief scientist, but he did not pull the political strings. Questions started to ping in McAllister's brain as to why Schuster had been told of his true purpose on-site, but apparently, the Chief Executive and political appointee had not.

Reynolds had not even been mentioned in the briefing papers. Odd.

Glancing to his left, he saw that the door to what he assumed to be Reynolds's office was open and over in the far corner, he caught sight of an old heavyweight safe, pushed under the bookshelves but otherwise not obscured from view in any way.

Also odd.

Seeing him looking at the room, Caryle got up from her desk, crossed over the carpet, closed the door to her boss's office and, smiling kindly, said that she had a lot to get on with until Mr Reynolds returned to the office tomorrow.

"Is he on holiday, then?" asked McAllister with a twinkle and his best attempt at what he thought was a winning smile.

"No," replied Caryle, doing her best to look like a schoolmistress, "he's been in Canberra talking to the big wigs. Now off with you," and with a shooing motion, ushered McAllister out of the door, closing it firmly behind him.

Well, that was interesting. "Interesting" seems to be the word of the moment. And safes everywhere. How odd. Perhaps odd was the more appropriate choice for popular description.

Having returned to his workstation and wrestled with the circuit board and diagrams for the rest of the morning, it was with some relief McAllister realised that it was nearly lunchtime. Just at that moment, Brows turned up at his side and invited him to the canteen for a break and to meet the rest of the lab team. McAllister fell in with the arrangement and, having joined the throng, secured some sandwiches and a cup of tea. He sat down with the rest of the group around a large table at the edge of the refectory.

Like most workplaces, the conversation swirled in and around numerous topics - particularly sport, and especially Aussie Rules football, which McAllister had to admit he knew nothing whatsoever about. They seemed like a reasonable and fairly unremarkable bunch of teammates. Most appeared to live very locally in either Salisbury or slightly further up the main road in the new Town of Elizabeth, most with their families.

Nothing much there, then. This assignment is clearly going to take a while.

McAllister made his goodbyes that evening, along with several others of the team. They invited him down to the pub for a drink, but he declined and feigned a return to the lab on the basis that he had forgotten something.

Instead of going into the secure section, he made his way to the other side of the building and headed for the staff toilets. It was 1710. He needed to wait a few minutes to ensure that the security staff had left the building before going into the security office for a scout round. He waited until 1730, and it seemed that there had been a quick exodus from the site – like most large workplaces – as soon as possible at the end of the working day. The empty silence descended, and McAllister slipped out of the toilets and moved down the hall to the security office.

Sure enough, they were prompt at leaving. Place in darkness.

He entered and started looking at the desks, papers, and books – in case there was anything of interest. He saw a tall cabinet with a defence lock mechanism over in the corner furthest from the door and made his way over to it. He mentally crossed his fingers and hoped that they hadn't bothered to change the standard default code on the dial. He entered the code and voila, it was a success. McAllister shook his head.

That's not good.

He had a rifle through the materials inside. Stuck in the back right hand corner, his glance fell on a dog-eared business card: "Jan de Klerk, Manager, Jindivik Winery, Nuriootpa, Barossa Valley, SA."

Why have that… ….

McAllister got no further before he felt the effects of the full blow to the back of his head. He acted instinctively and pumped his right arm backwards with full force into the body of his assailant. A grunt of pain.

Landed well then.

Turning quickly, he kicked out at the groin, hands moving quickly towards the area he expected the eyes/face to be – looking to get a finger into the eye socket. The assailant was strong and fit: they exchanged blow for blow, careering around the security office, smashing into desks, papers blowing around and falling to the ground. McAllister managed to get his assailant in a headlock and smashed it full force into the open metal door of the cabinet. He took a hard blow himself to the solar plexus, and both men stumbled in the dark, falling to the floor. McAllister felt a strong grip around his throat, and he chopped upwards with clenched fists and arms to push the chin and head of his assailant away: he didn't want any chance of having his neck snapped. Leaping to his feet, McAllister tackled the assailant, grabbing him around the waist and pushing him forcefully into the window, which shattered under the impact.

At that, the assailant lashed out with a wicked left hook, catching McAllister square on the chin. He took an involuntary step back, and his adversary leaped through the broken window and started sprinting across the car park.

McAllister gave chase. He was a fit man and started to make ground on his prey. They ran across the car park, through the green recreation area at the front of the site, and out towards the main Elizabeth Highway. McAllister watched in horror as, just at that moment, a large double-storeyed artic filled with a cargo of sheep swept along the road, the driver not paying particular attention. It hit the assailant straight on. The body was dragged along the ground under the truck for several hundred yards before the artic could come to a halt.

McAllister rushed over to the scene, but what was left of the body was unrecognisable. He saw a dismembered arm stuck between the tyre and the wheel arch of the front axle. McAllister's mind was reeling, but there was definitely something here that he knew he should be "seeing," but he wasn't just at that moment. Hopefully, it would come to him later. There was no opportunity to search what was left before the extremely shaken driver of the truck came down the side to see for himself what had happened.

Not wishing to be caught at the scene, McAllister said he had just left work and saw the incident from the roadside and that the bloke had just run out in front of the truck. McAllister said he would go and call the Police. The driver nodded numbly.

McAllister left the scene. He had thought of parking Englebert in the Woolies car park earlier in the day so that it wouldn't flag that he was still on site after everyone else had left. There was one thing that Englebert was not, and that was discreet. He doubled back to the shopping centre, and quietly drove away from the site. As he did so, heading up towards the turn-off for Salisbury East, a Police car with sirens wailing and blue lights flashing passed him at great speed on the opposite side of the road.

Driving carefully back to Weemala Road, McAllister reflected that he had let his guard down and he needed to be more careful. This was only his first day, and someone had decided to have a good go at him. Which also meant that someone already knew that he was not what he was pretending to be.

Chapter 5

He poured himself a stiff drink when he got back to the house and then went and sorted out the damage.

Nothing too major: cuts, bruises – a couple were nasty, but at least nothing was broken. Probably have a stinking headache in the morning. Obviously, my assailant had expected me to go down with the first bash to the back of the head. Ouch!

He went back into the lounge and rang Dave, arranging to go down and see him. McAllister needed to talk and find out the latest news about Lucy Andrews.

The mood at the house on Jacaranda Drive was sombre. Over a beer in the shed (which Dave explained was his man cave escape, so it was kitted out with a guitar, amps, a fridge (duly stocked) and some comfy slouchy chairs), Dave explained that a full-scale search was now underway for Lucy. There were no leads as yet, and no-one seemed to have any idea as to where she might be or what had happened to her – or why she had disappeared. The investigation was very much ongoing.

With that out of the way, Dave looked at McAllister, who was sitting slightly slumped in the armchair out in the shed.

"So what happened then, mate?" he asked. "Looks like you had a pretty shit first day."

McAllister smiled ruefully and gave Dave a potted version of the day's events. Dave snorted with laughter at the description of Brows but shook his head with disappointment at the disclosure that the security lock on the cabinet door had not been properly set despite the recent break-in.

He looked thoughtful at the reference to Norman Reynolds.

Almost as an afterthought, McAllister remembered the business card he had seen, but Dave didn't know the guy or the winery.

With Dave's promise to keep him updated on the Lucy investigation, McAllister left Jacaranda Drive and returned home, going straight to bed. He was bushed. Obviously, jet lag and the fight at the site had taken their toll.

This was turning into one hell of a gig.

He gratefully let sleep embrace him.

Chapter 6

The phone rang incessantly, demanding attention. Still half asleep and without moving his head from the pillow, McAllister picked up the receiver and grunted something that sounded vaguely like a "yes" into the mouthpiece while he tried to pull his thoughts together.

"Mike, it's Banjo," came the response. "Be ready in 10 minutes – I'm coming over to get you. The boss has called us down to the Port immediately. A development, he said. Don't have any more at the moment, but we had better get going."

McAllister immediately sprang awake and leaped out of bed. After an extremely fast shower, he was dressed seven minutes later. He had time to quickly make a thermos of coffee, grab two cups from the shelf, throw his jacket on and head towards the front door just as a loud knock erupted. Opening the door, Banjo was on the step – clearly very agitated. McAllister noted it was still dark and asked what time it was: 0315 came the response.

They got in the Holden and moved smartly away from the house, heading off in the direction of Adelaide. Before getting to the centre, they followed signposts for Port Adelaide and McAllister began to feel his anxiety levels creeping higher. Banjo was in no mood for conversation, and they rocketed along into the Port in almost complete silence.

They were stopped at the gatehouse at the entry to the Port itself. Banjo showed his ID – they were waved through, the officer on duty indicating that they should follow the concourse to the left of the main warehouses in front of them and follow it until they reached the Police checkpoint.

They drew up at the holding area sealed off with Police ticker tape. There were officers everywhere – both SA Police and RAAF Provosts – all with torches and walkie-talkies. There was a hum of activity.

A tall, well-built man walked over to them and nodded grimly.

"Banjo." Turning to McAllister, "And you must be Mike McAllister. Hear you're observing the RAAF Police on secondment from the UK."

So that's the cover line being given to the local cops.

"I'm DCI Mark Papodoulus – South Australian Police. Good to see you, but sorry it is on a night like tonight. Move yourselves – the launch is waiting to take you out to the site."

Dave grabbed McAllister by the arm and they threaded their way through the large number of military and civilian police vehicles now parked on the quayside. They made their way over to the SA Police Launch, "M.V.Archie Badenoch," which was moored alongside.

The man McAllister presumed was the captain welcomed them aboard and immediately gave the order to cast off. They cut away from the quay and headed out into the river entrance, with the two men now ensconced in the covered salon in the mid-section of the craft.

McAllister looked out of the windows of the salon and, dropping away to the portside through the darkness, saw the wharf emblazoned with lights, turning some of the myriad colonial buildings into a grim, distorted relief.

Both depressing and menacing all at the same time.

One of the Police officers who had been up in the wheelhouse came and introduced himself as Ken Fielding. He started pointing out some of the local landmarks to McAllister, explaining that the Port River is the western branch of the largest tidal estuary on the eastern side of Gulf St.Vincent. It has been used as a shipping channel since the beginning of European colonisation of the area in the mid-1830s. Even now, in the mid-1970s, it was still a busy place, although there was a sense that its heyday had well and truly passed.

The advent of containerisation had clearly done the area no favours at all, but the old buildings of the Colonial era still held a sense of decayed elegance.

McAllister found his guide to be a no-nonsense straight talker with pale blue eyes and a strong, square jaw.

During all of this, Banjo said nothing and just stared out of the window. When Ken had gone back to the wheelhouse, he broke the silence and said, "Just so you know, his eldest daughter works at the DSTO so you might want to keep an eye out for her: Caryle – "With a y," and he grinned sadly.

McAllister said nothing. He realised he had already met her and thought she could be an extremely useful contact and his own link to the SA Police if things ever got difficult.

All too soon, it seemed, the throb of the engine lessened and the speed of the vessel dropped away as she was navigated over towards what McAllister took to be the shoreline. There seemed to be a couple of inflatable-type boats bobbing around towards a group of trees. When McAllister asked about the trees, Ken responded that they were mangroves – this was the edge of the swamp country. They would need to get into the small inflatable that he was about to take off the front of the vessel by the wheelhouse and go in closer to the other small craft.

Once the inflatable had been lashed alongside and despite the swell, McAllister and Paterson gingerly made their way over the side.

The small outboard motor ferried them towards the other craft, who made way for them whilst still managing to train their searchlights on the scene in front of them.

As they approached, McAllister felt his stomach turn, even though he was not known for being squeamish.

Draped across the boughs of several of one of the larger mangrove trees right at the edge of the water and silhouetted by the bobbing Police lamps was the pale, limp body of a female. She was naked, and her skin glistened in the moonlight. What hair she had left appeared to be a dark red, although great chunks of it were missing and the skin on her skull was hanging off in a large sheet. She had numerous welts and cuts – most of which did not appear to be caused by being caught up in the mangroves. From the shape and extent of the bruising on her skin, she appeared to have been systematically beaten with a long, hard object.

Perhaps a pipe or a very large cosh.

In addition, there were a couple of really horrible, violent slashes across her breasts and stomach. One eye had gone completely, and the other appeared to be half-eaten. What remained was a bloody gel-like mess. A large blue swimmer crab chose that moment to come crawling out of what was left of the wide open mouth. The grotesque image appalled him.

McAllister reflected that his mother had been right when she had once said to him that there is no dignity in death. The scene before him bore that out with unflinching accuracy.

There were two further things that were inescapable. This woman had been held captive prior to her landing in the water – the welts and bruising around her wrists were clear to see, in addition to some of the other injuries he had already noted. Secondly, even with the extensive disfiguration, the body was undoubtedly that of the missing Lucy Andrews.

Chapter 7

The civilian and military Police officers in the inflatable boats worked together with a sombre efficiency and in almost total silence to remove Lucy's body from the scene of her impalement. A dive team arrived to search the river bed and mangrove area in case anything of evidential value could be located, but they were not hopeful of finding much. The body was eventually released from the clutches of the swamp and zipped into a body bag.

A Coroner had been brought out from the City to inspect and certify death. Lucy would be taken immediately to the morgue for a proper autopsy to be undertaken.

Banjo and McAllister's boat turned back towards the Police launch, and they climbed aboard, shaken and angry at what they had witnessed. When they reached the quayside, DCI Papadoulus met them and explained he had arranged for Dave to work as part of a joint team with his own officers on this murder enquiry. He had cleared it with RAAF high command.

That clearly presented McAllister with some difficulties in that he was meant to be at the DSTO in a couple of hours for "normal" work, and if the Lucy investigation got some legs, then it might mean that Dave was tied up quite a bit. That could leave him exposed if his own investigation started to progress.

On the way back to Weemala Road, he agreed with Banjo that if any information that might help with the Lucy Inquiry came to light in his own investigation, he would send it over straight away. If any really big problems emerged, then he would have to get a message to him somehow. McAllister remembered that it had been suggested that he go up to Woomera the following week anyway to observe the weapons trials, which was an added complication.

Returning to the murder of Lucy, they agreed that the biggest question of all was why she had met such an end – what was it that her captors had wanted to know?

They went into the house and McAllister pulled out a large bottle of Bushmills whiskey that he had brought over from the UK in his bergen, which was still dumped in the lounge. He poured them both a stiff drink.

"To Lucy" was the first toast.

McAllister didn't bother going back to bed at all. He knew that sleep was going to elude him, and it wouldn't be long before he was due at the DSTO anyway. He showered again and went to work as normal. Having completely forgotten about his own dramas the evening before, he was initially surprised to be met with looks of concern as he arrived at his workstation, as Brows and some of his other colleagues took in McAllister's battered face. He had not been at the bench long when Dr Schuster appeared and asked McAllister to accompany him. They left the work area and went down towards the security office.

McAllister whistled to himself silently. In the daylight, it was certainly one hell of a mess. Stuff was everywhere; the window, of course, was broken, and shards of glass were all over the place. He smiled grimly as he took in the head dent in the cupboard door. The Police were diligently going about their job, moving things, bagging items, dusting things, and generally trying to make some sense of the chaos. Jugs was sitting in the corridor just outside the room, and he looked at McAllister – or, in particular, McAllister's face – with some concern.

"Don't tell me you were involved in this?" asked Jugs, incredulously.

"No, not me," replied McAllister, looking directly back at him. "Got involved in a bit of a fight down the pub, that's all," he said.

Jugs looked slightly relieved; Dr.Schuster, standing next to McAllister, looked slightly disapproving but added, "Yes, it seems erm, erm, Toby here found this lot when he clocked on this morning, and the Police were here very quickly indeed. It really is most inconvenient and has put the whole routine for the entire site out of kilter."

McAllister stared at him.

What an odd response.

Turning to Jugs, he asked whether he had any idea what the intruder was after and whether anything had gone missing. Jugs shrugged and said that he didn't know – they only held unclassified materials there, "Duty rotas, that sort of stuff," and he hadn't really looked at what was, or was not, there – his first thought had been to secure the scene and call the Cops.

A small, wiry man in a crumpled Police uniform came out of the security office and ushered McAllister and Dr Schuster further down the corridor, out of earshot of Jugs. He introduced himself as Sergeant First Class Barker of the South Australian Police. Speaking directly to Dr Schuster in the first instance, he went through the usual questions.

Dr. Schuster was co-operative but not particularly forthcoming; indeed, McAllister almost described the scientist's demeanour as being sullen. He was not particularly engaging, and nor did he appear overly concerned at this latest turn of events on the site. Feeling he was not getting anywhere, Sergeant Barker dismissed Dr Schuster and turned his attention to McAllister.

Out of the corner of his eye, McAllister could see that the scientist was moving as slowly as he possibly could down the corridor to try and hear what McAllister was going to say.

Schuster is almost lurking: surely not?

Again, that word popped into his head: odd.

It was clear that the scene was being dusted for fingerprints, and as McAllister had not worn gloves the night before, those would be found. In addition, he would have to explain the cuts and bruises. The "pub brawl" answer would not stand up to scrutiny, not least because the Police would check their records and find that there hadn't been such a brawl in Salisbury or probably Elizabeth that evening. He decided that there was not much option but to "come clean." He thought ruefully of his favourite television programme at the moment, Starsky & Hutch – he was sure that they would have come up with a convincing explanation that did not involve "spilling the beans."

Barker was standing waiting for his answer. McAllister apologised and said he had missed the question but suggested that it would probably be best if he popped into

52

the Station a bit later on and had a private chat. Barker looked surprised, with his eyebrows creasing together in the middle. He rubbed his hand over his eyes – he was clearly very tired and had not welcomed this change to what he had assumed was a routine question session. Reluctantly, the Police officer agreed and McAllister said he would be down at the Salisbury Police Station at 15:00 that afternoon.

As he walked past, he nodded to Jugs, who was still sitting in the corridor, and returned to his workstation. As soon as he could, he made his excuses to take a break and went out of the front of the building and down the main road to the nearest pay phone. There, he rang Dave Paterson and explained the problem. Dave said he would handle it.

Chapter 8

Exactly on time, McAllister walked through the glass swing door of Salisbury Police Station and asked for Barker. A uniformed officer sat behind the main reception desk, immediately got up from his seat, came round to the side security door and asked McAllister to "please come this way, sir." – McAllister noted the "sir" in particular and inwardly smirked.

He was escorted up three flights of stairs to the Chief Superintendent's office. Passing quickly through the outer office, where the Chief's Secretary was hard at work, they knocked on the inner door and a loud "enter" issued from inside.

McAllister was ushered in and the door closed behind him. Involuntarily, he thought back to RAF St Mawgan and the dark, dingy mausoleum of an office as he took in the tastefully, if modestly, furnished room before him that was clean, bright, and welcoming.

Same routine, but very different gravy.

A large, muscular man behind the desk immediately stood up and introduced himself as Chief Superintendent James and indicated a vacant chair in front of the desk. Sergeant Barker was also present in the room and had moved to stand nearer the door. The only other occupant, sitting on the other chair in front of the desk, was a youngish woman with shoulder-length hair with blonde highlights, slim, not particularly tall but certainly not short (guessed McAllister). She was wearing a navy blue suit and high heels. Turning to look at him, he realised she had a pleasant, neat sort of face – not the obviously false overly, "Aren't I just fantastic," type: more genuinely handsome with a calm strength about her.

Those green/grey eyes of hers have the capacity to see into your soul.

Not having the faintest idea who she was, he nodded politely and she smiled and then turned his attention back to the Chief Superintendent, who opened the conversation in a confident, business-like fashion.

"Thank you very much indeed for coming to the station this afternoon, Mr McAllister – we are most grateful to you for handling the matter so discreetly. Your colleague here, Miss Wilson, has filled us in on the details and I am pleased to say that we have no further questions for you at this stage."

McAllister tried to hide his surprise.

Okaaay. Silence is probably the best policy until I work out what the hell is going on.

He simply nodded his head in acknowledgement, smiled, and made to stand up.

"But just before you go, Mr McAllister," came the booming voice; "just one thing, if I may?"

McAllister's gaze flicked to Miss Wilson, who was looking steadily at the Chief Superintendent.

"Please be careful. You appear to be turning up in all the wrong places just at the moment, and we have a lot going on here just now. There was the previous break-in at the DSTO, then last night's little "show" with some as yet unidentified person having been squashed under an artic lorry to put not too fine a point on it, and now we have a murdered WRAAF officer to contend with."

McAllister nodded and said, "Please don't be concerned, Chief Superintendent. I'm sure all will be well. In any event, I will be out of your hair as of the weekend as I am going up to Woomera for a while for some trial testing, so hopefully, that will give you and the lads some respite."

James smiled. "Well, enjoy your trip to the Outback, but please be careful." The smile faded. "We have no idea what is going on here at the moment. You need someone to watch your back. I understand that appropriate arrangements are being made in that regard."

This was news to McAllister, who said nothing and got to his feet. Barker took a large sidestep to the left to let him pass; Miss Wilson stood up, shook hands with James, and followed him into the corridor.

Once out of the building, she asked McAllister if he could give her a lift back to the City, and they both got into Englebert.

As they pulled out of the car park, McAllister couldn't help but notice the Red Datsun cherry that pulled out shortly after them. He pointed it out to his companion, who jotted down the registration number on the back of what appeared to be an old till receipt unearthed from her handbag and said she would look into it.

"By the way," he said, "what do I call you?"

She looked coolly at him.

"Terri," she said.

That puts me in my place, then. Nothing doing there. What a waste.

Not wishing to alert the Datsun driver to the fact that he had been clocked, McAllister drove straight into the City and dropped his passenger at the main railway station. As she was getting out of the car, Terri Wilson turned to McAllister and looked him straight in the eye.

"Be careful, McAllister. There is something else going on here that we don't know about beyond the problems at the DSTO. Watch your back. You have been authorised to draw a personal sidearm from the armoury at Woomera when you get there – completely under the radar, needless to say. I will ring you with the results on the Datsun if there is anything of interest, but keep your eyes and your ears open in Woomera. It is being arranged for Paterson to accompany you – he won't be working with the SA Police on the murder investigation. I need him with you not least because he is too close to the subject matter – although I'm sure you have guessed that already."

Without saying anything further, she turned sharply on her very high but quite sexy heels and disappeared up the steps into the mainline train station.

McAllister pulled away from the kerb, silently cursing himself for not having picked up on the signals in relation to Banjo and Lucy.

None of my business. Wouldn't be the first or last time close working relationships had gone further than the "working."

Probably for the best that Banjo was coming to Woomera on

a number of grounds. He reflected that they got on well and that Banjo may need a bit of a mate away from his usual haunts as the reality of the evening's events really hit home.

McAllister sighed.

Life is never straightforward, is it?

Having arrived back home without any further sightings of the Datsun, McAllister decided to have a hot bath, a light meal and then hit the sack. He was absolutely whacked .

Not really surprising bearing in mind my first 72 hours in Australia has not exactly been relaxing. Jet lag is also definitely in there somewhere.

He grinned at himself in the bathroom mirror, although the bruising on his face looked made it look more like a grimace.

Pouring himself a stiff whiskey and putting his transistor radio on the toilet seat next to the bath, he stepped into the rising bubbling water, allowing the warmth to seep through his bones. He had found some bubble bath that Lucy had left for him, and he had tipped a generous amount in so there was froth everywhere.

A bit like her bubbly personality.

The radio was pounding out some light pop music, and he closed his eyes, letting whiskey and the heat do their work and allowing his mind to wander.

He tried to keep away from the mangrove image and turned it instead towards the security office.

What have I missed?

Unbidden, the image of the severed arm lodged in the truck's

58

wheel arch came into his head.

Suddenly, McAllister's eyes popped open: he realised what it was that had worried him on the evening. The arm was wearing a bracelet that looked very similar to the one that the prisoner on the aircraft had worn on the way out.

Surely not?

He made a mental note to ring Dave first thing in the morning.

Having wallowed in the bath until his skin had gone wrinkly and his glass was definitely empty, McAllister threw on a robe and wandered back to the kitchen. He rifled through the fridge to see what else Lucy had left for him. There were some eggs, cheese, and onions – he could make himself an omelette, he thought. Then he spied a bottle in the door with a champagne-like cork but labelled "Cham-Pine."

How have I missed this?

He read the label:

"A refreshing cocktail of lightly bubbling champagne from the Barossa Valley, mixed with the freshest pineapple juice from our own plantations in Queensland – a great way to combine your celebration with the best Australian homegrown produce."

Sounds good.

He promptly opened the bottle, pouring a large glass of the yellow-coloured bubbly mixture. Taking a long swallow, McAllister had to admit that it really was very refreshing, and on a hot day, especially at something like a bar-b-que, this would be just the ticket. He looked back down at the label and noted that it was made and distributed by the Jindivik Winery, Nuriootpa, Barossa Valley, SA. He recalled the business card he had found at the back of the security cabinet the night before.

Well, there's a coincidence – don't like those. The Jindivik Winery makes another appearance. Might be worth a run out to the Barossa to have a look. Another thing to add to the list to talk to Dave about. He sighed.

The list just kept getting longer.

Chapter 9

The next couple of days passed uneventfully, interrupted only by the updates each evening from Dave as to the progress – or lack of – on the Lucy investigation and from Jugs (unofficially at coffee break) as to the progress on the security office break-in. The only news of any note was that the bracelet that McAllister had noticed on the severed arm must have been lost at the scene or in transit to the morgue because it was no longer on the body or in a separate effects bag—a bit of a mystery. McAllister was disappointed at that.

I know what I saw. It was so distinctive that it must have meant something.

McAllister was informed by Brows that they would be flying up to Woomera first thing on Monday morning, leaving from RAAF Edinburgh for the short hop; they would not be back for about ten days, perhaps longer. It was announced that Dave Paterson would be their RAAF Provost escort for the trip, and McAllister found himself to be slightly relieved to have a friendly face with him on that part of the journey. It also showed him – as if proof were needed – the extent of Terri Wilson's authority and influence.

Those arrangements having been settled, McAllister suggested a trip up to the Barossa Valley to wander around and learn some more about winemaking, which might be just the thing. Dave readily agreed and they set off on the Saturday morning.

Nuriootpa is the major commercial centre and largest town of the Barossa Valley, sitting about an hour's drive north of

Salisbury East. It is situated at the north end of the Valley, near the Stuart Highway, which is the main trunk route leading north to Port Augusta, Woomera, Coober Pedy and eventually the Northern Territory. Vineyards surround the town, with some of the best-known South Australian wineries being based in the area.

Although the State of South Australia is unusual in its Colonial history in that it was originally established as a freely settled, planned British province rather than a convict settlement, the area around the Barossa Valley also has a strong German influence, having experienced a large influx of settlers in the 1840s. It was largely they who established the first wineries here, recognising the excellent and almost perfect grape growing conditions of the area.

As they drove into the Valley, McAllister noticed a number of Lutheran Churches and various old German names for some of the homesteads and realised how strong these links have remained over the generations.

Nuriootpa itself had wide roads, beautiful stone-built houses with bull-nosed verandahs, and some even had grape vines growing on the outside. McAllister freely admitted that he loved Cornwall and some of the areas back in the UK, such as Pembrokeshire in West Wales, for example, but he had to admit that this had a colonial charm and beauty all of its own.

Dave explained that many of the wineries ran tours so that visitors could walk around and ask questions, learn about wine and then enjoy a tasting session with the opportunity to purchase some of the produce afterward. They both thought that sounded like a great plan.

After joining the walk-around tour at one of the largest

Wineries and then enjoying some lunch, they found the Jindivik Winery slightly out of town on the road to Tanunda.

The roadside sign said that tours for the public ran on Saturday afternoons only, and no booking was required. Looking at each other, it seemed like too good an opportunity to miss and so they turned up the dirt road track following the signs. The track took them through acres of grapevines across soft undulating land until, at the brow of a very small rise, they looked down upon the homestead that appeared to be at the centre of a large but orderly collection of vats, silos and outbuildings.

They parked where indicated and walked over to the main entrance.

They paid their nominal entrance fee and were asked to wait with the rest of the small group that were gathering for the tour.

Whilst waiting, McAllister looked around the high-ceilinged stone building, with the usual photographs and drawings of the Winery as it had developed since it was established – apparently in 1854.

Dave and McAllister looked at each other as a stunning woman appeared and called the group together. Standing just over 6'0 in height even without her heels – blonde, blue-eyed, big busted and with strong Germanic features, she seemed to personify every German stereotype. Having served in Germany, McAllister had seen plenty of them.

Statuesque: *that is the word to describe her: statuesque.*

She introduced herself as Anika de Klerk, the wife of the general manager of the site.

Another look passed between the two men.

She did not have an obviously Australian accent: it was quite clipped on certain words. McAllister tried to place it.

Perhaps a South African tinge in there? Could it also fit with the "de Klerk" bit?

With impressive organisation, she ushered the group from one part of the tour to the next, never appearing to be rushed nor to allow dawdling. Her narrative was informative and fluent, and despite himself, McAllister found he was enjoying this experience rather more than he had done at the much larger site earlier in the day. "Jindivik," he learned, was the Aboriginal phrase for "hunted" and had been chosen because that was how the original founders of the Winery had felt themselves to be when they had fled from Prussian Silesia in the late 1840s.

Interesting.

Anika went on to say that the present owners were, in fact, South Africans being descended from the Maritz family of Maritz Rebellion fame, who had bought the business from the previous owners just after the War.

As with most tours of this kind, several members of the group had questions at the end of the walkabout. McAllister put his hand up, and in due course, Anika de Klerk indicated to him. He asked how the Cham-Pine product had come about. Anika politely explained that the present owners had wanted something new by way of diversification, and this seemed like the perfect opportunity. They had diversified into pineapple farming up in Queensland to ensure their supply lines and to keep the product 100% Australian (much nodding of approval from the group met this comment), so it had proved to be an excellent business initiative in its own right.

She pointed to the heavily loaded trestle tables to the right of the group, confirming that Cham-Pine was one of the products available for taste testing and purchase now that the tour was coming to an end.

However, she added, before finally wrapping up, she was proud to announce that Cham-Pine (and more generally, the Jindivik Winery) was going to be one of the preferred sponsors for an extremely important, high-profile visit to South Australia in the Spring of 1977. "I can't tell you more at the moment," she twinkled, "but it really is huge, and we are all so excited."

There was much-animated chatter, followed by a short round of applause and a rush by the majority of the group towards the Cham-Pine end of the serving tables.

Again, the two men looked at each other.

Having sampled the tasters themselves, McAllister and Dave walked out of the cool gloom of the stone buildings into the not much warmer Winter's afternoon. It was dry, but there was a stiff breeze blowing.

"Let's stretch our legs," suggested McAllister, and the two men started off towards some of the vineyards that sprawled in every direction.

"Do you know what the high-profile visit that she was referring to is?" he asked Dave.

"No, mate, no one has said anything publicly at the moment.

Haven't even had an internal note with a hint of what is on the cards. I will ask some discreet questions when we get back and see what I can unearth. What did you make of the rest of it?"

McAllister stopped walking for a moment and looked over the vines without seeing them.

"There are so many things that don't add up," he said. "Why a business card in a security office that deals with sensitive Government work? Is this something – or is it absolutely nothing? How does it fit in with the burglaries at the DSTO? And Lucy's murder – what about that? And the missing bracelet – same as the one your prisoner was wearing on the way out here: what is this all about?"

Dave had also stopped walking, and he looked quietly at his feet. After a few minutes of silence, Dave raised his head and looked at McAllister. He said, "You know about Lucy and me, don't you?" McAllister just shrugged. "It's life, mate," he said, "but I am sorry that you have lost her. She seemed like a great girl."

"Yeah, she was," replied Dave. "Great fun. Fuck knows what she got herself into – or what someone else thought she had got herself into. She never said anything to me about being worried or concerned about anything, so there is absolutely nothing that I can link to: it's driving me fucking nuts."

They stood in silence again for a few more minutes, both lost in thought.

Whilst the two men had their conversation out amongst the vines, back in the private office area of the Winery, Anika de Klerk threw herself into one of the leather club chairs in her husband's office, kicked off her favourite needle-thin stilettos and threw her long legs over the arm of the chair.

"Phew," she said. "thank goodness that is over. The group today were so *boring*."

She looked over at her husband, who was sitting behind a large glass-topped desk. To his right was a large bronze of a bare-breasted woman in a seductive pose, but apart from the furniture and a telephone on the desk, there were no other personal items or clutter of any kind. It was almost sterile.

A bit like him, she thought idly, as he did not bother looking up from the papers in front of him or acknowledge her conversation in any way.

Jan de Klerk was mid 60s, going to paunch and almost entirely bald. She wondered what she had seen in him, then laughed to herself: the *only* thing he had ever had going for him, of course, and that was money and heaps of it.

She continued with her one-sided conversation: "I did get a question about the Cham-Pine today, and I did tell the group about the sponsorship arrangements for the forthcoming high-profile event – without mentioning any details, of course......" at which point she suddenly realised that her husband's pen had stopped moving and he was sitting silently waiting for her to finish.

She stopped talking.

He looked up at her through the thin, wire-edged spectacles that he wore all of the time, but there was a menace there. She knew that glint. He might be sterile in so many ways, she thought, but he was also quite violent when he wanted to be. And she was afraid.

Albeit not as afraid of her husband as she was of Him –
"Gifblaar" as he liked to be called by his cronies. Now there
really was one sadistic, arrogant son of a bitch, she thought.

Moving slowly to her feet, she moved over to the desk,
unbuttoning her blouse as she did so in order that he would
have a good view of her ample breasts. That usually got him
distracted. She perched on the desk and placed her hands on
her husband's face, turning his head towards her.

"Oh, my sweet Jan," she said in her best kitten voice, "don't
worry about all of that now, darling." She thought she had
succeeded, but then he suddenly and viciously slapped her
hand away and pushed her off the desk so that she fell to the
floor.

"You must be more careful, Anika," he said in a low voice
but breathing heavily.

"We do not want to give our competitors more notice than
necessary of our success in this arena. Please do not mention
it publicly again until Gifblaar himself has decided that the
time is right and has given the go-ahead for a formal
announcement by the Marketing Department."

She stood up, adjusted herself, and buttoned her blouse back
up again.

"Very well, husband," she responded in her most demure
voice.

"I understand," and with that, she put her shoes back on and
left the office.

Her husband sat behind the desk, torn between hate and an

erotic desire for her.

It is just as well you most certainly do not - and must not - understand anything. Tonight's punishment will be a real and justified pleasure to deliver.

For the first time that day, his face contorted into what he considered to be a smile and he returned to the papers in front of him.

Chapter 10

The room was dark and cold. It had a concrete floor. Very little light penetrated from the narrowest of slit windows high up against the roof line, but she could just about make out the outline across the ceiling of the large pipes, which appeared to be heating ducts of some kind.

She found it impossible to tell whether it was night or day and she had lost track of how long she thought she had been incarcerated here.

She was bitterly cold, wearing nothing but the clothes she had on when she had been grabbed by the two men.

They had said nothing to her, either during the abduction or since. Such food and water as was supplied was given to her silently: no words were spoken, despite her pleas to understand what was going on and why they had taken her.

It always seemed to be the same two men who brought her food. She couldn't be sure, though, as they were always hooded and wore gloves. But they looked to be about the same build.

There were no sanitary arrangements. She had been left to her own devices in that regard. Bearing in mind that she was chained to what appeared to be a large tank of some kind and her movement was almost totally restricted, her own devices did not amount to much.

She was filthy, tired, hungry, and frightened.

And alone.

Totally alone.

The silence was expansive and all-encompassing. It shrieked at her during the endless hours.

Her ears strained for the slightest sound of the boots on the hallway outside the room where she was being kept, and which usually presaged the arrival of the two men. That at least broke the silence, but she was always gripped in equal measure by hope and relief on the one hand that *someone* had not forgotten her and that her release was imminent and the crawling sense of fear on the other that, at some stage, probably quite soon now, they would come and she would either be killed or be taken to face whatever this was all about.

No doubt that she would then wish she was back here in her silent isolation, she thought grimly.

She groped in her increasingly jumbled mind for that phrase that her mother had used now and again: "Be careful what you wish for, young lady, be careful what you wish for."

The warning sounded like a clarion call in her brain.

Chapter 11

McAllister reported as requested at 0900 Monday morning at RAAF Edinburgh and met up with his colleagues from the DSTO. Brows was there already, getting everyone organised and ready for the short flight up to Woomera. He was busy clucking around like an old hen. McAllister realised that, in fairness, these were civilians not used to a military-style despatch, so he stood quietly at the back of the group and continued to observe the goings on.

Dr Schuster then arrived, together with an imposing, well-built man that McAllister put as being in his late 50s or early 60s. The man had a full head of thick, iron grey hair, and although not particularly tall, he was immaculately dressed in a suit and tie, and he certainly had some charisma. Without him even uttering a word, the previously chattering group quickly fell silent and looked at the newcomer, virtually ignoring a pale, tired, and crumpled Dr. Schuster.

"Good morning, everyone," boomed the newcomer.

Voice to match the persona.

"Thanks as always for arriving promptly. Short flight up to the site this morning; we should be there by about 1130 at the latest. Normal arrangements for accommodation, meals, etc. will apply. The only change is that on this trip, we will be accompanied by an RAAF Provost Officer, who will be looking after all of our security needs."

With that, he turned and introduced Banjo to the group. Eyes widened, and mouths opened in a silent "oh," but no one said anything. This clearly was not part of the usual routine. This was a highly classified project, so no one should have been surprised at the visible security uplift – not least in light of the break-in and the subsequent "events" in the security office, both of which were common gossip amongst the staff.

Banjo and McAllister made eye contact but did not make any other sign of recognition, Banjo's eyes continuing to sweep over the remainder of the group before him.

Once on the aircraft, McAllister was seated next to Stephen "Chips" McInerney. McInerney had come by his eponymous nickname not because of his love of fried food but because of his work (and love for) integrated circuits, known as microchips. McAllister remembered reading somewhere that these circuits had first been created in the US in about 1958/1959, and the years since then had seen this field develop into a whole specialism of its own: and Stephen McInerney was right at the heart of that burgeoning specialism.

So gossip had it, he was one of the hottest rising young stars in the field, considered to be "going places." It was rumoured he had been offered a job with a new start-up company by the name of Apple Computers over in California, and McAllister reflected that it seemed that the world was on the brink of another revolution – this time a technological one – which would probably see daily living completely change in currently unimaginable ways within 30 years.

Who knows? We might even have phones that we can use anywhere and which are completely mobile, and ways of accessing information that we can only dream about today. Thunderbirds come to life!

He laughed to himself as he happily recalled the 1960s

children's programme.

Perhaps we should be calling Chips McInerney "Brains" instead, in honour of the brilliant character in the series.

Another silent chuckle.

Whilst McInerney poured over what appeared to be the latest technical magazine he had pulled from his bag, McAllister put his head back against the seat rest and closed his eyes. The drum of the engines and the general chatter around him gradually droned out, and before he knew it, the pilot was announcing that they were coming into land.

Startled awake, McAllister looked out of the window of the rapidly descending aircraft and took in his first look at Woomera and the wild, empty expanse of The Outback.

They were only about 270 miles north-west of Adelaide, but it could have been a different world and McAllister had been told that this was actually regarded as the start of the Far North of the State. Long gone were the green, lazy parklands bordering the River Torrens and the neatly manicured suburbs emerging around the State capital.

The area was totally flat as far as the eye could see, and apart from one highway and a clutch of houses and buildings on the base itself, there appeared to be an abundance of nothingness but dust, heat haze, and scrubby trees and bushes.

Definitely not the place to get lost in – or perhaps it was if you knew what you were doing. Even in the winter, it still looked hot out there. Don't fancy it in the middle of summer: the sun's anvil, make no mistake about that.

On landing, the group quickly left the aircraft, heading for the small building that served as the first port of call for those arriving at the base. From there, everyone piled onto the waiting bus and moved out to the accommodation units on the outskirts of the village itself. It turned out that McAllister and Chips McInerney were to share a unit, and the bus dropped them by the gate where a wooden sign proudly announced their new lodgings as "The Shack."

A quick survey of the accommodation revealed a neat and tidy three-bedroomed bungalow, weather-boarded outside, with the bare essentials for living in this sort of climate – namely, a ceiling fan, fly screens on the doors and windows, a generator and a fridge. It was sparsely furnished, but that didn't trouble McAllister, who had never bothered much with such comforts. He nevertheless quickly nabbed what he considered to be the largest and most comfortable of the bedrooms much to Chip's obvious dismay.

"Who was the bloke on the aircraft with us this morning, then, Chips?" he asked, once they had stowed their kit and made a quick cup of tea before heading back to the main base.

"Oh, you mean the Chief Executive – Norman Reynolds?" replied Chips. "Very impressive, he is, even for a politician."

"A politician?" enquired McAllister.

"Yes, of course," said Chips. "Schuster and the other seniors think they run the project, but of course, they don't: the Australian and UK Governments do – and so there has to be a head politico somewhere in the equation, and Mr. Reynolds is it."

Caryle (with a "y"s) reference to Reynolds having been with the bigwigs in Canberra came back to him, and he thought again how odd it had been that no mention of Reynolds had been made in his briefing paper and that it was Schuster that he was asked to report to. For the first time, it occurred to McAllister that perhaps the "report to" was merely a convenience for getting him into the DSTO in the first place, and perhaps it was really *him* keeping an eye on Schuster - not the other way around. That would keep the political element out of things rather neatly.

More food for thought.

Nodding his thanks to his companion and finishing their tea quickly, both men then moved outside to meet the minibus that was coming up the main street to take them back over to the base.

When they reached the site, Dr. Schuster took McAllister to one side and said that rather than join in the general hubbub in the laboratories, and as this was his first visit to the base, a personalised tour had been arranged for him.

Just at that moment, a tall, slim lady, who McAllister placed roughly in her mid-20s, walked in. She was wearing desert boots, a non-descript pair of cargo trousers, and a tee-shirt. Her light brown hair was pulled back into a neck-based ponytail and grey eyes descended on McAllister, who suddenly felt a moment of recognition.

That's bizarre. I never forget a face and I know I have never met this lady before. But...there is something definitely familiar about her.

She continued to calmly observe him whilst his thought

process worked through.

"Everything ok, Mr McAllister?" she asked with a grin.

"Er, yes," stuttered Mc Allister, embarrassed at having been caught out in his musings.

"Sorry, I thought for one moment I had met you before, and it rather threw me. My apologies. Please call me Mike."

She laughed – a light, straightforward laugh.

"Hi, Mike," she said. "I'm Alison Fielding – but you can call me Ali. You have probably met my sister, Caryle (with a y). She works down at the DSTO."

Bingo.

"Or my Dad, Ken – who works for the South Australia Police."

"A whole Police and Defence dynasty of South Australians, then?" he asked with a laugh. Thinking of his impression of Ken's straightforward, no-nonsense style, it was clear that there were some obvious family traits here if ever he had seen some.

"Nah," she said. "I just work in the office. I leave all the running around stuff to my Dad and my cousin, who is in the RAAF."

With that, she turned on her heel and moved towards the sliding doors. They moved out down the steps and into the dusty roadway at the front of the building to commence the tour, which, all in all, took about three hours. At the end of it, McAllister had to confess he had not realised the size or extent of the complex.

It transpired that the RAAF Woomera Rocket Range (previously the Anglo-Australian Long Range Weapons Establishment) was a major site comprising both Australian military and civilian aerospace. It had had various names over the years, but the main parameters of its operation had not changed. It had a large land area of over 47000 square miles and was the largest land-based test range in the Western World.

That's roughly half the size of the entire United Kingdom! That's mind-boggling!

It had a dedicated prohibited area and restricted airspace, all of which enabled the Australian and UK governments (together with some projects with the US/NASA such as the NASA Skylark and participation in the Mercury and Gemini space programmes in the early 1960s, for example) to devise and test a variety of new rocket based weapons in relative peace and solitude from the outside world.

The RAAF base had been expanded over the years since 1947 to support the range. It was now a fully equipped military airfield incorporating a dual runway.

The three hours spent in Ali's company passed quickly. She was clearly very knowledgeable about the site and had answered all of his questions in what he quickly came to understand was her straightforward, quite direct style.

She's great company.

At the end of the tour, they went over to the canteen to grab a sandwich and a cup of tea before McAllister had to report to his designated office, which he was sharing with several others from the DSTO team. It was noisy and busy in the canteen, and it was clear that the testing trip had generated a lot of excitement.

Between bites of the sandwich, Ali gave him a quick rundown of the facilities available in the town, which he could use whilst he was at the base. It turned out that there was a community swimming pool with exclusive RAAF base use on Wednesday afternoons, a couple of local shops for any "stuff" he might require, and the Town Hall, which doubled as a general meeting hall and a dance/music venue usually when local jazz group Bill and his Bongs were playing.

Really? Bill and his Bongs? That is eye-wateringly bad.

A couple of the RAAF guys had managed to obtain a large screen and had set up a drive-in movie centre just on the outskirts of the town, with new releases coming up on the supply aircraft. It was usually the highlight of the Town's month when a big blockbuster arrived, Ali informed him, "Although the sound can be a bit dodgy on occasion."

That sounds like great fun.

"Apparently, the next film will be "Where Eagles Dare" with Richard Burton and Clint Eastwood," McAllister smiled. Obviously, "new release" was an elastic description here, as the film had been out in the UK for about 6 – 7 years.

If he wanted a game of pool and a beer, then apparently a shack called Crazy Pete's was the place to go, but, she added with a laugh, it could "get a bit crazy out there as the name suggests, so don't go alone, and keep your eyes open."

Sounds like my sort of place.

With that, Ali dusted herself down and got up from her seat. "Well, Mike, good to meet you. Hope you found the wander around interesting, and if you need anything, just ask for me in the office. Otherwise, hope you enjoy your time here."

And with that, she left the canteen.

I like her. She is one of those dependable people who don't flap in a crisis or have histrionics at the least little thing. Together with Banjo, I think I would be able to rely on her should things get sticky.

And something in the back of his mind was telling him that "sticky" was probably going to be the understatement of the year.

Chapter 12

In the days that followed, McAllister found that he was falling into something of a routine. There were some good parts and not-so-good parts.

The good parts were that, when returning from his initial walkabout with Ali on his first day here, he discovered that Banjo was the third person to be sharing The Shack with him and Chips McInerney. Definitely good news all around.

He had also quickly realised that he was going to have far more latitude here to do what he wanted than originally anticipated, which meant that he could hopefully poke about a bit and talk to some of the others on the team. He was concerned that his investigation was not really progressing and time was passing. Suddenly, the couple of weeks that they were going to be up here did not seem very long at all.

That all made it easy to fall into a routine every day: an early morning run of between 5 and 10 miles around the town and the base, followed by a shower, a quick breakfast and then down to work.

The downside was that everyone knew everyone else *and* their business.

Rather like the Valleys back home in Wales. I will have to be careful when talking to anyone. "Small town syndrome" will be magnified here because of the geographical isolation.

This was brought home to him when he popped into the small shop in the main high street to get a few provisions on his second day in town.

Walking from the dusty main street, he stepped onto the wooden boards of the verandah which covered the front of the shop and through the glass door, a little bell tinkled. He was transported back to his boyhood in Newport when visiting the local sweet shop: it was the same bell sound and the same feeling of warm, chaotic cosiness that he had felt then unexpectedly enveloped him.

The man behind the counter was in late middle age, with wire-framed glasses and brushed over grey hair. He watched McAllister closely as he made his choices of items.

As McAllister placed the things on the highly polished counter, the man opened the conversation.

"New in town, eh?"

"Yup," said McAllister.

"Well, I'm Burt Williams. Have run this place with my wife Vera for the last thirty years. If we haven't got it, I can usually get it for you." and he grinned and winked in a manner that he clearly thought was an 'all blokes together' type conspiracy.

"Good to meet you, Burt; thanks for that."

"And you must be Banjo's mate, the new Pommie, Mike McAllister," Burt half stated and half asked.

"Indeed – news obviously travels fast around here," McAllister responded with a gentle smile.

Burt paused mid-way through ringing up the purchases on the old-fashioned till and pulled absentmindedly at his not inconsiderably sized nose "You any relation to old Huw McAllister over in Coober Pedy?" he asked.

"No idea," replied McAllister, genuinely surprised. "What does he do then?"

Burt looked at him with no little astonishment. "Well, what most people do in that neck of the woods, Mike: mine's opals."

"Right," said McAllister.

Interesting. Unlikely, as I have never heard of anyone called Huw. I'll have to write and ask my sister about that. She'll know the family history of anyone does. Could be a bit of a laugh.

"Thanks for that, Burt. See you again soon," and with that, he picked up his meagre purchases, turned from the quiet darkness of the shop and stepped out into the warmth of the main street.

When he got back to the bungalow that evening, Chips and Banjo were both there. He asked about obtaining a car so that he could get out and about a bit. Both of his companions felt about laughing.

"You don't want a prissy car out here, mate," said Banjo.

It was good to see him laughing – he had not been his usual self over the last few days, which was understandable, but it was nevertheless good to see a flash of the old humour.

"The best thing is for you to take out a pool vehicle – a jeep or a ute. This is a tough country and it needs tough vehicles to get around. Definitely four-wheel drive. We keep a pool ready down at the base. There are some general ground rules that you must follow as well, however poncy they sound. I'll come down with you in the morning and we can sort something out.

Banjo was, as always, as good as his word and the two men turned up at the base the following morning and the arrangements were made. The pool mechanic, whom McAllister quickly learned was called Keith – or Greasy to his friends - had been adamant, however, that he had to agree to follow the rules before he would let him have the keys.

Banjo was right about that, then.

McAllister was handed a leaflet, which he had to read and sign and essentially promise:

- Never to go out alone;

- To log his journey before departing so that someone knew where he was going and when he was expected to arrive;

- To always call in when he had reached the destination so that they knew he was safe and when he was leaving to start his return journey;

- Always have a full fuel tank plus full spare jerry can in the back;

- To have a plentiful supply of drinking water ("there ain't any out here, mate unless you know where to look for it and you don't") and food;

Almost as an afterthought, Keith added that there was a pack of maps in the back and if he was authorised to draw a firearm from the armoury, then McAllister would be well advised to take that too.

All a bit dramatic and over the top.

His wide-eyed knowing look over to Banjo on reading all of this and listening to the warnings met with a completely unsympathetic expression from his colleague, causing McAllister to pause and think about things again.

Remembering my own reaction on seeing the vast expanse of nothingness from the aircraft window on arrival, the fact that I have already been in one fight at the DSTO, I don't know the country and haven't the faintest idea what is actually going on in terms of the investigation, perhaps it would be wise to reconsider. None of these things cost anything, but they could just save my life.

He good humouredly signed the chit and was promptly handed the keys to a Land Rover Defender. McAllister was delighted. He had driven so many of these in the past that it was like meeting an old friend. Looking in the back, he saw the extra kit that Keith had warned him he would be required to take with him and keep topped up at all times.

He drove the Defender back to the main parking area near the base buildings, and just as he was getting out of it, another vehicle, a white Ford Falcon XB, drew up. Ali got out, and she waved and smiled.

They walked back to the buildings together. He asked how far Coober Pedy was from here, and she informed him that it was "about 235 miles drive up the main Stuart Highway, Highway A87. Going roughly north. About three or so driving hours – probably more."

She didn't ask why; he didn't elaborate.

She left him at the doors of the cafeteria with her usual cheery "See ya around, Mike,"

He sighed, feeling like he was treading water.

Perhaps a quick trip up to this place, Coober Pedy, is what I need. Might clarify my mind a bit and set me off on a new line of investigation. Things seemed to have stalled on so many fronts. Still no further updates about Lucy Andrews; nothing further on the break-in or the blueprints. Everything amounts to a big fat nothing. Yes, a trip up through the wildness of the desert to Coober Pedy would probably do me some good. It would at least afford me some thinking time.

The next couple of days literally trundled along, and on Thursday evening, Banjo suggested that the three of them go out to Crazy Pete's to show McAllister what that was all about – grab a game of pool and some beers.

Chips declined: he had a paper to submit for Mr Reynolds apparently and some phone calls to make. McAllister wondered idly whether any of those phone calls were to California about the rumoured job offer, but he didn't ask. No doubt he would find out in due course.

McAllister thought it sounded like a bit of a laugh and after a quick shower and change, the two of them set off into the fast-gathering desert dusk.

The full darkness of night fell quickly here, and McAllister was glad Banjo was driving: after turning off the bitumen highway not long after leaving the base, he soon felt completely disorientated.

A keen stargazer, however, he was soon lost in the colossal sky that opened above him.

Another thing to investigate properly whilst I am here.

The first indication they were getting close to their destination was when a row of old oil drums, smothered in white paint, started appearing down the side of the track. Banjo nodded to the silent white guardians and told McAllister that Pete had had to put those in because of the number of crew from the base who – after a fun-filled evening at the Bar – couldn't find the road again. They laughed, although McAllister was slightly relieved to think he wasn't the only one who might lose his way out here quite easily.

Breaching the crest of a small rise, Crazy Pete's appeared in a blaze of light below them. An eponymous neon sign across the length of the roof line of the building, complete with pink flashing bulbs and what appeared to be some sort of cowboy figure leaning on a kangaroo, announced that they had arrived.

This is completely nuts: *a cross between Blazing Saddles and Skippy*. He laughed to himself.

The car park (or, more accurately, the parking area) was a mess of vehicles left higgledy-piggledy, and in keeping with what was obviously the accepted standard, Banjo threw the car into what appeared to be a spare space and they got out.

McAllister automatically did what he always did on occasions like this and his eyes quickly swept the other vehicles already there to see if there was anyone he knew already in.

Banjo was right again: the favourite sort of vehicles out here were either Utes or Land Rovers.

However, in their keenness to get into the bar and get a beer,

McAllister was not as thorough as he usually was and he missed the dark red Datsun Cherry that was sitting quietly unattended in the darkest corner of the yard, next to the cabin wall.

Chapter 13

They stepped through the door and were met with a raucous blast of laughter, noise and general hubbub. The pool table appeared to be getting good use, as was the dart board, and McAllister immediately felt at home. This was his sort of place. Hard-working blokes in jeans, enjoying a beer and a fag, after a tough week.

They worked their way over to the bar and grabbed a couple of vacant stools next to a large middle-aged man, clearly the worse for wear, who was clinging to his half-drunk pint for grim death. He wore no shirt, only a singlet that had clearly seen a busy day as it was covered in sweat and dust, together with non-descript jeans with great streaks of oil on them. He was waxing lyrical to anyone who would listen about the politicians and the state of the country.

Different narrative from home, but same theme.

Banjo got the beers in, and a menu (such as it was), and having drunk a few good slugs, they turned and looked at the rest of the room. *Usual mix. Apart from the Aussie twang, you could be anywhere.*

As is the way with such places, the fight – when it started – appeared to be over nothing much at all. Spilled beer, it seemed. The lads of the town started chest pumping up to each other and before long, punches were being thrown. McAllister and Banjo sat quietly at the bar, letting it all unfold. As far as they could see, there were no RAAF personnel involved so they had no jurisdiction anyway. Best to let the boys fight it out.

Tables were turned over, chairs broken, loose teeth flew, noses were mashed and blood was spattered.

That was until the sound of a pump action shotgun being fired through the ceiling of the cabin echoed through the din.

McAllister and Banjo turned from their seats to see a slightly built but wiry man, all of 5'5" or 5'6" at a push, standing near the doorway wearing an old Akubra hat that was almost as big as he was. Around his shoulders draped what appeared to be a thick bullwhip. Despite his slight stature, the figure he cut silhouetted in the light was quite intimidating and McAllister immediately got the feeling that he would be extremely effective in a fight. The shotgun had certainly gained the attention of the brawling mob: punches were held mid-throw, and all faces turned to the doorway.

"Crazy Pete," whispered Banjo.

"Now youze lot know the rules here," the man announced in a broad Aussie accent.

"Have a good time by all means, but anything you damage you pay for. If you tear that pool table covering, I will tear your head off your necks and shove your dicks down yer windpipes – get it?" There was a quiet but collective nod from the crowd.

"You know that I get a bit crazy when I get upset, and we don't want that, do we?" he asked, glaring around the now-subdued audience. He was met with mildly nervous shakes of the head from most of those in front of him.

"Then get this fucking mess cleared up, you lazy lot and if you can't enjoy yourselves properly, then get out. If you want a fight, then go down The Pit and sort it out properly,"

At this point, the drunk sitting next to Banjo and McAllister quietly and majestically slid off his stool, finally succumbing to his alcohol intake.

The spell was broken, and the previously warring factions separated themselves, picked up the overturned chairs and tables, cleared up the broken glass and one guy even asked the barmaid for a cloth to wipe up the spills. McAllister couldn't hide his smile – *wipe up the spills? What sort of a place was this?*

As he turned to take a slug of his beer, which miraculously was still intact on the bar, he felt more than heard someone behind him.

"Think that's funny, mister, do ya?"

The silence that returned to the cabin was palpable.

McAllister replaced his beer on the bar and slowly turned in his seat. He looked down at Crazy Pete and was met with hard, dark eyes that clearly had seen and done a lot in their lifetime. No messing; no quarter. This was a serious player, regardless of his age or size. Not a good enemy to have.

"No offence," said McAllister.

"Glad to hear it, Pommie brain. I run my shed my way, get it? Don't like it? Fuck off back to the City."

McAllister had many talents; he also had many good character traits, but unfortunately, patience was not one of them and he knew that his buttons were starting to be pushed.

Banjo, realising the danger, intervened. "Sorry, Pete," he said – "he's only just over on the boat if you know what I mean, and still getting the lie of the land,"

Pete's expression didn't change.

After a short pause, he simply grunted and said, "Mind my words, mister: you won't get a second chance."

Nodding to Banjo, but his eyes never leaving McAllister's face, Crazy Pete turned on his heel and went back out the front door.

There was an audible sigh of relief amongst the gathered customers. Some decided to call it a night, but a hardcore remained.

"You wouldn't believe he only has one leg, would you?" said Banjo in a conspiratorial whisper.

"You kidding me?" replied McAllister.

"Nope – lost it overseas somewhere when serving with the SAS in the UK as part of the Australian detachment over there."

McAllister couldn't help but give a rueful smile at the thought of the tough little Aussie losing anything as if it was lost luggage – let alone a leg.

Before McAllister could return to the joy of his pint, a large bull of a man sidled over towards the bar.

"Well, seems you didn't have the balls to have a go at Pete, then, or any of the rest of us for that matter," he smirked. "That's the problem with you English Poms – no balls at all and a load of whining into the bargain. Whine, whine, whine. That's all you do,"

Before he could finish, McAllister's fist met his jaw and the brawl erupted again – this time with McAllister and Bull at the centre of it.

One of the customers started a book on the fight's outcome, and dollar bills started changing hands as the bets were laid. The rest of the men present quickly formed a circle around the brawling pair, and the noise level started rising again as the excitement and the blood started to flow.

Both men were seemingly possessed. They exchanged blow for blow, kick for kick. When one was on the floor, the other managed to extract themselves and turn the tables, and it was the other using their core strength to bring the other one down.

It was hard fought, and the crowd cheered them on. McAllister eventually managed to get his thumbs over the eyes of the man now pinned beneath him and, through clenched and bloody teeth, growled "Get this fuck head: I ain't English. I'm Welsh, and that doesn't make me a Pom, and I don't whine. Ok?"

The man beneath him was clearly in pain, but he moved his head enough to let McAllister know that he got the point and the fight was over.

They separated, gasping and sweating. The crowd went wild and there was a two-way rush – one half went to the guy running the book on the outcome of the fight; the other rushed to the bar to get another drink. Business was brisk in both directions.

Banjo, who had let McAllister fight his own fight, took him by the arm and suggested that they make a discreet exit. "No way," said a still very heated McAllister. "Going to finish my beer," and with that, he made his way through the throng back over to the bar, stood his bar stool back up and plonked himself down on it. As he went to take a strong pull on his pint, one of his teeth finally gave up the ghost and plopped into the amber liquid. He was not amused but fished it out and carried on with his drink.

He noted that Bull had quickly disappeared into the throng.

Before he could finally drain his glass, a large, fat, balding man approached him.

"Good evening, young sir," he smiled. McAllister immediately took a dislike to him. "My name is Brandon. If you ever want to make a quick bob or two, give me a shout – Maxine behind the bar will get in touch with me. I run a fight club down at The Pit. Usually, once a month. If you are interested, I can set you up with a couple of bouts. Bare knuckles; no rules. Interested?"

"Thanks, but no thanks," responded McAllister.

"Ok," replied Brandon. "But think about it, and if you change your mind, let me know. There's good money to be made to the right fighters,"

With that, he turned and left the shed.

McAllister signalled to the barmaid and asked if she had any Bushmills; Maxine said nothing but passed him a half-drunk bottle and two glasses.

I knew I liked this place.

McAllister grimaced as he and Banjo slugged some of the whiskey down. Not long after, Banjo finally got McAllister out of Crazy Pete's and they started to make their way back to The Shack. The white-painted oil drums stood out against the pitch black, and McAllister sat brooding and quiet in the passenger seat, content to let Banjo get them back.

"Sorry to add to the fun of the night," said Banjo, "but I think we have got some company" and he nodded behind.

McAllister turned in his seat as they bumped over the uneven ground, and at first, he couldn't see a thing. Then he realised as his eyes adjusted that he could just about make out the outline of a vehicle following them – no lights, but very definitely following them.

Or was it? Anyone leaving the pub would have to come this way, and their own headlights were very effective. Perhaps they were just happy to follow them.

As soon as he thought it, McAllister realised how unlikely that sounded.

"Let's find out who they are," said Banjo. With that, he killed the headlights and swung the Ute off the track. They were quickly swallowed by the desert night. He stopped the vehicle and turned the windows down to hear what was going on. Sound travelled fast across the desert.

The vehicle following them had clearly not expected the change of approach, and McAllister and Banjo heard It come to a stop almost as if the driver was trying to decide what to do. After a wait of several minutes, which seemed like a lifetime in the darkness, they saw headlights switch on, and the other car grope its way towards the main highway. They remained stationary until the car was far enough ahead for them to fall in behind them, this time becoming the cat in the chase game.

Just as they reached the main highway, the car turned away from the base and McAllister properly caught sight of the vehicle for the first time. He was stunned to see that it was a

Datsun Cherry and two people were silhouetted inside. Banjo and McAllister looked at each other and immediately turned to follow the car.

They flicked on their headlights, and the Datsun was clearly illuminated in front of them.

The chase was on.

"Same plates!" shouted McAllister over the noise of the engine;

"There's a two-way in the bag just behind your seat," shouted Banjo in response: "Call it in and ask for assistance. We are on the main A87, northbound," McAllister did so, not once taking his eyes from the Datsun. It might be small, he thought, but it could certainly shift and it was giving the Ute a run for its money.

As he rummaged around in the bag, he found not only the radio but also a couple of RAAF issue L9A1 Browning Hi-Power side arms and two Colt M16A1 assault rifles, together with a supply of ammunition for each. There were also a few hand grenades. "Came loaded for bear, then Banjo," said McAllister, more as a statement than a question.

Banjo simply nodded and hung grimly on. He was pushing the Ute as fast as it would go, and it was taking all of his concentration to remain on the main highway – no lighting, of course, only his headlights picking out the scurrying Datsun up ahead.

Having made the call, McAllister checked the chambers on the side arms and made sure both were loaded with the safety on. He didn't want to blow his leg off at this stage.

That really would be the icing on the cake.

Involuntarily, a picture of Crazy Pete flashed through his mind and despite himself, he smiled. He went through the same procedure for the assault rifles, placing those down next to him in the footwell. Having made his preparations, he cradled the side arms on his lap and let Banjo concentrate on the chase at hand.

It seemed that they were gaining, albeit slightly.

Something ghostly grey moved suddenly to his right in his peripheral vision; McAllister's head switched immediately to try and see what it was, but it had disappeared back into the darkness.

He flicked his head back to the front, shouting as he did so that there could be further incoming from two o'clock.

Just seconds later, the Datsun seemed to come to a juddering stop, the boot catapulting over the front of the car so that it literally somersaulted in the air. It landed with a huge crash on its roof and almost immediately, flames started licking at what was left of the wreckage.

Banjo brought the Ute to a halt a safe distance away, and both men raced over to the by-now-burning vehicle.

McAllister observed the extensive and bloody remains of a very large grey kangaroo scattered over the roadway. The Datsun would not have stood a chance against such a large, compact, moving obstacle.

No wonder it catapulted upon impact.

The silhouettes he had seen earlier were indeed two people who were now trapped upside down in the burning car.

McAllister tried to fight through the growing flames to reach the handle on what had been the passenger side. As he did so, the man in the passenger seat, who was hanging upside down, turned his head towards him. The blood was pouring down from a massive blow to the front of his head. His dark eyes bore into McAllister, who stopped short. The man grinned at him and pushed the button on the door down to lock himself and his companion into the vehicle. As he did so, McAllister noted the wooden bracelet that dangled from the man's wrist.

Again?

Banjo raced round from the other side and said that the car was locked and he couldn't get near enough to smash the windows and get the driver out. He thought that the driver was dead anyway.

There was an ominous crackle, and McAllister just succeeded in grabbing Banjo and throwing them both to the ground before a huge fireball erupted. The fabric of the Datsun and its inhabitants were gobbled up by the flames almost immediately.

Through the fug and dizziness created by the explosion, Police wailers sounded dimly in the distance. McAllister and Banjo were slowly picking themselves up from the floor as the Police cars (one civilian and one from the Base) arrived on the scene.

This was going to be a long night. And what in hell's name had they been transporting? The Datsun should never have blown up as it had done, despite the severity of the collision with the kangaroo.

Coober Pedy was going to have to wait after all.

Chapter 14

The next few hours were filled with detailed conversations – often repeated depending on the enquirer – and lots of paperwork. There was a general hubbub of noise and activity in the Provost HQ at the Base, coupled with a significant number of crumpled plastic coffee cups and fag ends. The air was generally smoke-filled, and only belatedly, someone opened a window to let some fresh air in.

Amidst the chaos, Terri Wilson walked in – unannounced and unaccompanied. She walked straight over to where McAllister was sitting and, clearing empty crisps packets, a full ashtray and other rubbish from the chair next to him, promptly sat down. The high heels were gone tonight and she was wearing a sensible but immaculately cut business-like trouser suit with what appeared to be flat brogues and was carrying a small attache case.

"Ok – what happened?" she asked, and McAllister gave her a very straightforward – if slightly edited – account of the evening's events.

She opened the case and pulled out a sheaf of papers.

She pushed a photograph in front of him and asked whether he recognised the man shown.

McAllister did. It was the man in the Datsun who had purposely locked the car doors so that neither he nor his companion could be rescued.

Wilson nodded. "I was so hoping you weren't going to say that, McAllister, but thank you for confirming. That is one

Hendrik Cronje, originally from South Africa. Has lived here in Australia since childhood, his family having emigrated here straight after the War. His surviving family are all based around Melbourne. Unfortunately, Hendrik fell into bad company; he started with the small fry stuff as an adolescent but has moved down the ladder to more serious offences in recent years, including manslaughter for which he served time, but his conviction was overturned on appeal and he was released eighteen months ago. He is believed to have links to some organised crime groups that we have an interest in. We have had difficulty keeping tabs on him since his release, as he is adept at dropping out of sight when he wants to."

"Two questions," said McAllister, at which Wilson sardonically raised an eyebrow as if to say, "Only two?!"

"First, he was wearing a wooden bracelet when I last saw him; it is very similar to the bracelet that the man who broke into the DSTO security office was wearing on the night we had our tussle there and very similar to the one being worn by the prisoner who came over on the transfer flight with me, Banjo and Lurch from Hong Kong. That cannot be a coincidence. What is the significance of that bracelet?"

Wilson looked thoughtful. "Don't know is the honest answer, McAllister. I'll look into that. And your second question?"

"Was he the registered keeper of the Datsun?"

"Can answer that one," Wilson responded. "No, he wasn't. That was registered to one Beatrice Langley at an address in Murray Bridge. A visit there shortly after you first drew my attention to the car has confirmed that Mrs. Langley was an elderly lady who sold it about a year ago. Can't take that enquiry further, as unfortunately, Mrs. Langley passed away earlier this year."

"A supplementary question then," added McAllister quickly. "Who was the other person in the Datsun tonight?"

"Don't know that either," responded Wilson; "the body was badly burned, so we will have to rely on dental records for identification. And before you ask, I will check whether that body was also wearing the bracelet,"

A rueful grin spread across McAllister's rather battered face, and he nodded to her. "What's the latest on the Lucy Andrews investigation?" he asked sombrely.

"Not a lot, unfortunately," Wilson replied kindly. "Cause of death is still unclear; there are some toxicology tests being run, but the experts seem fairly doubtful that those will produce anything concrete. At the moment there is very little else for us to go on. I suggest you get back to The Shack, McAllister, get those wounds cleaned up and then get some rest. I will be in touch again when I have anything further to report,"

Sounds like a good idea.

With that, she got up, collected her papers back into the attache case, nodded goodbye and walked out of the room as quietly and undramatically as her arrival had been.

Banjo wandered over, looking pretty done in himself, and asked if he was ready to go, as they had just been released from any further questioning or paperwork tonight. Gratefully, they both left the Base, making the journey back to The Shack in double quick time. All was quiet on their arrival – Chips was obviously sleeping soundly, as the place was in darkness – and after a quick shower and general patch-up, McAllister dropped into his bunk, rather relieved to have got to the end of another day.

Over and over again, the face of Hendrik Cronje grinning at him from the locked door of the Datsun came back to him – haunting him, taunting him – until Cronje's face started contorting into that of a dead Lucy Andrews. Finally, a very disturbed, restless sleep overtook him.

Chapter 15

When they eventually came for her, she knew she had been right to be careful about what she had wished for.

Fear gripped her completely.

She was taken to a sterile-looking room. It certainly did not have a whole load of furniture from what she could see – which was very little. The lighting had been set to shine into her eyes and cast the others in the room in darkness.

What is this - some old movie? It's certainly got all the cliches.

The voice that came from the darkness behind the lights was male. It told her that she had been taken prisoner by mistake, that he was very sorry that she had been put into these circumstances. He was going to make it up to her, and she was going to be moved to much better accommodation so that she could rest and recuperate before going home.

Struggling with her words, she almost shouted that she didn't care about rest and recuperation; she just wanted to go home.

With a sanctimonious clicking of the tongue, the voice behind the lights said that was not possible. She would need some proper food, sleep, and medication and only then would she be taken back.

"What do you want?" she screamed in the darkness.

The only reply was silence, followed by the movement of the two hooded men beside her who stood her back up from her chair and, still handcuffed, walked/stumbled her out of a side door.

She was taken down a long corridor until they reached the end.

A large metal door slid sideways, and she was taken into the new room. It was impossible to grasp how different this accommodation was from her previous location.

Light flooded in from some large windows, looking out onto what appeared to be a private indoor garden of tropical plants and palms that jostled for position against the glass. It was so bright that the light hurt her eyes. She realised she had become accustomed to the gloom of her previous incarceration and it would take her a while to learn to see properly again.

She felt her handcuffs being removed, and she heard rather than saw her captors leaving the room without a word. The metal door had closed as quietly as it had opened, and as she looked around, she realised that although the trappings had changed, she was nevertheless still a prisoner.

Her eyes fell upon what appeared to be a bathroom and without further ado, she took off what remained of her filthy, stained clothing and walked into the shower enclosure. The hot water and soap that had been provided was bliss, and she stood immobile in the cubicle for a long time – just letting the clean feel of the hot water cascade over her.

When she was eventually finished, she found soft fluffy towels and a clean cotton robe ready in the bathroom. All the toiletries she could need had also been provided, and she immediately used the toothbrush and paste that had been left.

What joy of joys! I would never have guessed that just cleaning my teeth and being able to shower and wash my hair would be such a treasure to be enjoyed and savoured. I will never take them for granted again.

Walking back into the main room, feeling the plush carpet under her bare feet for the first time, she walked towards the low coffee table. A tray had appeared.

Or had it been there all along, and I just didn't see it?

It seemed that there was a pot of hot coffee, some rolls, butter, marmalade and some fresh fruit. She plunged in hungrily.

The next couple of days passed in the same way. There was no television or radio in her new accommodation, so she was still isolated from the world outside but as she felt so tired, she had to confess that she had little interest anyway. It seemed that the voice behind the lights had been true to his word, and she was now receiving much better treatment. Hopefully, she would be able to go home in a day or so, and this would all be a horrible nightmare.

On what she thought was the third or fourth morning, breakfast was brought to her room as usual. This time, however, there were also some clean, new clothes brought for her. She was handed a printed note which told her to enjoy her breakfast, and then get dressed and be ready to leave – she was going home today.

It took several minutes for the words to sink in. "Going home" – she burst into tears at the thought.

She finished her breakfast and quickly got showered and changed.

She was just ready when the metal door slid back and her

two guardians appeared. They placed a hood over her head and then took an arm each and escorted her out into what she presumed was the passageway that she had entered by. She was frightened by the hood.

Why had that been necessary?

They seemed to arrive at some sort of garage, as she could smell exhaust fumes and petrol. One of her captors placed a hand on her head and pushed her down and to the right – presumably to get into a car. Her presumption was correct, and she felt herself sink into soft leather seats. From her position, she thought she had been placed in the back as she could hear the front door of the vehicle open and the rocking of the car as a large person got into the seat in front of her.

The car moved off.

Despite her pleas to know where they were and where they were taking her, no one said anything. The journey was conducted in total silence.

Her fear levels rose.

She found it impossible to guesstimate how long they had been travelling. She was conscious of the growing noise of other traffic nearby, and it sounded as though the route they were taking was getting busy. The vehicle took a number of turns during the course of the journey until, suddenly, it slowed to a stop.

Whoever was in front of her quickly got out of the car and opened the door next to her. He pulled her out of the vehicle and told her that she could remove the hood in five minutes. They would know if she disobeyed, and the consequences for her and her family would be "serious," The voice was gruff, and she suspected that the man had attempted to disguise it.

With that, he got back in the car and she heard it drive off.

She waited for what she thought was enough time for "them" to get clear and then she ripped the hood from her head.

She found herself standing on a small strip of lawn in what appeared to be a commercial service yard. As her mind cranked into gear, she realised that she was actually standing at the back of the new Woolworths supermarket in Salisbury, so she was just around the corner from the DSTO building.

"Dad," she thought, and immediately, she started a stumbling run along the service yard, around the corner towards the Main North Road and the grassed area leading to the DSTO building.

Chapter 16

Having showered, shaved and breakfasted, McAllister and Banjo had gone back into the base at Woomera to start another day of paperwork and no doubt face more unending questions.

By 11.00, they were seated in Dr Schuster's private office. He seemed extremely irritable and looked dreadful. He had large, dark circles under his eyes, and such hair as he had was oily and hadn't seen a wash or comb for several days. His white coat looked grubby and crumpled. Something was clearly amiss.

"Are you ok, Dr Schuster?" asked McAllister carefully.

"Yes, yes, why?"

"Bluntly? You don't look it. Do you want to tell us what is actually worrying you?" McAllister sat quietly, looking at the obvious internal wrangling that the man opposite him was going through.

"There's nothing, McAllister. Just a few problems getting ready for the trials, that's all. Obviously, with all the attention from Canberra and London, it is a bit pressured at the moment,"

Banjo said nothing and looked at Schuster thoughtfully.

McAllister's mind flicked back to the office in Salisbury, and for some reason, the photograph on the desk came into his mind.

"How's your daughter doing?" he asked.

Schuster looked up at him, his eyes widening. His face was ashen. If he had looked bad before, he now looked positively awful. He was obviously very, very afraid and McAllister looked at him with concern.

Such was the tension that had exploded unbidden into the room, it took several moments before any of them realised that the phone was ringing.

It kept ringing insistently.

"I need to take this call," stumbled the scientist, grabbling for the receiver on his desk.

"Yes" he almost barked into the handle. Almost immediately, his whole body went rigid, and his eyes widened as though he could scarcely believe his ears. He was overtaken by a terrible shaking, and his hand went to his glasses, pushing them absentmindedly up his forehead so that they perched precariously on his dregs of oily hair.

"Thank God," he stuttered into the phone. "Thank you for letting me know. I will arrange to come back immediately,"

He replaced the receiver, and McAllister was appalled to see that large, fat tears were coursing down the scientist's face. The man before him seemed to crumple as he put elbows on to the desk, placed his head in his hands and sobbed. The sobs were deep and dreadful to hear, a testament to long-suppressed anguish.

When the worst of the storm had passed, Schuster tried to pull himself together. As he tried to stand up, he looked up and seeming to belatedly remember the question McAllister had asked him, said that his daughter was very well and that she had just arrived at the DSTO in Salisbury. He needed to get down there immediately and would have to sort out a flight.

"Why didn't you tell me that she was missing?" asked McAllister, guessing the true position.

"Because they threatened to kill her if I told anyone," replied Schuster in a wretchedly defeated voice. "I know you will have lots of questions, but I just can't deal with them now,"

Banjo got up from his seat and said that he would organise things. He left the room. McAllister helped the shaken man in front of him towards a chair on his side of the desk and said he would get him a cup of tea so that he could calm down and hopefully, by then, Banjo would be back and there would be news on the flight. Schuster clearly had no energy left for a fight, and he sank gratefully into the seat that McAllister pushed towards him, clasping and unclasping his hands, the tears still falling and clearly in emotional tatters.

As he left the room to get the promised cup of tea, McAllister's mind was churning.

At least that possibly answers one issue, but there are still so many others. None of it makes any sense. What the hell is going on here?

Chapter 17

Having organised the flight back to RAAF Edinburgh for Dr. Schuster for later that afternoon, Banjo eventually found McAllister in the armoury. He was chatting to Steve Bathurst, the Base armourer, and had just secured himself a personal sidearm – as directed by the one and only Terri Wilson. He had fired a number of rounds in the shooting range, just to keep his eye in, and had just finished when Banjo arrived to update him.

Thanking the armourer for his time and generally taking their leave, the two men left the bunker. Grateful to get some fresh air into his lungs both after the emotional events of earlier in the day and to get the pungent but somehow comforting stench of cordite from the shooting range out of his nostrils, McAllister stood quietly for a few minutes.

Banjo filled the silence by confirming that Dr Schuster was going back to Salisbury on a special flight at 1600, so he should be home about 1800 all being well. He added that the scientist had been given a week's compassionate leave, but that would not preclude him from answering questions in the meantime – just that he would not have to return to Woomera for the rest of the trials programme.

McAllister still said nothing but nodded his understanding.

"We will have to go back on Monday to see him – and his daughter - to start the debriefing, but at the moment, she is apparently being checked over by the medics. The initial report is that she appears to be in reasonably good shape, notwithstanding her abduction. We will go down on the red-eye on Monday morning,"

Again, McAllister said nothing but nodded.

Slowly, he said, "In that case, Banjo, I want to go up to Coober Pedy tomorrow. Just want a change of scenery whilst I am up here,"

"What on earth do you want to go there for?" asked his friend.

"Just a change, as I say. Need to clear my head a bit. It is all so claustrophobic up here, and we don't seem to be making progress on anything – although hopefully, now that Miss Schuster is home safe and reasonably well, we might start getting to the bottom of things,"

"Do you want some company?" asked Banjo.

"Thanks, but no thanks. Not this time. I am not going to be very good company, and as I say, my head just needs a good sort out,"

"Okay, mate," said Banjo. "Just make sure you don't forget the rules about the Land Rover – they are there for a reason – and make sure you have a firearm on you anyway. Do you know anyone up there?"

"Nope. Just going with the flow," he replied.

"Well, if you speak nicely to Alison in the office, she might have a contact who will give you a safe and clean bed for the night. Don't expect there to be loads of hotels or motels available because there aren't. You really are out in the wilds there – it exists purely for the opal mines and as a staging post for the sheep ranchers, so it really is tough. Besides, I would prefer to know that you had access to a telephone or radio set just in case anything happens. The way this case is going, you just never know and having you completely off grid won't help.

If you do get into trouble, just remember that all the sheep stations and cattle ranches out here will have radio sets as it is their lifeline and most will usually help you out if you are in a bind."

"Thanks, Banjo. Really appreciate that. I will speak to Alison as you have suggested and will let you know tonight where I will be heading. And yes," he added with a small smile touching his face for the first time that day, "I will let you know when I get there safely,"

With that, they parted and McAllister walked back to the main administrative buildings, where he sought out Alison. As Banjo had correctly predicted, having checked her Filofax, she did indeed have a contact in Coober Pedy. She even put a call in to make sure that his anticipated host had space to take him.

"That's all sorted then," she said with a smile. "Kaz McNamara will look after you. As you get towards the outskirts of Coober Pedy going north on the Stuart Highway, you need to hang a left when you see the wooden sign "Paradise Acres,"

"I beg your pardon," said McAllister, thinking that this had been a long day after a short night, and he must have misheard.

She laughed again.

"Paradise Acres," Alison repeated. "Somehow, I think you will enjoy it there. It's about two miles down a dust track, so make sure you don't get there as it's turning to dusk – you won't ever find it,"

"Ok," said McAllister, will do. "And thanks, Alison, really appreciate your help,"

"Everything ok?" she asked.

"Yup. Just need to clear my head. It's been a bit of a whirlwind ever since I got to Australia, and I just need to stand back and look at things with a different eye" he replied.

She looked at him calmly, and again, he felt those eyes searching his face intently.

"Okay" she said. "Your flight back to Salisbury on Monday leaves at 0600, so please make sure you are back in good time for that,"

He gave her a mock salute, coupled with one of his lazy grins, and he turned and left the office.

"Paradise Acres? Cryin' out loud, what is this going to be?

For the first time that day, he felt his mood genuinely start to lighten and he realised he was really looking forward to getting out of the hothouse and having some time to himself.

Chapter 18

The reunion with her father was, understandably, emotional for them both. She could not remember the last time she had felt so emotionally close to him, and certainly not since her mother had died some four years before. She was grateful to be home, and she promised herself that she would never get cross or short-tempered with her father ever again and would never complain at his rules and concerns for her well-being, which she had previously categorised as "fussing" or "nosy parkering." She was grateful now that someone loved her enough to have been so worried for her – as clearly her father had been. She was shocked at the change in him and was just glad to be able to hold him tight. They stood for what seemed like a long time, clinging together in the middle of the lounge, each reluctant to let go and break the spell.

There was a Police guard, of course, but they had said that they would keep a discreet distance outside and allow the Schusters some privacy. The questions would start in the morning.

Neither of them wanted to discuss the details of what had happened; both were just rejoicing in the pleasure of being together again.

Having bumbled comfortably about in the kitchen together, putting a light supper on, and having had a couple of glasses of wine, they eventually sat down on the sofa in quiet companionship. The TV was on, but neither was paying particular attention. Both were lost in the warmth and comfort of being safely home together.

The first indication that all was not well was when she felt her stomach starting to gurgle. She suddenly needed to relieve her bowels and rushed to the bathroom. This was followed quickly by a fit of vomiting, and she began to feel extremely unwell. Her father rushed to the front door to find the Police guard, who was nowhere to be seen. He rushed outside onto the front lawn, anxiously calling for the Police, but receiving no answer, he went back into the house to call the emergency services, but the line was disconnected.

Beside himself, he ran back outside and went to his neighbour, his desperation rising.

"I can't remember their name."

Answering his frantic knocking on their front door and seeing his distress, they agreed to call the ambulance.

He went back to his own home to find his daughter now vomiting repeatedly over the toilet bowl. She was desperately trying to get back onto the toilet to relieve her bowels again. He went and found a bowl from the kitchen, and she continued vomiting into it. As he got her off the toilet to clean herself between spasms, he noticed that the stools were bloodstained.

Putting her back on the toilet, with the bowl lodged somewhat precariously in her lap, he answered the knocking at the front door, hoping against hope that it was the ambulance. In fact, it was his neighbour, confirming that they had called and the ambulance would be there as soon as it could, but it was likely to be about half an hour "because they are short of crews tonight."

When the crew finally arrived, Schuster knew that things

were not good. He saw the glances exchanged by the two ambulance men, who quickly got a drip into his daughter's arm. They placed her on a trolley and got her into the back of the ambulance, saying they were taking her to Modbury Hospital. He was slightly relieved, as this was much closer than the one in Adelaide, and it had only been built about three years ago, so it was state of the art with really modern facilities.

He said he would follow on in his car.

The wait at the hospital was lengthy. A consultant eventually came to see him and asked a series of questions about what his daughter had eaten in the last 24 – 36 hours, whether she had any allergies, etc., etc. No information was forthcoming in return, and it seemed to him that the medics were purposely keeping their cards close to their chest.

He was desperately tired and very worried.

He stayed there all night and must have dozed off in the chair in the hallway because he suddenly became aware of a lot of activity centred upon his daughter's room.

Another consultant then came to see him and told him that his daughter's condition had worsened and that they were doing all that they could to stabilise her. However, she now seemed to be suffering from liver failure, and she was very seriously ill. He should go in and see her, he was told.

At some stage, the Police arrived. He was asked where his Police guard was, and he explained that when his daughter had been taken ill, the guard could not be found, so he didn't know.

Events became a blur.

Everything crystallised, however when, at 1133 am that Saturday morning, a solemn-faced doctor came towards him and told him that he was sorry, but his daughter – his beloved Zoe – had passed away. At this stage, they did not know the cause of death, but there would have to be a full autopsy.

He could not take it all in.

Only a few hours ago he had been elated to have his daughter home. Now, she was dead.

He could not process it.

He nodded numbly to the doctor in front of him and turned to go.

The Police Officer, now with him, spoke to him, but it was as if he was underwater. The words were jumbled and he could not make sense of them. He was guided down to the car park, where he was put into a Police car and driven home. He couldn't be bothered to worry about his own car still in the hospital car park.

Again, the officer said something to him that did not make any sense to him.

He just walked into the hall, closed the front door and was overwhelmed by the silence of the house and the enormity of his loss.

Having found a bottle of whisky at the back of a cupboard in the kitchen, he went and sat back on the sofa, recalling how wonderful their last night had been. He drank several glasses of the warming liquid.

He got up and walked through the internal door from the laundry into the garage.

Fumbling around, he opened his old metal box that was kept in the corner and unwrapped his pistol. The DSTO had insisted that he have a personal firearm at home "in case you ever need it," but he had refused to keep it in the house. It had, therefore, been put away in a corner.

Well, I need it now.

He loaded the chamber, pointed the barrel under his chin and pulled the trigger.

Chapter 19

Oblivious to the events unfolding in Salisbury, McAllister set off for Coober Pedy at 0500 on the Saturday morning. As he hit the road in the Defender, dawn started to break and he felt a sense of release and freedom that he had not felt since arriving on site.

Woomera had been quite claustrophobic, but then, in fairness, it had been a fairly intense, emotional start to his stay here.

The Stuart Highway opened up before him, and he pushed on as quickly as he could. It wasn't long before he passed the site of the crash on Thursday night. The wreckage had been removed, but the road surface was still charred and burnt. He shivered, the face of Hendrik Cronje coming back to him yet again.

He revelled in the sparse emptiness that opened up before him, and he felt the pressures of the investigation starting to ebb away and his mind clear.

The miles clicked past, and for a long time, he was the only vehicle on the road. As he got further north, large artic lorries with three, four and sometimes five trailers behind, full of sheep or cattle, started passing him going south.

They can certainly shift; they are so long they *look like road trains.*

He soon realised there were no road houses or food places to stop at – or none that he had found yet. A pull-in at the side of the road where he could take a break was the best he could do.

As he turned off the engine of the Defender, all he could hear were the chicadas chirruping and the wild expanse of nothingness that was the beginning of the Far North area of South Australia enveloped him.

The warmth of the July sun was starting to break through, and he relaxed in the driver's seat with the doors open to capture what breeze there was.

His mind started to work, reviewing everything from the bracelets to the murder of Lucy Andrews, the loss of the plans, the abduction of Zoe Schuster, the break-in at the security office and the role (if any) of the Jindivik Winery in all of this. It made no sense, and without realising it, he fell into a warm, comfortable sleep.

He came awake with a start as he felt and heard something land on the bonnet of the Defender. As his eyes focussed, he found himself looking into the nodding head of a fairly large, beautifully coloured bird. Its sharp black eyes seemed to assess him coolly, and as McAllister moved in his seat, the bird quickly flew off.

Some sort of parrot.

He realised that he knew nothing about the creatures that lived here. *Better do some homework.*

As he turned the key in the ignition and noise suddenly flooded the air, a flock of the same coloured birds that had been quietly sitting in a nearby tree observing him took to flight. It was a magnificent sight.

McAllister smiled and headed on towards Coober Pedy,

realising that he was now much later than he had anticipated.

As Alison had promised, the sign for Paradise Acres was a rather battered wooden sign sitting at an angle on the side of the road about three miles outside of Coober Pedy town. He followed the undulating track and gave thanks for the fact that he had the Land Rover. The dust was everywhere already, and the track was extremely bumpy.

A further mile and a half passed when he saw another similarly weather-beaten sign pointing off to the right. Following it, he bounced along until he came to a halt by some swings and a see-saw. He couldn't see a house – just some rock in front of him and not a lot else. He got out of the vehicle and looked around.

At that, a noise behind him made him turn and from the rock, a door had opened.

A tall, jolly woman approached him.

"G'day – you must be Mike," she said.

He smiled. "Kaz, I presume?"

"That's me," she said. "Come on down. I'll get the kettle on."

Without further ado, she turned and led the way back to the door in the rock. He was immediately met with a set of steps that went down into the bedrock and a large living area opened up before him.

She went over to the corner and put the kettle on the hob. The single light bulb in the middle of the room had been fixed by hooking the wire across the walls and ceiling, and although sparse, the living room was comfortably furnished.

It was dry and cool, and McAllister suddenly realised that the heat here in the summer must be absolutely ferocious.

Whilst making the tea in an old battered teapot that she said her mum had brought over with her from Ireland, she filled McAllister in on the fact that most of the homes up here were built underground because of the heat; she explained water was sparse as they only have a very low rainfall, and that most of the work up here was linked to the opal mine. In response to his question about the swings and seesaw outside, Kaz explained that she had five children with ages ranging from 3 to 19: all of them were still at home, and her husband worked at the mine. Schooling was done in the town in the fairly new school buildings, and a new pre-school, or "Kindy" as she called it, had started just a couple of years before, so her youngest would be starting there in August as soon as she was four.

"A tough life then, Kaz," he said thoughtfully.

"Well, you get used to it, but it certainly isn't for the faint-hearted. My eldest son has already started working for the mine, but I don't know if he will stay up here."

She gestured to him to sit at the dining room table that was at one end of the large cavernous space.

"What brings you here then, Mike?" she asked as she put the steaming mugs of tea in front of them.

"Just taking the chance to look around a bit whilst I am here. I was told that there is someone else up here with the same name as me, so thought I might just have a dig around and see if there is some long lost relation here waiting to be discovered" he said smiling.

"McAllister – that right?" she asked. "You from Wales, by any chance?"

He looked at her jolly face and her long auburn hair.

The heat must play havoc with her pale skin.

"Yes, as a matter of fact," he replied. "Newport."

"Hah," she laughed.

"You might want to call in on old Huw then. Don't know if he *is* anything to do with your family, but he is certainly a McAllister and is also from Wales. You might find him down at The Old Colonial in town a bit later on if you are interested."

"Thanks for that, Kaz. I will."

Just at that moment, noise erupted from the door and stairs and in a flurry of bags and arguing, three children arrived. McAllister noted they were all auburn-haired, and he had no doubt that these were the middle three. With the change in noise level, the youngest member of the family came wandering out from what was obviously her bedroom off the living area, rubbing the sleep from her eyes, which opened wide as she spied the stranger sitting and talking with her mother.

The other children took absolutely no notice whatsoever as they engulfed their mother in hugs and kisses and a series of demands, from milk and biscuits to help with their maths. It was a wonderful homely feeling, and McAllister suddenly missed his own family back in Wales. *Must call Mum and Dad when I get back to Woomera.*

Having been shown to his room, which was a small but well-

124

equipped space carved into the side of the cavern and which was obviously kept for unexpected visitors, he dumped his bag and told Kaz he was going into the town.

She gave him directions, and said that as he was going to be back after dark, then she would get her husband, Eamonn, to put a light out at the turning off the highway. She also said that she would send a call out to the base at Woomera to let them know that he had arrived safely.

McAllister said he was grateful and headed off, leaving Kaz to the happy cacophony of demands from her family.

Chapter 20

The trip into the actual township of Coober Pedy was uneventful. The harsh, arid landscape that surrounded the town was a testament to the challenges the severe temperatures must bring to the townsfolk. He parked the Land Rover and wandered down the main street noticing the Post office, the general store and a few other small shops that had a variety of things of interest.

On the other side of the road, he saw The Old Colonial.

It could only have been a pub.

He grinned as he walked on over.

A huge ceiling fan laconically tried to stir the air, and there were a number of hard, tough-looking men whom he presumed were from the mine, busy downing pints.

Over in the corner of the bar, there was one guy sitting on his own with a pint in front of him. He had a tousled mop of salt and pepper hair that had obviously been almost jet black in his younger days, but when he looked up, his bright blue eyes were clear and direct. For some reason, McAllister just knew that this was Huw. He went over to the bar and stood next to him. The man's gaze never left him.

In for a penny.

He ordered a beer and turned to the man.

"You don't happen to be Huw McAllister, do you?" he asked.

"Depends who's asking," came the reply, not unkindly. The

eyes twinkled even though the face remained calm.

"Well, my name is also McAllister – Mike, from Newport in South Wales. And I just wondered if there is any connection?"

"Newport, you say? Well, now, I haven't thought about that neck of the woods for a very long time. Why would any connection interest a young'un like you?"

"Someone asked me if I knew you; I said I didn't, but as it is a reasonably unusual name, and as I was passing this way, I just thought I would ask – that's all," replied McAllister.

"Fair dooze, mate. And yeah, as it happens, I did come from Newport but a long time ago now. Who's ya, Dad?"

"Rhys McAllister – he married my Mum, Hannah Taylor, just after the War."

At this, his companion burst out laughing, slapping his thigh with his hand. Clearly delighted, he almost shouted, "Yeah, I know, mate: I was at the wedding – last thing I did before I left the Old Country. Well, I never. So you are Hannah and Rhys' boy. Any others?"

"Just my sister who is three years younger than me," McAllister replied.

"This calls for a celebration," said Huw, and promptly ordered more beers with whisky chasers. "I knew you had to be something to do with the family the minute you walked through the door," he said. "You are the spitting image of your grandfather. Mind you, probably never met him, did ya?"

McAllister shook his head.

"Shame. Had a bad War himself: the First lot, that is. He always said that the only good thing that ever came out of it was that he was nursed by your Gran, Anika, and they fell in love and got married in 1918. That's when they moved back to Pembrokeshire, of course. Caused one hell of a stink with her people, apparently, but there you go.."

Pembrokeshire? Didn't know we had any connection there.

Huw was clearly enjoying himself hugely, and he asked. "So how long you up here for then?"

"Just overnight," replied McAllister.

"Crikey – then we'd better get our skates on, lad." And with that, Huw McAllister downed three-quarters of a pint of beer in two swallows, threw back the whisky chaser, and beckoned McAllister off his chair and to follow him.

"Um, where are we going?" asked McAllister.

"Over to the mine – we might just catch him," replied Huw over his shoulder.

"Who?" ventured McAllister.

"Well, your uncle Geraint of course lad. Don't tell me you don't know about him either? Goodness me, has your Dad not told you anything about our family?" and with that, he strode out of the doors and jumped into a battered white pickup truck parked virtually right outside the pub.

They bounced along the dirt roads for several miles, with Huw happily chattering away about reminiscences of the Old Country, and they gradually hove into view of a large mine. Huw drove straight through the entrance gates towards what appeared to be an office building. He jumped out of the truck, and strode towards the main door and disappeared. McAllister followed.

Just inside the door, Huw had found another man and was talking to him in an animated fashion. As McAllister entered, both of them turned and looked at him. The second man had a similar reaction to Huw's original response at the pub, and they immediately walked over to meet him. Introductions were made, and the second man – bearing a very close resemblance to Huw but slightly younger – was Geraint McAllister.

All three then returned to the pickup truck, and they drove back to the town – and The Old Colonial, where more drinks were ordered and downed.

It turned out that Geraint was four years younger than Huw, but both had emigrated to Australia in 1950 to start a new life after the War. He dabbled in opal mining as he had an open opal field down on his Station (as he called it).

To much grinning, thigh slapping and general good humour McAllister asked what that was, and Geraint explained that he had about 2,500 square miles of sheep Station just north of Andamooka "about 300 miles by road from here over towards the Flinders Rangers and Lake Torrens." When he had enough opals to make the trip worthwhile, he travelled over to see Huw and the "bloke at the Mine" to sell them.

And, happily, this was one of those occasions.

The door to the bar opened, and no one took any notice until a booming voice rang out: "Is there a bloke here by the name of Mike McAllister?"

Silence settled amongst the gathered customers, and all eyes turned to the three McAllister men sitting at the table in the corner.

The man asking stood about 6'6' and was built like an ox. He had a huge beer belly that hung over his trousers, but the giveaway was that he was wearing a Police uniform.

McAllister groaned inwardly.

"Here," he called out.

The Police Officer turned and strode towards him. As soon as he reached the table, he leaned down and, lowering his voice, said: "Mike? Kaz McNamara has been on the blower. Apparently" – and at this, he further lowered his voice conspiratorially – "Woomera needs you to call in urgently. You can come with me over to the Station if that would help?"

The silence in the Bar was almost palpable as McAllister got up out of his seat, nodded to his two Uncles, who were both looking slightly stunned and walked out of the room with the Police Officer.

They walked down the street about 100 yards and then crossed over to a small side road where there was a prefab building with "South Australian Police" on a round light stuck on the outside.

On his call in, McAllister was informed of the events in Salisbury that afternoon and the deaths of both Zoe and Dr Stephen Schuster. He was told to get back to Woomera as soon as possible tomorrow. "Too late today," was the message, "but you are needed back here pronto, so leave at first light, and don't spare the horses."

When he finally left the Police Station, he was relieved to walk out into the early evening dusk and take in some fresh air. He hadn't realised how stuffy it had been inside.

Mind you, not exactly a joyous call.

He thought back to the last time he had seen Dr Schuster. How tired and emotionally wrung out he had looked. He recalled the obvious relief when the telephone call had come through.

And now this.

What on earth was going on?

It took him a few seconds to realise that he was being observed – quietly and unobtrusively - by his two newfound uncles, who were leaning against the bonnet of the pickup he had travelled in earlier. Both had their hats on and were looking at him with genuine concern and almost palpable bewilderment.

"Look, matey, my place is only up the road – why don't we go there and you can fill us in on what is going on?" said Huw.

McAllister simply nodded in agreement, and all three men got into the truck. The "only up the road" drive was, in fact, about 10 miles out of town in the opposite direction to Kaz MacNamara's place, but not on the A87 – the ute had swung off the main highway onto The Kempe Road towards Oodnadatta. Trying to make conversation, Huw nodded to their right: "See that, Mike: that is the boundary of the Woomera Range – stretches all the way back to Woomera itself and I guess you know where that is."

McAllister was genuinely surprised. Even though he had been told how large the Range was, there was nothing like seeing the physical manifestation of the boundaries to clarify the mind. It seemed endless, and he realised that the chain link fence that formed the boundary must have taken years to build. Either that, or a very large number of men and machines. Even then, it would not have been a quick job.

Again, he nodded.

There was no more discussion until they turned off The Kempe Road, leaving the Range fence behind in the distance, and started moving towards some large mounds of rock. As with Paradise Acres, McAllister soon learned that these mounds were, in fact, the top of homes built underground. They finally stopped, and both of McAllister's uncles got out.

McAllister followed, and all three men strode towards the mound at the end of the row, where an old Land Rover was parked outside. They walked in the door which was almost hidden by the rubble outside, and made their way down into the main house itself. This was much smaller than Kaz MacNamara's place.

But then she does have a family to accommodate.

This place shrieked that his uncle Huw lived alone.

There were absolutely no home comforts at all, no soft furnishings, no small "feminine touches," as his Mum called them. Just an old arm chair by the range over in the corner, a small sofa that had obviously seen better days, a table with two chairs and an old lamp.

There were two other things, however, that had pride of

place in the room: one was a large old Westinghouse refrigerator; the other was a piece of wooden furniture that looked suspiciously like an old radiogram. His gran had one back in Newport, and he thought that he could see the similarity.

How on earth did he keep that in any sort of condition out here?

Huw saw him looking at it, and he walked over and lifted the lid. "See you are admiring my beauty," he said cheerfully.

"Yup. Won her off Wally Warburton down at The Old Colonial in a poker game one night. Fantastic she is. Even got some records. Do you like Nat King Cole? Or Glenn Miller? I can get the ABC radio on a good day, but that's about it." His eyes had lit up as he had run through the pleasures of the radiogram, and he was clearly waiting for McAllister to say something complimentary. He obliged and said he did like both Nat King Cole and Glenn Miller. Before he could say anything else, Uncle Huw had pulled out the battered sleeve of the long play record and had put the record itself on the turntable, having deftly turned the unit on, almost without McAllister having noticed. The strains of "Moonlight Serenade" promptly echoed through the house.

Uncle Geraint had made himself at home, and by the time McAllister turned back to the main part of the room, three beers had materialised out of the fridge and were opened and standing on the table. "Right, young fella," he said; "time for a serious chat. What's really going on, and what the hell are you doing in Woomera?"

As he revealed that he was an RAF Police Officer here on secondment from the UK and that he had genuinely driven up to see if the McAllister he had heard about was related, the eyebrows above the two pairs of piercing blue eyes that had been watching him intently had been rising. The two brothers looked at each other.

"You in some sort of trouble?" asked Huw.

"Not exactly, " said McAllister, "although I must confess that there seem to have been some challenging events since I got here. Sorry, I can't say more – I do hope you understand."

Huw looked pensively down at the beer bottle that was by now in his hand.

"Look, lad, I was in the last lot. Spent several years as a guest of the Japanese up on the Burmese railroad when my Army unit was overrun and taken prisoner in Singapore. I don't like people very much, and I keep myself to myself. But I wasn't born yesterday. I've met men who had a certain stamp about them. Wherever they went, trouble followed. And you have that stamp all over you. That and the bruises on your face and arms. So you might like to try again."

He took another long swig of his beer and looked very directly at McAllister.

"I genuinely can't say much, I'm afraid," said McAllister. "But there seem to be lots of things happening – which may or may not be connected. And my task is to try and unpick all of that, and stop whatever it is from happening. And I genuinely don't know what that "whatever" actually is. In the couple of weeks that I have been here in Australia, there has been a theft of secret material, a second break-in at the same place, and five people are dead – one of them in the most horrible of circumstances after being held prisoner, and two after a car chase where they hit a kangaroo and crashed and burned."

"So you were involved in that little number up on the Stuart then?" interjected Geraint.

"How do you know about that?" asked McAllister.

Geraint laughed. "Big news around these parts, lad. Especially when the cops are all over it like a dose of the clap. You armed?"

McAllister nodded.

"Just as well," continued Geraint. "Sounds like you might be needing it. I take it you are back off to Woomera in the morning, then?"

Again, McAllister nodded.

"Then you had better get back to Kaz's place pronto. It will be getting dark before you get there. But listen: if you ever need any help, you can always put a call in to Huw here over the radio. Or to me at the homestead on Beltana Station, just north of Andamooka township. Don't bother with that idiot Jacko at the Cop Shop: it will take him all day to make up his mind about what he thinks he can do to help you. We can always round some of the lads up to help should you ever be in a jam."

McAllister was genuinely grateful and said so.

Quickly finishing their beers and taking their leave, Huw and McAllister left Geraint to the fridge and Glenn Miller and went back outside to the ute. Darkness was falling, and not for the first time, McAllister was glad not to be doing this part of the journey on his own. They quickly got back to town, and McAllister went to retrieve his Land Rover, which was still parked on the main street almost opposite The Old Colonial, where he had left it earlier that afternoon.

"You be ok to find your way back to the MacNamaras?" asked Huw

McAllister nodded and thanked his uncle, saying that he would be in touch as soon as he could and they could perhaps have a proper get-together. Huw simply nodded, gunned the pickup, swung a U-turn in the middle of the main road, and drove off back toward his place.

McAllister got in the Land Rover and headed out southbound on the A87. Kaz MacNamara had been as good as her word, and he saw the blazing oil drum on the right-hand side of the road next to the "Paradise Acres" sign, and which was obviously the marker that she had asked her husband to put out for him.

He turned off the main road and headed onwards.

This was no joke of a journey in the dark.

McAllister bounced along the track, the old Land Rover squeaking and groaning at the terrain, and he was relieved when another burning oil drum appeared. Before long, he was back by the swings and see-saw at the front of Kaz's place. This time, a white, fairly battered ute was standing in front of the entrance. McAllister knocked, and Kaz opened the door. She ushered him into the lounge, where the entire MacNamara clan seemed to have congregated: she made the introductions, particularly to her husband, Eamonn and whom McAllister thanked for the signposting.

He was directed to a chair at the table, and with that, a joyous, noisy, fun-filled meal started. Everyone seemed to talk all at once, and there was the usual banter between the children. It made a wonderfully homely, friendly break from the drama and the tense events of the last couple of weeks. McAllister felt the wave of weariness start to sweep over him, and with Kaz promising to call Huw and then Woomera on the radio as soon as she had cleared away, he was packed off to his room where, having simply taken his boots off, he sunk gratefully onto the deceptively plump mattress and fell promptly asleep.

He woke the following morning to almost pitch dark – there were no lights of any kind on in his bedroom and no windows, of course. He looked at the luminescent dial of his wrist watch, which announced that the time was 0400.

Best get moving.

He groped around in his holdall next to the bed for the small flashlight that he always carried with him. He had a quick slosh of a wash in the basin on the stand in the room with the water kindly left in the jug for him, changed into a fresh shirt and jeans, and repacked his small holdall. He noted the time was now 0415.

He quietly opened the door to his room and made his way into the lounge. Kaz had left a small night light on for him so that he could find his way easily, and he moved up the steps to the front door and let himself out into the almost cold morning. The sky was streaking with the early dawn which was apparently not far off, and as he got into the driving seat of the Land Rover, he wondered what this day would bring.

He gunned the Land Rover into life and made his way

somewhat gingerly down the track. As he turned right onto the main highway, he realised that there could be no rest stops admiring the local wildlife today – it would be pedal to the metal all the way.

Chapter 21

McAllister drove into the car park at Woomera nearly four hours later. He had pushed the old Land Rover as fast as she would go, and he hadn't stopped on the way down from Coober Pedy. He had relished the trip – it had certainly allowed him time to get some of his thoughts in order.

He quickly made his way into the main administration area, noting as he did so that Alison was already in office – he saw her Ford Falcon in the car park.

Thank goodness for that. Some calm heads may well be needed.

His little voices were chirping big time.

He walked into the main office being used for the investigation into the car crash to find a number of mobile notice boards had blossomed since he was last in here.

Was it only 36 hours or so ago?

There was now a blizzard of photographs, written details, arrows pointing between different pieces of information, and right in the middle, an enlarged photograph of Hendrik Cronje.

And next to it, one of Chips McInerney.

What? Why is his photograph up on the board with Cronje?

As he stood in front of the photographs, trying to assimilate this information, he heard a cough behind him.

"He was the other body in the car," she said. He turned and saw Terri Wilson behind him, observing his reaction.

"But we left him at The Shack asleep when we went down to Crazy Pete's," he said. "How is he linked in with all of this?"

"We don't yet know exactly," she said. "But it was definitely him in the car with Cronje. Dental records have confirmed it. We are looking into his recent work and his background to see what we can find; we don't know how he met Cronje or what the link is there, but it was definitely him."

"A possible, then, for taking the blueprints from the DSTO," responded McAllister.

"Yes," she said. "A possible," McAllister noted, however, that she looked doubtful.

"And the bracelet?"

"Doesn't look as though McInerney had one; when Cronje's body was retrieved from the vehicle, the bracelet was still on the arm and it is currently being examined. We aren't sure what it is yet, but I will let you know as soon as we have some news."

"And what happened with Dr Schuster?" asked McAllister.

Terri Wilson calmly and succinctly explained the situation as far as they had been able to piece it together. And no, she said, they did not know what had happened to the Police guard posted to his house – the officer had disappeared; and no, they did not know that he had a firearm at home; and no, they did not know where his daughter had been held,[delete] hostage.

"What did she actually die of?" asked McAllister.

"The toxicology guys aren't sure, but it looks like a slow-working – inevitably fatal – poison, possibly plant-based. Should have the final results on that as well later on this morning."

McAllister felt his shoulders slump as he took in the magnitude of everything that had been happening whilst he had been up in Coober Pedy. He had only been gone a short time, and yet the world seemed to have gone completely mad.

"Get back to The Shack," she continued. "SA Police have done a search of McInerney's room: go back with Banjo and go through it again, just in case they have missed something. I have called for the phone records, incidentally, so you don't need to put that in hand."

McAllister nodded.

"Is there any truth in the rumour that he was in the running for a job at a new start-up computer company in the US?" asked McAllister.

"Didn't know about that," she replied: "Do you know where and which company?"

"I think it was in California; a new company called Apple Computers. But it was only a rumour – I don't have anything definite from Chips, just cafeteria gossip."

Terri Wilson nodded and jotted something down on her hand with her pen. "Will look into that as well. The phone records might help in that regard. Let me know if you find anything. In any event, report back here at 1300. We will regroup then and decide what action to take next – hopefully, the various toxicology results will be back by then."

He nodded, and she turned away without further ado.

Banjo walked in and immediately made his way over. Nodding towards the board, he said, "So you have been filled in then?"

McAllister nodded and relayed Miss Wilson's orders.

They left together, got into the Land Rover and were back at The Shack within 5 minutes.

Chapter 22

The South Australian Police search appeared to have been reasonably thorough, if extremely untidy. As they entered The Shack, a jumble of furniture and possessions met them. Items were in no particular order – and did not even appear to be in any particular room order, either.

Almost as though the place had been ransacked.

"Do you know who was leading this search?" McAllister asked Banjo.

"No – but I'll find out. This isn't their usual style at all," and with that, he rummaged around the items on the floor and managed to find the telephone. Fortunately, it was still connected, and he immediately called the office. They would find out and come back to him, they said.

"I'll get the camera from the truck," he added and returned very shortly afterward with a Polaroid. "I think we'll take a couple of snaps, just in case," and with that, he pointed the camera at the mess in the living room and kitchen and took a photograph of each, the developing print emerging seconds later from the front of the camera. As Banjo took more photographs, McAllister lined them up on the window sill to dry so that they could then touch them safely without leaving fingerprints all over the face of the images.

Once that had been done, they moved into what had been Chips' room. That was even worse than the rest of the house. They decided to work methodically clockwise from the door and, having taken the "starting position" photo, went through what turned out to be a very small collection of personal items and clothing.

"Not much here," commented Banjo.

"Mmm," replied McAllister. "Almost as if he wasn't coming back and that he cleared out in a hurry. Nearly all his clothes are gone, save for a few items that he either missed or didn't need anymore."

"Certainly got that feel about it," agreed Banjo, and the search progressed.

They finally moved the bed and the small, empty wardrobe.

There was a stack of magazines under the bed. McAllister picked them up and started flicking through the pages. An unusual mix. Some of the top shelf stuff, but also a lot of computing and science magazines mixed in together with the odd "Homes and Gardens" type publication. He recalled Chips reading some sort of technical magazine on the plane when they had come up to Woomera on that first day, so he paid more attention to those. As he ruffled through the pages, a piece of paper fell from the folds with one line of typewritten text:

8573619875928632189537139416l

He turned the piece of paper over – it was blank. There was nothing else. Just the list of numbers.

He called out to Banjo, who came over to him and peered over his shoulder at the piece of paper. After taking the usual photograph, McAllister folded the paper up and placed it in his wallet for safekeeping.

"We'll need to log this in when we get back," he said. Banjo nodded.

Nothing else emerged from their search. They took the opportunity to put things roughly in order back in the lounge, but other than that, they agreed they would head straight back to the base and find Terri Wilson.

As McAllister was retrieving the now-dry Polaroids from the window ledge, the phone rang. Banjo picked it up. He said nothing but grunted in response to whoever was on the other end and then hung up.

"That was Fred up in the base office," he said. "The search here was led by Sergeant First Class Ian Mitchener. I know him – an excellent officer. This is definitely not his style. Do you think this place could have been turned over *after* the Police search?"

"Quite honestly, mate," replied McAllister. "Nothing would surprise me about this anymore. It certainly is a mess, and I have never seen a Police scene left in such a state. Where is Mitchener?"

"We might get lucky and find him at the Base. Let's go."

And with that, they hurried out to the truck and got back to the main base area as fast as they could. They hurtled through the main doors and up to the office.

Alison was there, busy dealing with a phone that appeared to never stop ringing, people waiting to speak to her and a number of piles of paper that she was heroically keeping in order.

She got to McAllister and Banjo as soon as she could.

"You are in luck," she said. McAllister knew he liked her. "He is up with Terri Wilson at the moment. They are in the dark office."

Seeing McAllister's bewilderment, Banjo said: "Don't worry. I know where that is. Thanks Ali"

McAllister nodded his thanks and both men turned and left the busy Alison to keep order in what was obviously a chaotic situation.

They raced up the stairs, through the main Provost office with its jungle of boards and straight through to an inconspicuous-looking door at the back of the room. Although McAllister had seen it before, he had assumed – wrongly, as it was turning out – that this was a store cupboard.

Banjo went straight to the door and tapped three times.

As if by magic, it opened, and a uniformed RAAF Provost officer was standing on the other side – duly armed and clearly ready for any attempt to enter without authority. He radioed in and was given permission to allow them access.

They moved into a small hallway, and the door was locked and bolted from the inside behind them. The Provost Officer then moved to another door on the right-hand side and opened it to reveal an inner hallway with a lift. They moved to the lift, and as the doors closed behind them, McAllister whispered to Banjo:

"This is all a bit James Bond, isn't it?"

Banjo laughed and said that McAllister had forgotten exactly what they were doing at Woomera.

"It isn't exactly the Magic Roundabout up here – at least not in the innocent sense," he replied. "We have to have strict security measures, but we don't like to advertise the fact."

McAllister made a bit of a thoughtful face, and the short journey downwards progressed in silence.

The lift stopped, doors opened and they walked out into another hallway. They were clearly now some way under the actual base, but McAllister had completely lost all sense of direction. They moved forward and opened another door on the left this time.

Again, they were met with a uniformed presence – another two RAAF Provosts, heavily armed this time, with both side arms and sub-machine pistols. They were searched and asked to officially "sign in," and one of the officers then called through on his radio... The doors opposite where they were standing clicked open.

Electronically operated then. This really is turning out to be quite an eye-opener.

They walked through the doorway into what was obviously a high-security briefing room. The doors closed behind them automatically. They were faced with a long, highly polished mahogany table – elliptical in shape – with high-backed executive chairs down either side.

If all the seats were taken, this sits about 24 people – with one for luck at the head of the table itself.

There was a large projection screen behind the table at the head of the room and a lectern with a microphone, presumably for when a larger audience was necessary.

The only seats that were occupied were seven at the furthest end: three on either side of the head position and the main seat itself, which McAllister noted was occupied by a man in a suit that he hadn't met before. The man had a closed, thin face and wore glasses. His suit was immaculate, and McAllister thought to himself that this was definitely some sort of spook.

The man was flanked by Norman Reynolds, Terri Wilson and a man he assumed to be the Base Commander Iain Carmichael – McAllister noted the scrambled egg on the RAAF hat placed carefully on the tabletop – on the one side; and three men in SA Police uniform on the other. Due to his insignia, McAllister realised that the man immediately on the Chairman's left was the Commissioner of the South Australian Police, Frank Taylor. To his left was none other than Chief Superintendent James, whom he had met in Salisbury.

That seems like a lifetime ago.

To his left again was the final participant, a more junior officer whom McAllister did not know.

Somewhat belatedly, McAllister realised that there was another man sitting quietly at the back of the room and who appeared to be taking no part in the discussions but who was watching intently.

"Thank you for joining us, gentlemen," said the man at the head of the table. McAllister decided to call him Head Shed. Seemed appropriate somehow.

He got the feeling this was going to take a while, not least when Head Shed indicated that they should take a seat.

Chapter 23

The discussion was well structured, and clearly, Head Shed had a strict meeting formula that he intended to keep to. Neither McAllister nor Banjo were asked to contribute much at all – other than confirming that Cronje and another had been in the Datsun the night of the accident and for McAllister to confirm the information in relation to the bracelets that he had already passed to Terri Wilson.

McAllister and Banjo did not learn much – whether the meat and drink of the meeting had already taken place before their arrival was a matter for debate – but what had become apparent was that the Australian Secret Service was heavily involved in all of this somehow.

In reaching the conclusion of the meeting, Head Shed finally turned to McAllister.

"Well, Sergeant McAllister. I will leave you in Miss Wilson's capable hands. You will remain involved in this matter, together with Paterson, and will report directly to her in all things. Is that clear?"

McAllister nodded and mumbled something approaching a "Yes sir."

Head Shed continued: "We are stretched at the moment, McAllister, so it will seem that you will both have to get on with it. You have the authority to draw whatever resources you need. We have a number of issues that we are looking into at a national and international level, but up here, you will essentially be our contingency against further developments. Is *that* clear?"

McAllister noted that both the Base Commander and the Commissioner of Police both looked skyward at that point. Clearly, there were internal politics at play here on top of everything else.

Again, McAllister nodded.

"Any questions?" rapped Head Shed.

"Er, yes, Sir," piped up McAllister. "What killed Lucy Andrews and was it the same cause of death for Zoe Schuster? I haven't heard the outcome of the toxicological tests."

There was a nasty, awkward little silence broken only by noisy teeth-sucking coming from the direction of Chief Superintendent James, who was rewarded with a severe stare both from Head Shed and the Commissioner.

Head Shed waved a hand towards Norman Reynolds, "Your bailiwick, I think?"

Bailiwick? What sort of character was this bloke?

Reynolds turned to the two junior officers, and his face was grave.

"It would seem that both the WRAAF officer and Miss Schuster were poisoned. Certainly Miss Andrews had been tortured prior to being killed; Miss Schuster seems to have been held captive but not physically injured in any way prior to her release. We are still not sure what the reason for both events is.

In the case of Miss Schuster, the toxicology reports have revealed a very unusual trace. We haven't come across it before, which is why it has taken some time for us to confirm what we are actually dealing with. We think it is a substance called Abrin, which is a natural poison found in the seeds of a plant called the Jequirity Pea. They are from the same horticultural family, Fabaceae, as our own Sturt's Desert Pea, which you may have seen as the emblem of South Australia."

At this point, Head Shed raised an irritated eyebrow, indicating that the conversation should move on pronto.

Reynolds duly took the hint as to who was actually in control of the room and continued.

"The peas are red in colour, with a black spot covering one end. In essence, Abrin is similar to Ricin. As with most things like this, it has been used in medical research as it would seem that it has the potential to do great good – in this instance, as a treatment to kill cancer cells. However, the not-so-good news is that it is a stable substance and can last for a long time in the environment, despite extreme conditions of heat or cold, and can be ground down to be made into a form of powder, mist, or pellet. And it is soluble in water.

It is tasteless and colourless, so if actively administered maliciously, the victim would have no idea that they were being poisoned. Main symptoms usually seem to appear after about 8 – 10 hours and include difficulties in breathing or swallowing and, depending on the method of exposure, vomiting and diarrhoea that may become bloody. Dehydration, low blood pressure and organ failure usually follow.

Death usually takes place within 36 – 72 hours of exposure. And, before you ask, no – there is no known antidote. For that matter, there is no known reliable test yet available to confirm whether or not a person has even been exposed to Abrin – which is why it has taken us so long to reach our current position."

Again, a solemn silence descended that remained unbroken for several minutes. Reynolds had removed his spectacles during his discourse and was now fiddling with one of the arms.

A deep sigh escaped from him, and he suddenly looked very tired as he continued:

"As far as we can tell, the cause of death for each of the women was different. Zoe Schuster was killed by the administration of Abrin – probably through food and/or drink, possibly also through water used to shower or bathe in. Her symptoms absolutely fit with that analysis. After some terrible treatment, initial indications suggest that Lucy Andrews was finally killed by an intravenous injection of strychnine. The one thing the deaths have in common, however, is that they were both extremely unpleasant for the victim."

No one said anything.

McAllister simply nodded.

Reynolds continued, almost as an afterthought. "We aren't certain, McAllister, but we think that the bracelets that you have reported may be made from dried Jequirity Peas. It is common in many tropical areas throughout the world, and some indigenous peoples have used dried peas to make beaded jewellery. If swallowed, the wearer can, of course, be exposed to abrin poisoning. Whether there would be enough pea pods in a bracelet to cause death, we don't yet know, but it is a possibility."

McAllister glanced at Banjo, who appeared very pale and drawn.

"Thanks for explaining," said McAllister. "If we see any more, then we will let you know straight away."

Reynolds nodded. Head Shed resumed control.

"Thank you both," he said.

"As you can tell, we are now in uncharted and somewhat dangerous territory. We have no idea if this is a lone-wolf scenario or an active terrorist group of some kind. The fact that several people involved appear to have similar bracelets would indicate the latter, but the extent of that organisation or group is completely unknown to us at this time. As a result, London and the UK MOD have authorised you, McAllister, to be kept on official secondment attached to our field team here and in Salisbury for another twelve months to be reviewed further if necessary. If things are tied up within that time, all well and good and you will return home at that point. Keep your eyes open, and report directly to Miss Wilson, as I have already said. Paterson will remain your key daily operational link man. Otherwise, you can talk to Alison Fielding in the main office. She is one of our Joint Intelligence Organisation field operatives, so you can trust her completely. And please be careful. Dismissed."

Paterson and McAllister stood up, both awkwardly saluted, and then left the room. They said nothing until they had made the reverse trip up through the lift, the corridors and out into the main admin building. They quickly headed outdoors to the car park and drew in large breaths of fresh air.

Although the briefing room downstairs had been well air-conditioned, the nature of the discussion had left a very unpleasant taste. They both lit up a fag and stood together in sad, if companionable, silence under one of the large trees that stood in the parking area.

Chapter 24

Just at that moment, the aforesaid Alison Fielding, Joint Intelligence Organisation (Australian Secret Service) field operative, walked across the car park towards them. McAllister and Banjo turned as she approached.

"So" said McAllister, "I wasn't so far off the mark in the first place then?" and he flashed a tired smile, which she returned. "I take it that Kaz MacNamara is also one of yours?"

"Yup. She sure is. Keeps her eyes and ears open for us in that neck of the woods. Sorry about that, but rules are rules. If you need anything, just ask.." Both men nodded.

"Thanks," said McAllister, "and actually there is. We need to have a word with Ian Mitchener who led the SAPOL search back at The Shack. Was he the other guy in the briefing? Unfortunately there weren't any formal introductions."

"Yes," she said. "Is there a problem?"

"Well, we don't know is the honest answer" said Banjo. "The state the place was left in just didn't look right for Ian's style. If I didn't know better, I would have said that the place was turned over *after* the formal Police search had been concluded. In which case, someone is definitely looking for something."

"Have you told Terri Wilson any of this?" asked Alison, looking quietly concerned.

"No – we haven't had a chance." Banjo replied. "And there's another thing. Were any tests done on the Datsun after the

155

accident, and by tests I am thinking mainly of explosives? The car certainly went up with a bang."

Alison looked steadily back at him. "Traces of PE-4 were found in the boot of the Datsun. The fact that it was PE-4, and not the US manufactured C4, leads us to think that there is probably a British connection here somewhere, whether directly or indirectly. I guess that's another reason that you have been retained on secondment" she added, looking directly at McAllister.

" Ok, thanks for the update" said McAllister. "We'll get going and sort out The Shack, and then see if we can come up with some sort of a plan. Can you let us know about seeing Ian Mitchener? Is Terri back on site in the morning?"

"As far as I know, yes she is and yes, I will see what I can arrange with Ian for you" replied Alison.

"Ok, then we will see you in the morning."

Nodding to her, both men turned and walked over to their truck.

As they got in, Banjo said: "Why didn't you tell her about the note that we found at The Shack?"

"Don't know," replied McAllister. "Just needed a bit of time to think about it I guess."

"Roger that" Banjo replied. "We'll stop off and get some beers and then we can try and relax a bit and think all of this through. That Abrin stuff gives me the willies," and he shuddered as though someone had just walked over his grave.

Sorting out The Shack did not take long – after all, it was

only a basic accommodation in the first place but it was homely enough, and it had been sad to see it in such a mess. Banjo found the BBQ, and got it set up out in the back yard, carefully positioning the Esky with the cold beers easily at hand to ease the cooking process.

McAllister grinned as he lounged in one of the garden chairs that had thoughtfully been provided with the unit. The sun was shining, which suited him just fine and had the circumstances been different, he would have been perfectly content sitting here with a mate drinking beer and enjoying a simple BBQ.

He got the note out of his wallet and read it a number of times. It made no sense to him at all.

"Do you have any people who specialise in codes up here?" he asked Banjo.

"Probably – never really have had to ask" he replied. "Why?"

"Oh, just that note. It's driving me nuts. It clearly means something but highly likely it is in some sort of code. My brain just won't sort it out at the moment. I am usually good with numbers but I just can't see the pattern on this one" he added somewhat ruefully.

"Sleep on it, mate" replied Banjo. "It's amazing what a good night's kip can do."

Raising his cold bottle to that, McAllister tried to let it go and enjoy the simplicity of the moment. But that was easier said than done. Images kept pushing themselves to the front of his mind – not least the grinning belligerent face of Hendrik Cronje as the Datsun had become engulfed in flames, and the grotesque image of Lucy Andrews draped amongst the mangroves.

This was definitely getting very nasty indeed.

It seemed as though there were going to be some tough times ahead.

Chapter 25

The rest of the DSTO Salisbury team returned back to the main site at the end of the trials testing, as planned. The death of Dr Schuster had sent shock waves through the close knit community, and it was a very subdued group who boarded the aircraft for the return flight. Details of the circumstances of the death had not been released, and the official line was that Dr Schuster had been depressed and worrying about the trials.

After much debate, it was decided by Head Shed that McAllister and Paterson would remain in Woomera and conduct further enquiries there, travelling – should the need arise – to conduct interviews or further investigations. It became clear very quickly that the authorities were extremely keen indeed to keep the developments on a strictly controlled "need to know" basis, and so discretion was the key word.

The weeks seemed to pass quickly but with little material progress on any part of the investigation. Every avenue that they tried, McAllister and Paterson came to a dead end. Anything that looked even remotely promising, was passed to Terri Wilson but they got little feed back – no doubt thanks in large part to Head Shed's desire to control both events and information as much as possible.

The phone records from The Shack had revealed little, other than that Chips McInerney had indeed been speaking with a US based company market, Big Byte, who were already specialising in micro-chips and data storage.

Cutting edge stuff, but that doesn't really take us any further. And not Apple Computers after all.

"Do you know anything about this firm, Big Byte?" he asked Paterson, one afternoon when they were still trawling through documents and records yet again – and yet again, coming up with nothing new.

"Nope. Sounds like a fast food joint to me!" Banjo replied laughing.

"Mmmm. Perhaps we ought to pull the company's incorporation records – just have a look at who is involved there: just in case there is any connection with Chips" replied McAllister. Banjo agreed, and they put together a formal request for the information and faxed it over to Terri Wilson for consideration. As the Company seemed to be based in California, she would need to pull strings with her US counterparts to get the information quickly.

Deciding that they could do nothing further that evening, they tidied everything away and left the building, agreeing to give Crazy Pete's another try.

Fortunately, their trip there on this occasion was far less eventful than the last and they had a pleasant evening, with a good game of pool thrown in. When they called it a night, they made their way back to The Shack. They still had not got used to the fact that Chips was no longer there, and the bungalow seemed very quiet and still.

That was until the telephone started ringing. It had that harsh, clamouring sound that McAllister always associated with impending trouble.

He answered with a gruff: "Yup." He said nothing further,

listening intently, but waving at Banjo to get his attention. When he hung up, he turned to Banjo who immediately realised that something had just happened.

"Well, mate, it looks like Big Byte might be a possible line of enquiry" said McAllister. "Apparently the Yanks have been looking at the company for other reasons - which weren't explained on the open line, obviously - but they are interested that one of our guys with a high level of security clearance and some connection with the company has been involved in incidents down here. Our request for information on Big Byte hit one of their red flags, and they are sending one of their FBI guys, who is currently on deployment in their station in Canberra, down to Adelaide to see us. We need to be on the red eye in the morning to meet him. So we need to get our kit together and be ready to move."

With that, they both set about getting ready for their unexpected departure.

When he finally got into bed that night, McAllister's mind was a jumble and he slept fitfully. Between cartoon images of a head taking big bites out of a hamburger, he kept seeing the line of numbers that had fallen from the magazine those weeks ago and which he and Banjo had still not disclosed to Terri Wilson.

Chapter 26

Kevin Tapping was 27 years old, and he was "going places." Recently appointed as the new – and youngest ever – deputy Security Manager for the Australian Intercontinental Bank, he had been posted to the South Australian Head Office in Adelaide to serve for a two year secondment. He was one of the first intake on the Bank's new accelerated promotion scheme, and providing he did well and kept his nose clean, a further climb up the Banking institutional ladder would be assured.

He was smartly turned out, and he looked the part of a busy but efficient Bank official. He was fairly tall at 6'4," with mid brown hair and he had a certain presence which so far had served him well since his arrival at the new office.

If he had to admit to it, he had initially been disappointed with his transfer from the East Coast down to Adelaide. Many – initially including himself – considered it to be a quiet Colonialesque backwater that was certainly not the centre of the Banking world that was rapidly emerging in Sydney and Melbourne, and was not where an ambitious young man would ideally want to be based.

That however had all changed that February night earlier in the year when he had met Caryle Fielding at a colleague's drinks party held on the banks of the River Torrens, overlooking the new Festival Theatre. It did not take many meetings for him to know that he was smitten, and their romance had deepened over the following months.

He looked at the picture of her that had pride of place on his desk, and silently asked her to send him some good luck because he felt he was going to need it this morning when he faced Old Grouchy.

Nervously he gathered his papers together and made his way down the carpeted corridor towards the end office. No one entered this inner sanctum without an appointment, and he had already had quite a tough time getting a slot in the old man's diary as it was.

He knocked on the outer door, and a sharp "Come in" issued from inside. Miss Hancock, Old Grouchy's secretary, looked over her horn-rimmed spectacles at him. He always got the impression that she disapproved of him – in fact, probably disapproved of anyone under the age of 50. She said nothing but pointed to an empty chair in the corner against the wall.

He obediently went over and sat down.

Almost immediately, a buzzer went off on Miss Hancock's desk, and she again fixed him with her glacial stare and indicated that he should enter the office. Throughout all of this, she uttered not a single word.

Kevin knocked on the door, and when a gruff voice responded, he entered. It was a huge office right on the corner of the building, with panoramic views of the City and the river.

So this is what the top job gets you. Wouldn't mind some of that.

"You like the view then, Tapping?" asked his boss in an extremely irritated tone. Without waiting for an answer, he beckoned Kevin forward and indicated a chair in front of his large mahogany desk.

Kevin, again, complied with the unspoken direction.

"Now, what is it that you want to bring to my attention? Miss Hancock tells me that you were anxious to see me quite quickly. So, spit it out. Time is money, lad, and the longer you spend in Banking, you will realise that."

The old man glared over his spectacles from beneath large, bushy white eyebrows at the younger man before him.

"Well, sir, as you know, the Security Manager, Mr Cox, is currently on leave. I therefore thought I should bring this to you directly. I was checking some of the transfer records for the Bank yesterday, as standard…"

Before he could finish, the Old Man almost shouted at him: "Who's standard, Mr Tapping? Who authorised you to do that?"

Kevin gulped. This was not going well. "Good business practice, sir; I try and ensure that we have an extra layer of due diligence built in to our security processes in order to try and protect our customers from any fraudulent activity – and the Bank too, of course," he added, almost as an afterthought.

The Old Man continued to glare at him.

"And?" he asked testily.

"Well, sir. I came across what seems to be an unusually large cash transfer from one of our clients, and before raising it with the company concerned directly, I thought that you should be aware, not least in case you have further information about the client that would allay any concerns." Kevin stumbled to an abrupt halt and waited whilst the Old

Man continued to stare at him wordlessly.

"And how much is "unusually large," may I ask?"

This was like being in the Head Master's office at school.

Kevin gulped again and continued: "The customer concerned is Jindivik Wineries in Nuriootpa, sir. They moved over AU$ 2,000,000 to an account with Pineapples'R'Us in Yeppoon, South Eastern Queensland.

Whilst there have been transfers before, nothing of this size has ever been sent. It seemed odd, and we have not had any prior warning or notification from the Winery."

Kevin realised that the Old Man was still looking at him.

"AU$2 million, you say?"

"Yes, sir."

"And there is something else, sir."

"Go on," said the Old Man.

"Jindivik Wineries has a flag from the Security Services. It came through on the security telex link three or four days ago. I have it here, sir." Kevin reached into his bundle of papers and handed the telex printout over the desk.

The Old Man quickly read the content.

"Right, Tapping. Well done in bringing this to my attention. Do not – I repeat, do not – contact the Winery at this stage. We will follow the instructions in the fax. Contact them as set out and arrange a meeting. Then let me know."

"Yes, sir" replied a relieved Kevin. "I'll get on it right away."

With that, Old Grouchy returned his attention to the papers on his desk and waved Kevin away.

Kevin needed no asking twice, and he duly left the office, returning past the gauntlet stare of Miss Hancock and rapidly retreated to his own office, where he heaved a huge sigh of relief, took off his jacket and released his tie.

Thank goodness that's over with.

He took a gulp from the mug of now stone-cold tea that was on his desk, before picking up the phone to dial the number on the telex.

Chapter 27

As per their orders, McAllister and Banjo caught the red-eye flight from Woomera and they landed at RAAF Edinburgh mid-morning. They immediately travelled into Adelaide to meet Terri Wilson at the address she had given them. They had not been to the address before, which was contained within a non-descript office block just off King William Street in the heart of the City.

Having passed through the various security features, they were eventually shown into a glass panelled office that had basic office furniture. McAllister noted that there was also a small fridge in the corner, and he went over to investigate – hoping to find himself a Coke.

Just as his hand alighted on the fridge, the main office door swung open and Terri Wilson accompanied by a man he didn't know, entered the office at a pace. They moved straight over to the desk and pulling out chairs, beckoned to McAllister and Banjo to sit down.

Papers were brought out of manila folders, and being able to read documents that were on table tops opposite him and, therefore, essentially upside down, meant that McAllister quickly realised that this material was Top Secret – Five Eyes only. That meant that it could only be shared with appropriately cleared officers from the Five Eyes group, namely the USA, UK, Canada, Australia and New Zealand. This was rapidly confirmed, as Terri Wilson explained exactly that to them and introduced her companion as Special Agent Jim Brock from the FBI. Courtesies having been observed, the group quickly settled down to the purpose of the meeting.

"Gentlemen," started the US Agent. "Thanks for getting here so quickly. I understand that you have been looking into Big Byte. Can you briefly outline for me why you have an interest in that corporation, and how that fits with your investigation? Miss Wilson here has already given me the bare bones, but I would like to hear it from you."

McAllister looked at the burly American and thought that whilst he was not particularly tall, he was certainly solid. He had calm, dark eyes to go with his dark hair, and there was nothing about him that was frivolous or unnecessary.

Mmm. Probably ex-Forces. We will soon see if he is truly a friend or foe.

Banjo succinctly outlined the position and how they had really followed a hunch to try and find out a bit more about Big Byte.

The Special Agent nodded.

"Thanks. Yup, that is about the position as I had understood it. Well, Big Byte is indeed a fairly new start-up. Only two years old and registered in the Cayman Islands. Part of the rapidly expanding technical set down in Silicon Valley, California. We have a lot of emerging firms down there centring upon computers, technology generally and microchips, so I am not surprised that your guy, McInerney, was looking to jump ship over there. It's sure going to be the face of the future.

However, we have this particular business flagged and when your request came through from Miss Wilson as to any information, we thought we had better come down and have

168

a bit of a discussion. The FBI has an interest because of some of the transactions the company has been undertaking with Panama and Russia. Odd bedfellows, you could say." He offered a lazy grin.

Texan, I reckon.

"Who are the key players in the business?" McAllister asked.

"Well, I have a list of names which I am happy to share with you. None of them mean anything to us, but we are checking with the Brits as well, just in case they have anything on them. We also think that this is just one arm of a whole conglomeration of companies that are interlinked. Now, there may be nothing suspicious in that at all. On the other hand – particularly bearing in mind events over here – there could be a web of companies that we are going to have to pick through to start getting to the heart of what is actually going on here."

Banjo and McAllister looked at each other.

"So, I have agreed with Miss Wilson here that we will continue to liaise and as and when we find out any further information in relation to Big Byte, then we will, of course, let you know. She has kindly confirmed that information will be shared on a reciprocal basis, and we really appreciate that close cooperation." Again, the lazy grin as he turned towards Terri Wilson.

"Here's my card – it has my direct line on it. Please feel free to call me in the event that anything further comes up," and handed a card to each of them.

"Thanks for coming down, Jim," said Terri. "As I mentioned to you, we are not sure what we are dealing with here, so any help you can give us would be really appreciated."

"No problem," he replied and stood up.

"I'll show myself out and will look forward to speaking to you again real soon." With that, he flashed another grin and made his way out of the office.

For a couple of minutes, no one said anything.

Terri Wilson then broke the silence by clearing her throat.

"Before you both go, there is something else that you need to know about that has only come through this morning. This is strictly within the three of us in this room, and I have not as yet shared it with the Americans."

McAllister and Banjo looked at her steadily.

"We have had a call from the Deputy Security Manager at the Australian Intercontinental Bank here in Adelaide. They were doing some standard due diligence checking and realised that one of their customers had moved an unusually large amount of money. Fortunately, the Manager had read the security warning telex or red notice, that we circulated to all of the financial institutions following on from the list of people or companies that could be of interest that you put together for me when we were up in Woomera. One of the businesses on that list was Jindivik Winery in Nuriootpa."

Terri realised that she now had their rapt attention. She continued:

"Apparently AU$2,000,000 was transferred to a company called – [and here she checked her [notes] – Pineapples'R'Us in Queensland. This was an unusually large transfer, and the company had not cleared it with the

170

Bank first. The Deputy Security Manager, Mr Kevin Tapping, fortunately, remembered our red notice and, before raising any concerns with the Winery, spoke to his Managing Director. That led to an alert to us. I want you both to go and see Mr Tapping as soon as possible – today, certainly, and find out as much as possible about the Winery and this transfer. $2 million is a lot of bottles of plonk in anyone's language."

"What is the background information on the Winery?" asked McAllister.

"We are still checking," she replied, "but it looks as though they were incorporated here in South Australia and have been trading for a number of years. We are not sure what the connection with the Queensland company is."

"Well, we might be able to shed a little bit of light on that," interjected McAllister, and he went on to explain about the visit that he and Banjo had paid to the site before they had gone up to Woomera and the Cham-Pine product.

Terri Wilson nodded thoughtfully.

"Ok," she said. "Interesting. Please see Mr Tapping and report back to me. We can then try and take it from there."

"What sort of clearance does this guy have?" asked Banjo.

"For once, in this case, we have had a bit of good luck," Terri Wilson replied. "Mr. Tapping is on the graduate accelerated promotion scheme that the Bank is trialling. As part of that scheme, we entered into an arrangement with them that all of those entrants would pass through security vetting from the outset so that, hopefully, there would be no nasty surprises for the Bank or for us in the wider sense later on down the line, perhaps when the individual is in a very senior position. It has also enabled us to talent spot from a very discreet distance and means that we are starting to forge some grassroots links with financial institutions, which could be invaluable in years to come.

The Australian Intercontinental Bank is the first to trial this approach as an organisational initiative, but we hope that it will expand to other companies and sectors. So the short answer to your question, Paterson, is that he has security clearance, albeit not to the highest levels. Whilst you will still obviously need to be slightly cautious in what you disclose at this stage, it is not the same situation that we may have faced had he not had any clearance at all."

She smiled at him. "Makes a change to have some good news, hey?"

"Oh, and one other thing. His girlfriend is Caryle Fielding from the DSTO in Salisbury. So, quietly elegant, don't you think? All things considered?" She smiled again.

With that, McAllister got up from the table and used the phone on the other desk in the office cum meeting room to call Mr Tapping, and arrangements were made for them to visit him that afternoon.

As they exited the building, McAllister and Paterson looked at each other and decided to go for something to eat in one of the coffee shops just round the corner in Rundle Mall whilst they had the chance.

As it was a pedestrianised area, it gave McAllister a good opportunity to really get the "feel" of one of the central areas of the City and as they drank their tea and ate their way through a selection of sandwiches, it occurred to them that this investigation was finally starting to show some signs of life. Could be dead ends, of course, they agreed, but nevertheless, at least something was starting to happen. It was, therefore, with a sense of growing anticipation that they walked around the corner to the Australian Intercontinental Bank for their appointment with Kevin Tapping.

Chapter 28

The meeting at the Bank went extremely well. Kevin Tapping had presented as an intelligent, competent guy who had anticipated some of the questions that they were going to ask him and had already prepared a lot of the paperwork. He was personable, quick on the uptake and didn't waste time.

The upshot of it was that Pineapples'R'Us appeared to be some sort of subsidiary or linked business with the Jindivik Winery – which of itself was no problem, especially bearing in mind the label on the Cham-Pine bottles confirming that they owned their own pineapple plantation in Queensland, but the size of the transfer was the thing that had caused the raised eyebrows.

Mr Tapping had already done some discreet digging in readiness for the meeting, and it seemed that the Queensland Company had a registered office in Beerwah, which, he informed them, was in the Glasshouse Mountains in South Eastern Queensland, in the heart of the pineapple growing region.

So, nothing unusual there, either.

There were three Directors of the Company registered: Jan Christiaan de Klerk (who had given an official address in the Barossa Valley, South Australia), Stephen John Fraser (from Caloundra, Queensland) and Michael Stephenson (from Mooloolaba, Queensland).

From an examination of the accounts held by the Jindivik Winery, Mr. Tapping had established that the next largest transfer of funds to any recipient within the last three years had been to a company by the name of Southern Star Logistics, but that had been nowhere near the amount of this particular payment.

He also disclosed that there were regular payments to the Queensland company by the Winery, and these went out on the 15th of every month and were the same amount every time: AU$120,000. So, all ways around, this latest transfer was definitely very odd.

He had also confirmed that the Australian Intercontinental Bank did not hold the accounts of Pineapples'R'Us. He was, therefore, unable to interrogate that end of the money trail, but could confirm that Jan Christiaan de Klerk was a current Director of Jindivik Wineries, and the main signatory on the account held with the Bank.

At the conclusion of the meeting, and after much discussion, it was agreed that there would be no approach to the Winery at this stage but a careful watch would be kept by Mr Tapping on all movements from the business accounts with the Bank. He would report on the telephone number he already had should there be any further suspicious transactions. He confirmed that he would do just that, and that he would be formally reporting to his Managing Director as to the outcome of the meeting this afternoon.

As they left the Bank's premises, McAllister and Paterson agreed that Kevin Tapping had made a very good impression, and if this was the calibre of those graduates selected for the accelerated promotion scheme, then the economic future for Australia certainly looked bright.

They decided to walk back to Terri Wilson's office and

report the outcome of the discussion, and ten minutes later, they were back in the office cum meeting room that they had been in when meeting with the FBI earlier that morning.

Terri Wilson came in not long after their arrival, and placing a sheaf of papers on the desk, immediately got down to business.

"I am glad that you came back to give me a bit of a debrief," she said, and McAllister and Banjo promptly outlined for her what they had found out and how the Bank would proceed. She nodded.

"Yes, that sounds like the most discreet way forward," she said.

"We will follow up on the information about the owners of Pineapples'R'Us, but in the meantime, it has been decided that you two will go straight up to Queensland to have a bit of a look around and see if anything unusual emerges. Even if it is only background information as with the Jindivik Winery visit, it could prove extremely helpful as we try and find out what is going on. Your flight leaves from RAAF Edinburgh at 0600 tomorrow morning, and you will collect a car from the pool at the base. You will need to find your own accommodation this time around, so here is a chit to draw some money for the trip," at which point she handed over an envelope to Paterson. "Needless to say, discretion is the word. In the event anything goes seriously wrong, then you can call me. If it is more urgent than that, you will have direct contact with the Base Commander at RAAF Amberley, which, for your information, McAllister is about 50 miles southwest of Brisbane. His number is also in the envelope. He will expect a code word so that he knows the call is legitimate and that code word is also in the envelope. As in true Mission Impossible fashion, when you have memorised the word and his number, please destroy the note." She grinned.

Both men nodded, stood up and Paterson said that they would call in when they got settled in Queensland.

They walked out of the building into the fresh air, and McAllister blew his cheeks out with a puff.

"Looks like you're getting a bit of a whistle-stop tour of Australia whilst you are here," laughed Banjo.

"Yeah, can't be bad," smiled McAllister. "How far is Queensland?" he asked.

Banjo laughed again and shook his head. "You Poms, I dunno. It's about a three-hour flight - possibly slightly more, depending on the aircraft. And before you ask, the Glasshouse Mountains are about another four or so hours by road north of that – and you will only have just started getting into Queensland proper."

McAllister nodded. "Quick beer then," and the two men strode companionably into the first Bar they came to on King William Street.

They emerged about an hour later and, chatting amiably, walked back to Banjo's Holden, which they had parked on a side road just off Rundle Mall before going into Terri Wilson's office earlier that morning after arriving back from Woomera.

Just as they reached the car, McAllister stopped dead in his tracks. He put out a hand and grabbed Banjo by the arm.

Staring at the car, he said, "Don't touch the car, Banjo."

"What are you talking about?" replied his friend, looking at the vehicle in a perplexed fashion.

"Don't know – but something's wrong."

McAllister's little warning voices had suddenly piped up big time. He didn't know exactly what it was, but there was definitely something different about the car. He told Banjo to stand to one side, and he gingerly started looking all around the vehicle. He got down on his hands and knees and looked under the car.

And there he saw it.

A block of what appeared to be PE-4, complete with a detonator in place, stuck onto the underside of the vehicle with what looked like duct tape.

McAllister stood up and, taking his friend by the arm, moved away from the vehicle.

"Get back to Terri Wilson. Tell her we have a suspect package underneath the Holden and we need to evacuate this whole area immediately and get her to call the Ordnance boys."

Banjo looked pale.

"You serious, mate?"

"Deadly. Now go. I have no idea if this thing has a timer on it or whether it is a tilt switch or pressure switch. Whatever the firing mechanism, it could go off at any time. I have seen enough of these in Northern Ireland to know that you don't mess and you don't waste time. Now go."

Banjo immediately left the scene.

McAllister was aware that the various shops in Rundle Mall looked as though they were getting ready to close, which meant that there would be a big influx of shop workers and office people who were leaving work very shortly. The area would be packed with innocent pedestrians who would get caught in the blast. Just at that moment, two Police Officers on foot patrol walked around the corner and McAllister ran towards them.

He pulled them back towards North Terrace, showed his military ID, explained the situation and asked them to call in urgently. They looked at him in a bewildered fashion.

This is Adelaide. We don't get that sort of thing here.

"Have you been drinking, sir?" asked the older of the two officers.

McAllister's patience was starting to wear thin.

"Please listen, officer. There is a bomb under that car. We need to start evacuating the area urgently."

Whilst his older colleague was engaging McAllister, the younger officer walked over towards the vehicle.

McAllister called out to him not to approach or touch the car under any circumstances, at which the young officer waved his hand in a relaxed manner but continued walking towards the vehicle.

"Look," said McAllister, turning back to the older officer. "I have shown you my military ID. This is no joke. I need you to call it in urgently. For God's sake, we are running out of time – the thing could go off at any moment without warning."

The older officer looked at him sceptically, and slowly got his notebook out of his breast pocket, and, speaking as if to a child, continued:

"Now then, sir, shall we run through this again? How much have you had to drink? I can smell it on your breath, so please don't deny it. I would advise you that wasting Police time is a criminal offence, and we don't take kindly to it hereabouts."

McAllister's patience snapped. He landed a huge punch on the officer's unsuspecting jaw. As the officer fell to the ground, McAllister picked up his radio and called in:

"Officer down, Officer down. Suspect bomb under a vehicle off Rundle Mall, next to Johnnie Martin's Department store. Repeat: Officer down. Call the Bomb Squad. Urgent assistance required."

McAllister had no idea if his message had been received, and he immediately turned on one knee towards the young officer, who was now crouching down on the pavement next to the car.

"Don't…." called out McAllister.

But the rest of his shout was drowned out by an enormous blast that lifted the Holden off its axles and shattered the windows of all of the surrounding shops and offices.

McAllister instinctively threw himself to the floor, covering the officer he had knocked down with as much of his body as he could and covering his own head with his hands. Debris and glass rained down all around, and the pressure wave from the blast played havoc with McAllister's ears.

He couldn't hear anything at all after the blast.

When the debris had stopped falling, he looked back, unaware that he had a large cut on the back of his head that was bleeding profusely, and glass shards were embedded in the back of his hands. There was nothing much left of the car and nothing at all of the young officer who had been examining it save for his blackened Police cap, which now lay sadly in the gutter.

What a waste. Another good man lost. I've seen too many of these already. What a dreadful waste.

The realisation then kicked in that of course, the bomb had been intended for him and Banjo, and McAllister felt his stomach turn and an icy resolve enter his blood.

We must have kicked the hornet's nest somewhere along the line. We just need to work out what we did that has upset these bastards so – and then nail them.

Chapter 29

The scene quickly turned from a stunned, split-second silent aftermath to a chaotic mix of Police and Ambulance sirens, screams and cries from injured people. Those who could, tried to make their way as far from the scene of the blast as possible.

McAllister started to pick himself up off the officer on the floor, who looked at him with wide, grateful eyes. He was trying to say something to McAllister who couldn't hear, and tried to stagger to his feet.

It seemed that, suddenly, people were all around him and there were flashing lights from various vehicles that had arrived quickly on the scene.

The next couple of hours were a blur for McAllister.

He remembered seeing Banjo's pale, worried face peering at him at one stage whilst he was still on the floor in the side road and then being put in the back of an ambulance. He had no idea where he was other than it was obviously a hospital. There seemed to be a lot going on as there seemed to be an air of calm busyness out in the main areas that he could see through the window in his room, and for once, McAllister was content to rest his head back on the clean pillow, close his eyes, empty his mind and try and let the throbbing headache lessen. The problem with that was that the last image of the young Policeman kneeling down against the vehicle, followed by the explosion, kept flashing into his mind.

This is going to be a bad one. I already have enough

problems with images from Northern Ireland. I don't need any more.

A nurse came into his room at that point, and noting that he was awake, immediately walked out again. She returned a few moments later with a Doctor, and McAllister could see Terri Wilson and Banjo hovering anxiously by the doorway.

The Doctor ran through the usual tests. McAllister nodded in what he hoped were all the right places. His hearing still had not returned properly, and it was almost as if he were swimming inside a goldfish bowl so that all of the sounds were warped and distorted. He thought he got the gist of what was being said to him, which essentially was that he would be kept in hospital overnight for observation.

With that, the doctor and nurse left the room. McAllister noted that they exchanged a few brief words with Wilson and Banjo out in the hall, and his two colleagues then entered the room.

Terri Wilson came near to the bed, and McAllister realised he still had a sense of smell. She was wearing perfume – he didn't know what it was, but it smelled expensive and lovely.

No doubt Chanel or Dior – it is definitely something classy. That would suit her style.

She was trying to say something to him.

He interrupted her.

"Sorry, can't hear you!" he shouted. "Ears are buggered at the moment."

She patted his arm and looked sympathetic.

Banjo had been scribbling on a piece of paper, and he turned it around and showed it to McAllister.

"U OK? Still got all your bits?"

Despite himself, McAllister laughed and gave a thumbs up.

Banjo wrote something else.

"Good. We will see you tomorrow. Pineapple chunks are off the menu."

McAllister nodded, and with that, his two companions turned to leave.

The nurse arrived with what looked to McAllister like an alarmingly large array of pills – most of which he realised were destined for him as she started handing them out to him with a drink of water. She was standing right next to the bed so that McAllister had no chance of "losing" anything in the bedclothes.

It wasn't long before a wave of tiredness swept over him and he did not have the energy to fight it. He closed his eyes, but a procession of faces passed him in his mind: Lucy Andrews, Zoe and Dr. Schuster, Hendrik Cronje, Chips McInerney and the young Police officer in Rundle Mall.

So many dead. I was right. This is going to be a bad one.

And then the list of numbers that had fallen from the magazine back in Woomera.

Still have not got to the bottom of that.

He finally slipped into a deep, thankfully dreamless sleep whilst the hospital hummed efficiently around him, dealing with what seemed to be a constant stream of casualties from the blast.

Chapter 30

The overnight observation in fact turned into three days, and as McAllister's strength returned, so did his anxiety to get out and start tracking down the bombers. Banjo had been in to see him several times but was tight lipped about the progress of the investigation into the bombing.

Clearly under orders not to say much.

On the second evening, McAllister had picked his moment and walked down to the patients' television room to try and find out what exactly was going on. He was aghast at the news coverage and the damage that had been caused to the centre of the City. Somehow – miraculously – the young Police Officer had been the only fatality. McAllister shook his head in disbelief when he heard that.

Terri Wilson and Banjo came in to see him on the third morning.

"Glad your hearing has largely returned," she said to him. He nodded.

"You and Banjo have had quite a time of things, so you are going up to Queensland as soon as you are discharged, but you are going to have four days R&R to enjoy some of our lovely country before picking up the trail again. Things are in hand down here." She smiled kindly at him.

"I want to help," he said tetchily. "Not go on holiday."

Her smile faded.

"You will do as you are told, McAllister. I need you completely fit and recovered, and coming back in too soon will not help anyone at all – least of all you. A few days in the Queensland sunshine will do you a world of good, and then you are in place to pick up the investigation."

At that point, and somewhat serendipitously, the Doctor walked in and confirmed that McAllister could be discharged straight away. The nurse would be in shortly with the pills he was to continue to take for the next five days, he added.

McAllister nodded and immediately threw back the bedclothes.

Paterson smothered a grin and looked at his feet. "Keen to get out of here" rather sprang into his mind.

"We'll wait for you outside. There are some new clothes in the bag," said Paterson, placing a bulging plastic carrier bag on the floor next to the bed.

It took McAllister slightly longer than he expected to get changed – everything seemed to ache, especially his head, which was still extremely tender. His arms wouldn't do quite what he wanted, either. But it was still only a few minutes later that he emerged from the sideward and made his way towards Paterson and Wilson. He thanked the nurses and the Doctor on his way out and was relieved when they finally stepped through the sliding doors into the fresh air.

It was a beautiful Spring morning in Adelaide, with the blossom on the trees, and the grass looking so fresh he had the notion he just wanted to take off his shoes and run barefoot through it.

"What's the date?" he asked Banjo as they moved towards a fairly large, non-descript black sedan car.

"12th September," replied Banjo.

"So I've been here in Australia for over three months?" asked McAllister.

"Yup – see what happens when you are having fun!" replied his friend.

Terri Wilson unlocked the car doors, and they climbed in. She drove them back to Weemala Road, and McAllister realised that he had not been "home" for some considerable time.

"What have you told the DSTO?" he asked Terri. "My cover is rather blown, don't you think?"

She watched him in the rearview mirror.

"Norman Reynolds, of course, knows, and your immediate supervisor there has also now been told. As far as the staff is concerned, you have remained in Woomera to make further preparations for the joint testing programme, which has been put back slightly. As you know, it should have taken place next month, but it will now happen in mid-late November/early December instead. You will be back there for that, so no one will be any the wiser."

She went on to give them their instructions, namely that they were to report to RAAF Edinburgh at 1400 that afternoon for the flight that would take them up to RAAF Amberley as originally planned. They would then pick up a rental car and head towards Mooloolaba, where accommodation had been rented for them for the few days of R&R that they were to enjoy.

"A chance to decompress," she said.

He nodded and sank back into the soft leather of the seat and stared out of the window. The rest of the journey was conducted in companionable silence.

Chapter 31

The flight to RAAF Amberley was unremarkable, and it passed in a blur for McAllister, who slipped into a doze.

Those damn pills.

They landed nearly four hours later, in the warm early evening sunshine in Queensland.

Banjo ushered him towards the side of the main building next to the runway, where they found a rental car waiting for them rather than the pool one they had originally been told to expect. A white Toyota Galant. They threw their bergens in the boot and immediately headed north.

"Where's this place we are going?" asked McAllister.

"Mooloolaba? Well, knowing that you love the beach, I thought you might like to take a look at a real beauty. Not the ones you think are great back in the UK, but a *real one.* Stunning sand, wide bay, great swimming. A few shacks and caravans, and what-have-you along the coast. There are some great places to eat. You'll enjoy it. On what we call the Sunshine Coast – for obvious reasons." Banjo's face split into a wide grin, and McAllister suddenly realised how tired his friend had been looking.

Perhaps it will do us some good after all.

The drive took them just over three hours to travel the 100 or so miles from the base, and they were lucky to get through the centre of Brisbane without too much trouble or traffic. McAllister looked at the city, which again seemed to be fairly new and growing rapidly, snaking along the banks of the Brisbane River.

Another beautiful city.

It was well into the evening by the time they arrived at the beach shack that had been rented for them. As they got out of the car and McAllister stretched, the only noises he could hear were the chicadas, which were busy chirruping away in the tropical warmth of the evening and the soft lap of the ocean.

Banjo called out to him, and he walked around the side of the house into the back garden. It seemed that they were right on the edge of the beach, and he could walk out of the bungalow and be in the sea in under a minute.

I can't wait to see this at sunrise in the morning.

The next few days fell into a relaxed rhythm of swimming, sunbathing, running along the untainted beach, eating, drinking beer, and making friends with some of the locals.

Banjo was right: I am in my element here.

On the third morning, McAllister had gone for his usual morning swim. He loved that quiet time, just as the sun was coming up and before the heat of the day started to build. Just him and the ocean. Fantastic.

It was a long swim that morning, and he came out of the sea feeling tired but mentally and physically refreshed. He found Banjo sitting in one of the chairs in the garden with the newspaper in front of him, chewing on the end of a pencil and looking perplexed.

"I just can't get this one," he announced as McAllister approached. "Kettle's only just boiled, by the way, if you want a brew, or there's a beer in the Esky."

McAllister threw himself into a chair on the other side of his friend and asked him what he was struggling with.

"Mmm. A word of five letters, with "g" as the third letter: A basic elementary number, is the clue," replied Banjo, who looked skyward as if seeking inspiration.

"An elementary number?" said McAllister. He thought for a few moments. "Let's see the crossword," he said, reaching for the paper.

He looked at the boxes.

He laughed. "I think you'll find that it's eight."

Banjo looked at him. "What do you mean, eight?"

"All elements have an atomic number, right? And one of the most basic elements is Oxygen. The atomic number of oxygen is 8, so the answer to your clue is: ...." McAllister suddenly stopped talking as his thoughts raced.

"Are you alright, mate?" asked Banjo, looking concerned.

"Banjo, have you got that list of numbers that we found back at The Shack?" McAllister asked.

"Yes, I left it in your wallet, which I retrieved from your stuff before they got rid of what was left of your clothes after the bombing."

With that, McAllister leaped out of the chair and rushed inside, coming back quickly, clutching his wallet. He found the piece of paper and sat down, taking up the pencil.

"I don't know, Banjo, but I think you might just have opened up the list of numbers."

Banjo looked perplexed.

"What are you talking about?"

McAllister started scribbling. Almost in triumph, he finally looked up at Banjo.

"I can't remember them all," he said, "but I am pretty sure that the key to that list is the atomic number of elements on the Periodic Table. Look," and he shared his hurried writing with his friend.

"I can't remember what 85 or 73 are, but 6 is Carbon, so "C," 19 is Potassium, so "K," 8 is Oxygen, and 7 is Nitrogen. See what that starts to give us:....."

Banjo read the top of the newspaper page.

85. 73. C. K. O. N.

"We need to find a library," said McAllister. "Then we can see if this idea really works."

They both jumped up, rushed into the house to get changed, and were in the Toyota within 10 minutes.

"I think that the nearest library will be in Buderim, just along the coast," Banjo said as he started the car. True to his word, they got to the town within 15 minutes and quickly found what they were looking for.

They raced through the doors, and a somewhat startled librarian looked up from her desk. She was in her late 50's, wearing a beige-coloured cardigan twin set, and she reminded McAllister of his gran back in Wales. A large name badge announced that this was Gwen.

Banjo turned on the charm, and within a few minutes, they

were shown to the children's science section. Gwen kindly even found the book that she thought would be of most assistance to them: "*The Earth and Its Elements,*" and sure enough, as they opened the book, virtually the very first page had a coloured reproduction of the Periodic Table.

They moved over to a desk nearby and quickly looked up the atomic numbers on the list. They followed it through, copying down the letters on their piece of paper:

85 73 6 19 8. 7

At Ta. C. K. O. N

5. 92. 86. 32. 18

B. U. Rn. Ge. Ar

9. 53. 7. 13. 94. 16 1

F. I. N. Al Pu S. H

The two men stared at what had appeared on the page.

"Attack on. Burn Gear. Final Push," read Banjo.

"Christ, we need to tell Terri Wilson. This proves that Chips was in on the whole thing and that he wasn't operating alone. This seems to suggest that he was actually taking instructions from someone else."

McAllister nodded in agreement.

Which attack? Was it the bombing in Adelaide (unlikely because of the timing of finding the note) or something else yet to come? Was it linked to the explosives in the boot of the Datsun that had gone up so spectacularly on the way back from Crazy Pete's?

His mind was racing.

They needed to get to a secure phone line quickly. They immediately called the Base Commander at RAAF Amberley and arranged to go back there straight away. The trip back down took less time than their original journey. The urgency pressed down on them, and McAllister and Paterson were anxious to get the word out as quickly as possible.

The Base Commander was ready for them as soon as they arrived, and without formality, they were shown into a secure communications room where they could make the call in private.

After a slightly awkward conversation where McAllister had to admit to not having disclosed the piece of paper earlier and why, Terri Wilson agreed that they should carry on with their planned visit to Pineapples' R'Us. "Further discussion about this can wait until you get back here," she added rather ominously.

Different countries, same earache.

Having completed the call and received their new instructions, the pair got back in the Galant and drove north to Mooloolaba. Again, it was early evening by the time they got there, and they slumped into the garden chairs with a cold beer in hand, in tired relief that at least now there might be something else to go on.

The phone conversation had confirmed that, unfortunately, nothing further had come in from Kevin Tapping at the bank whilst they had been in Queensland, so they would just have to keep looking for other threads to try and pull.

They looked at the map together and decided on a plan of

action for the following day. They would be heading for Beerwah in the Glasshouse Mountains to see what light the pineapple business could shed, if any, on this increasingly complex picture that was starting to unfold. And that was about the extent of the plan.

Let's see what happens when we shake the pineapple tree.

That night, he slept fitfully, plagued by weird dreams. The bomb blast featured a string of numbers doing a cartoon-style can-can dance around a very large pineapple. The final gruesome image of Lucy Andrews also came to the forefront of his mind but was quickly overtaken by the darkly smiling face of Hendrik Cronje, as the Datsun had been engulfed in flames.

Chapter 32

He sat in his favourite rocking chair on the verandah, overlooking the rows of vines covering the hillside in front of him. The chair was his only possession from "the old days." It had belonged to his grandfather, and it still seemed embued with the old man's strength, grit, and passionate belief in his God and his Country - a Boer to the core. He stroked the old wooden arm fondly, almost without thinking about it.

Time had passed since he had committed himself so fully to The Cause, and he thought back to Gough Island, where he had renewed his vows, as it were. It seemed like such a long time ago now, but he had remained faithful throughout, and his meticulous planning meant that, at last, he felt that he was drawing near to his final goal.

The arrival and meddling of the two military policemen was an unexpected nuisance, and the bungled car bomb was extremely irritating. However, there would undoubtedly be another occasion. He had come too far and through too much to allow his plans to be derailed now.

Quite simply, there was just too much at stake.

As his grandmother used to say to him, "Old foes cast long shadows," and he was determined to be the longest shadow of all.

PART II

"He hails from Snowy River, up by Kosciusko's side,

Where the hills are twice as steep and twice as rough,

Where a horse's hoofs strike firelight from the flint stones every stride,

The man that holds his own is good enough.

And the Snowy River riders on the mountains make their home,

Where the river runs those giant hills between;

I have seen full many horsemen since I first commenced to roam,

But nowhere yet such horsemen have I seen."

Extract from: The Man from Snowy River, A B Banjo Paterson

Chapter 33

The trip out to Beerwah showcased some fantastic scenery up in the Glasshouse Mountains and surrounds, but apart from learning a lot about pineapple cultivation and production and the new moves that were afoot in terms of eco-tourism, McAllister and Paterson unearthed very little of any obvious note that would further their investigations.

They asked as many questions as they could without arousing suspicion or appearing to be irritating pineapple obsessionists on the almost obligatory tour around the plantation and elicited that the bottles for Cham-Pine were produced by Simply Bottles in Toowoomba, Queensland; their logistics and distribution across Australia (firstly to Jindivik Winery for the actual bottling and then onwards to the various sales outlets) were handled by Direct Logistics, based in Melbourne, Victoria; and it seemed that they even utilised one particular fuel company, looking at the fuel pumps that were dotted around the lorry yard and all of which were ablaze with the "Southern Star Fuels" name and logo.

After reviewing the day, McAllister and Paterson agreed that they could do no more than go back to RAAF Amberley the following day, call into Terri Wilson, give her a short report and give her the names of the various companies that they had come across. Perhaps further checks through the FBI and/or Kevin Tapping at the Bank might come up with something. It looked as though they would then need to head back to Woomera and re-group.

One final night in Mooloolaba was, therefore, on the cards

before heading south again in the morning. They discussed whether they needed to fly back or whether they could drive it.

"You up for a bit of an adventure then and the chance to see the real Outback?" he asked.

"Count me in" laughed McAllister. "You should have known the answer to a question like that by now."

Laughing, Banjo replied, "You Poms. Like I have said to you before, this is a Big Country. Do you have any idea how far it is?"

"No – but I guess you are going to tell me that it is quite a long way," replied McAllister.

"Yes, mate. If we share the driving it will probably take us about five or six days to do the journey allowing for the track, and including the stopover in Toowoomba. Providing nothing goes wrong. We are probably looking at about 2000 miles or just over all in. You up for that? You'll see some great country mind, as we go through the Great Dividing Range and then right out to the border. We will need to change the car though, so suggest we leave the rental at the Base and get ourselves a pool ute: we definitely need a four wheel drive with a roo bar."

"A what?" asked McAllister.

"A roo bar! So that if you hit a kangaroo, it doesn't total your front. If that Datsun had had one the night we gave chase coming out of Crazy Pete's, it wouldn't have had all of the damage that it took. So a roo bar is a necessity for that sort of country."

McAllister simply laughed, and thought how lucky he had been to be allocated Banjo to work with. He was more like a mate already.

So easily could have been Lurch, and I certainly don't think I would have enjoyed the trip as much as I have.

Having bought some steaks and beers on the way back to the beach shack, they were looking forward to a last bar-b-que looking at the waves. They pulled up outside the beach shack, and realised straight away that something was wrong.

"Mate: look at the window in the front there. We didn't leave the curtain like that, did we?" asked Paterson. McAllister was immediately aware, and agreed: something did not look right.

They cautiously checked the exterior of the building; they could not hear any unusual sounds from inside the house and entered with caution.

Whilst the place had not been turned over, as such, it was clear that it had been searched. Things had been moved, and the dust and sand on the floor had been disturbed.

"Someone searching for something," said McAllister, wondering at the same time if it could be the list of numbers that was still in his pocket.

"Ok, let's get this cleared up, have some grub and get ready to move out first thing in the morning. We will set up a couple of welcome tricks, so that if they try and come back tonight, we should have some warning."

Paterson agreed, and they set about having a clean up. They called in to the Base to tell them that they were coming in the following morning; "Arrangements would be made" was the response.

Chapter 34

Having enjoyed a quiet and companionable bar-b-que, with McAllister taking the chance to have a last swim off the beach, they settled down to what was an uneventful night.

They set off early, just after dawn, to make the most of the morning. McAllister was sorry to leave this little slice of paradise and as they drew away, he promised himself that he would come back here.

They kept a lookout in case they were being tailed, but there was nothing obvious and they threaded their way back down to Brisbane, through the City and back to the Base where they reported in as expected. Terri Wilson confirmed that she would check the various company names, and let them know if there was anything of interest.

She agreed that they could take the road trip, calling in to Simply Bottles at Toowoomba on the way – although even the phone line couldn't hide the smile when they broached the subject to her.

"You can have seven days to get back to Woomera," she said. "That should allow for the stopover in Toowoomba, and should coincide quite nicely with the return of the advance party for the trials testing. I take it you are going to come down the Birdsville Track?" she asked Banjo.

"Yup: thought that might be a good way to get back; hopefully, they won't be expecting that either – off the usual trail a bit and all that," he added.

"Ok. Call in when you get to Birdsville. You know the

201

contact there don't you?" she said, and Banjo confirmed he had all the information he needed. "I'll also let Kaz McNamara in Coober Pedy know that you will be on the Track, so that the usual lookout can be kept."

McAllister and Paterson grinned at each other, and promised to call in should they get anything interesting in the meantime.

As agreed the night before, they changed vehicles, took on board all the necessary supplies and arranged for the rental to be returned.

"Hopefully, this should be a fun trip" said Banjo. "Fingers crossed, hey mate. Right – next stop Toowoomba."

They followed the National Highway 54 westwards and after about an hour and a half, rolled into the township of Toowoomba. It was much larger than McAllister had expected, and Banjo informed him that, as far as he knew, it was just about the second most populous inland place in Queensland. Occupying the crest of the Great Dividing Range in the Darling Downs area of Queensland, it was certainly positioned brilliantly for moving stuff across country and some of the scenery was, as Banjo had predicted, quite stunning.

It wasn't long before they saw the signs to Simply Bottles on the outskirts of the town.

Obviously for the lorry drivers, trying to keep them off the main drag.

They stopped for a milkshake and a custard tart (both of which were American sized rather than what McAllister was used to back in the UK) at a small truck stop cum diner, on the other side of the road to the bottle factory. Their booth in the diner gave them perfect line of sight to the entry of the factory, and what was immediately clear to them was that this was a busy industry. Trucks were rolling in and out nearly the entire time, and a high proportion of them had the Jindivik Wineries or the Cham-Pine logo on their side awnings.

Business in Nuriootpa is clearly booming.

Having asked the waitress in the diner whether the bottle factory had any sort of guided tours, she said they did but they were out of luck, because they had been suspended for the time being. She didn't know why.

They were discussing what to do next, when a large black sedan car slowed down on the highway, and then turned into the bottle factory yard. A tall, unmistakeable figure got out of the car. Neither man spoke for a few minutes.

It was Lurch.

He looked cautiously round, his eyes taking in everything around him. Although he glanced at the diner some distance away, it was only in passing and he did not seem to take any particular notice of it. Having buttoned up his jacket, he walked in towards what was presumably the office area.

"What's he doing here?" asked McAllister.

"Dunno. Wasn't aware he was doing anything on this particular job. In fact I haven't spoken to him at all since we came back from Hong Kong – largely because I haven't seen him," replied Banjo. "He has kept right out of my way – which is just how I like it."

"Who was that guy you brought back – I keep meaning to ask?" said McAllister.

"A right hard nut that one. Nasty piece of work. Goes by the name of Roberto Milanese. Real name: Fred Robertson. Obviously didn't think that sounded exotic enough! He has been involved in some very nasty jobs, largely down in Melbourne, which included the death of one our blokes. Hence our interest. It then turned out he has been in cahoots with the Chinese Tongs, and was trying to set up some Organised Crime group over here to bring in illicit drugs. We managed to get an Extradition Warrant, and bring him back. As I say, nasty piece of work who runs with others of the same brand. I was glad to be rid of him when we landed at Adelaide." Said Banjo.

McAllister thought back to that very first day, and the impression he had that Banjo had indeed been relieved to get the prisoner in the back of the van.

Not far wrong, then.

"Don't think I ever told you that he committed suicide in prison?" added Banjo.

McAllister looked surprised. "Any idea why he would do that?" he asked.

"Nope. Probably afraid that the Tongs would get him to him inside – no prisoners, all that sort of shit."

McAllister nodded. "What was the bracelet all about then?"

"He claimed it was his religious rosary and he was entitled to keep it in order to pursue his faith. We put it upstairs to the Big Wigs, and they – reluctantly, I have to say – agreed. That's why he had it on him."

"Where is it now?"

Banjo looked at him. "No idea, mate – why?"

"I just wondered if we could get it over to Norman Reynolds for tests to be done on it – just in case it is one of the same batch that we were discussing back in Woomera," said McAllister.

"Remind me to ask Terri, boss lady, when we next speak to her, will ya?" Banjo said, and turned his face back to the window with a worried expression. He was sure they would have told him if Lurch was going to be on the plot, but nothing had been said. He turned back to McAllister and said:

"Mike, I think we need to be even more careful. I wouldn't mind betting that it was Lurch who turned the bungalow over yesterday. I didn't know he was going to be on patch, and it's just the sort of thing he would be quite happy to do. I'm probably jumping to conclusions, but as far as I know, he shouldn't be here and I would rather be safe than sorry."

McAllister looked at his friend.

Not like Banjo to express concerns like this – he usually just quietly makes the necessary arrangements, like the night they chased the Datsun and he had everything already packed in the back of the car.

"Ok – then if that's the case, I think we give Simply Bottles a miss. Let Lurch do whatever it is he is up to, and whilst he is in there, we will make a quiet exit."

Banjo nodded; they finished up, paid the bill and quietly left the diner, resolving to put as many miles as possible between them and Toowoomba.

Chapter 35

Banjo continued to drive, and so McAllister was free to enjoy the magnificent scenery that was unfolding. What became clear as they started to descend from the Range was that the townships they were passing through were becoming smaller and more isolated the further west they went.

The drays and transportation in the mid-1800s out here must have been hard graft.

At Banjo's suggestion, they were heading for Charleville, which he said was about 380 miles from Toowoomba. "It would be quite a crack" he said "but we need to put some distance between us and Lurch – not that I think he will be expecting us to go west, or even that we need to be worried about him, but even so."

They rolled into Charleville early evening, and for the first time, McAllister started to get a sense of how big and lonely this Country could actually be. Banjo gave him a quick update on the key history points of the town (not least that Cobb & Co had started a coach building business here back in the 1880s, and that Qantas had started their second scheduled flight service from here early in 1922 – reminding McAllister that Qantas actually stands for: Queensland and Northern Territory Air Service).

McAllister laughed. "Thanks for the history lesson, matey, but let's leave it there for now, find a beer and some grub, and get our heads down for a few hours. We need to be on the road before first light in the morning."

They found a small guest house in the town, that also served dinner – they said they would not need any breakfast in the morning, much to the landlady's concern – and after a hot bath, McAllister fell into a plump, clean bed that was absolute bliss. He was soon asleep and despite the turn of events during the day, was – for once – not bedevilled by horrible dreams.

The following morning they were up and gone before dawn had broken, and Banjo confirmed that they had about 600 miles to cover before they got to Birdsville, and they really needed to be there before dark. They shared the driving, only stopping now and again for a comfort break, to eat some of the sandwiches that the landlady at the Charleville guest house had kindly left out for them and to let the radiator cool down a bit. Not that there seemed to be any problem, "but you can never be certain and I would rather give it a breather than cane it to death, " said Banjo.

They finally rolled into the main street of Birdsville just after 1730, so they had made good time. They got out of the ute, which was now covered in dust, and walked towards the iconic Birdsville Hotel, which stood on the corner of the main crossroads and had done so since the 1870s. They ordered a jug of beer and downed a couple of pints each.

Rather like Crazy Pete's it had that air of a somewhat bygone era. All of the customers in the bar were men, noticed McAllister, and there was the gently whirring ceiling fan going above the almost obligatory mahogany bar top. They didn't do rooms any more, said the barmaid, but if they spoke to Wally over in the corner (and at this she nodded vaguely in the direction of an old guy sitting on his own), he might be able to help: "He has a homestead about an hour out of town, and sometimes takes guests" she added.

They wandered over to where Wally was sitting, and after some discussion over a few more pints, it was agreed that they could take a couple of beds in one of the outhouses that he kept for occasional visitors. They followed him out of town, and turned north on what appeared to be the main track heading (so the signs said) towards Bedourie, some 150 miles away.

After about half an hour, they turned off onto a side track, where a tired sign "Arcadia Station" pointed onwards. After another 15 minutes, they approached the old homestead. Although tired, it still looked in good condition. The obligatory bore hole windmill and water tank stood in the main yard, and there was a certain olde world charm about the house.

Wally got out of his vehicle and pointed to the several outhouses lying to the side and rear of the main house.

"There ya go, boys," he said. "Ya might prefer the small second one."

"Thanks, Wally," said Banjo. "We will be gone early in the morning." Wally looked at them through a crinkled face. "That's just fine; go when you want. I ain't expecting any other guests, so you won't be disturbing anyone else." He smiled and turned away, walking back towards the homestead.

They got their bags out of the ute and made for the second building, as Wally had suggested. When they walked in, they thought they had made a mistake. It was like walking into a museum. The walls had been covered with various photographs and memorabilia: Wally had been in the Royal Australian Navy at some stage in his life. Photographs of ships, shipmates, flags, insignia – they were all here, laid out like a tapestry to the past. It seemed he had served in the War and had been on the Atlantic Convoys rather than in the Far East. It was an impressive collection of information and historical artefacts. How it had managed to survive the heat of the Outback, they couldn't imagine and for a moment, McAllister was transported back to his uncle's underground house in Coober Pedy and the stereogram where he had wondered the exact same thing.

The door opened behind them, and they found Wally watching them with a keen interest.

"Thought this might be more up your street, lads," he said, with a grin. "What are ya: Army?"

Banjo laughed. "Nah – we've got more brains. Air Force."

It was Wally's turn to laugh. "Knew yewze had to be something. Yew in trouble of any kind? Yew based in Woomera?."

McAllister's turn to answer: "Why do you think we are based there?"

"Well, you ain't headin' towards Ipswich and the big base there not least because you came into Town from the East; there ain't nothin' further north or nothin' that makes sense anyways; you ain't goin' West 'cos there's nothing out there but the Simpson until you get to Alice Springs and I just can't see yew wantin' to do that, which means you got to go south. If you had been goin' straight to Adelaide, you would probably have gone further south on the main highway routes before cutting across, which says to me that I'm right about Woomera."

McAllister smiled quietly. This guy may be old, but he hadn't missed a trick.

"Yes, we are based there, Wally, but we thought we would take the scenic route back."

"Ok." The hard, world-weary stare was back. "Anything I should be looking out for?"

"Shouldn't be" replied Banjo, "but if we could use your radio to put a call through to the Base, that would be great."

"No problem: come up to the main house when you are ready," and with that, he turned and left the cabin.

They wandered over to the house about half an hour later. It was immaculate inside – everything was neat and clean, and nothing was out of place. Nicely framed photographs were on the table in the main sitting room, and there was a wedding photograph on the little table next to what was obviously the old man's favourite chair. Over in the corner, taking up a large portion of the wall, was the radio set. Above it were various maps of the area, and notes to remind Wally of certain things, and a calendar for the year 1969.

Clearly not bothered about keeping that up to date.

Wally saw him looking at it and said, "I keep it there because I like the pictures. Tea?" McAllister grinned and nodded his thanks as Banjo set up on the radio.

"What's your handle, Wally?" he called out, hoping it wasn't going to be their location.

"Just Arcadia Station," came the reply.

Banjo's heart sank.

"Then I'm not sure we should use that," he said. Quietly, he hoped that Lurch and whoever else he was working with – by this stage, Banjo was almost certain it wasn't really his RAAF Provost colleagues, but hadn't yet admitted that to McAllister – did not have access to the radio. Even as he thought it, he knew that was a forlorn hope and they now had to work on the assumption that if he did, then he would hear any transmission and would know exactly where they were.

Wally came to the doorway with the empty teapot in hand.

"So there is something I should be aware of," he said, matter of factly.

"It doesn't matter what the detail is, and I can assure you we are not in any trouble. But there is some sort of a plan afoot – we don't yet know what the objective is – but it involves some secret missile plans for the Navy, so we are being extra cautious," said Banjo, looking extremely embarrassed.

Wally's eyes gleamed. With that, he took the mic and sent out a general broadcast, saying that he had been having some problems with sheep rustlers – anyone seeing anything or anyone suspicious in the area, please call in and let him know.

Almost as soon as the message was finished, the radio crackled back into life with messages of concern and confirmation from some of the neighbouring sheep and cattle stations that they would be keeping their eyes open.

"There you go, lads," said Wally with a smile. "Woomera might not know, but all the local homesteads and stations will now be on watch. I see you have a CB in the ute, so if I hear or see anything after you leave tomorrow, then I will call you. Is there anyone else that it would help for me to contact should something go awry?."

"Yes," said McAllister. "can you call Kaz McNamara at Paradise Acres just outside of Coober Pedy? She will know what to do. And thanks, Wally," said McAllister, "but please be careful. We don't know much about what we are up against except that they are not particularly nice people."

"Never are," replied Wally, and he turned away to make the tea.

Tea turned into sharing a simple meal together, and the evening passed in companionable chatter. When they stood to leave, it was with genuine regret on all sides.

"Don't worry," said Wally. "We'll have eyes out. Just look after yourselves."

When they left early the next morning, Wally was already up and waved them off from the verandah. When they'd gone, he walked back inside and straight over to the radio set.

Chapter 36

Kevin Tapping was still at his desk at the Bank, working methodically through a bundle of transfer reports that his Secretary had brought to him earlier that afternoon. Amongst them he had found another large transfer to Pineapples'R'Us, and had rung Terri Wilson to let her know the details. But something was troubling him.

This had all the hallmarks of a much larger web of shell companies, but he couldn't seem to follow the trail.

With a start, he realised the time and hurriedly shuffled his papers together, put them into the safe and left his office – almost at a run. He had completely forgotten that he was meant to be having dinner with Caryle this evening, and he should be picking her up in – looking desperately at his watch – about ten minutes. Hopefully she would understand. He rang her. She did.

He got through the Adelaide traffic and raced into his flat in Christie's Beach. He was a keen surfer when he got the chance, and the flat had seemed like the ideal location for him when he first came down here. He showered and changed and quickly drove out to Salisbury East. All in all, he was about 45 minutes late for their date – not too bad considering all of the delays.

He had even found time to pick up some flowers for Caryle as a "sorry" on the way, and when she walked into the room, he thought she looked lovely. He realised he really was very smitten indeed. They left without incident and got to the restaurant that he had booked. Caryle had thoughtfully called ahead to say that they would be late, and after collecting some drinks at the bar, they were ushered to their table in the corner.

"Sorry again for being so late," he started.

"Doesn't matter, as long as you are ok" she said, looking at him thoughtfully and reading the signs.

He started fiddling with his beer glass, looking down at it. His mind was a jumble, and he wasn't sure that he should have come out for dinner this evening after all. He did not think that he was going to be very good company.

The waiter took their order, and a few minutes later, he returned with an iced wine bucket with the foil-wrapped neck of a bottle showing above the rim.

"I didn't order that," said Kevin, slightly startled.

"Oh, I know, sir," said the waiter, "but this is a complimentary bottle we are giving to all of our customers on Wednesday evenings. Part of a local promotion where we are trying to support local businesses. At the moment, that is the Jinidivik Winery at Nuriootpa. Hopefully you will really enjoy this special vintage that they have produced: Cham-Pine." The waiter showed him the bottle proudly, and was clearly waiting for Kevin to nod and make some sort of pleasantry.

He didn't.

He simply sat staring at the bottle.

Caryle intervened and rescued the situation: "That's a lovely idea, thank you," she said. "Please pour away," and the waiter, somewhat anxiously, did just that.

When the waiter had gone, Caryle decided to tackle things head-on.

"Ok, Kevin, what's going on? You haven't been yourself for the past few weeks, and you looked like you had seen a ghost just now when the waiter pulled that bottle out of the bucket. Time to have a chat."

Kevin looked down at his placemat and sighed deeply.

"Yes, I think so – but not here. We'll have dinner, and then we can talk."

"Ok," she said. And with that, they settled down to a very quiet dinner that they seemed to get through quite quickly.

Just as they were leaving the restaurant, a cheery voice rang out across the other diners:

"Well, hello, Kevin: haven't seen you for absolutely ages? How are you?"

Caryle and Kevin turned to see an extremely tall, bespectacled man, standing approximately 6'7," striding across the restaurant towards them.

"Good heavens," said Kevin, somewhat taken aback. "I haven't seen you since University. How are you?

The man invited them over to his table to meet his new wife and have a quick drink, brushing aside their protestations that it would be an intrusion and that they "really did need to be going."

Manners won out, and they walked over together to the table.

The man then introduced himself as Simon Hurdle-Jenkins, an old friend of Kevin's from their University days, and then introduced his new wife (who blushed at that description), Rose. Caryle and Kevin sat down. Kevin said it was great to see them, but they really could only stay for one drink – they were already meant to be somewhere else and were running late. Simon laughed. "Not a problem; let's just exchange numbers and cards, and we can perhaps catch up properly at another time?" "Perfect," said Kevin. "So what are you doing now?" he asked.

Slight pause. A laugh.

"Well, if I told you that, I would have to shoot you," replied Simon.

Kevin's face drained of colour, and Simon realised he had unintentionally put his foot in it.

"Sorry Kevin," he said. "Didn't mean to frighten you there. Just joking.

I am doing some detailed forensic accounting analysis for one of the big firms in the City. Nothing exotic," and with that, he handed over his business card.

"Sorry Simon, it's been a long day. Here's my card in return. I'm at the Australian Intercontinental Bank. I'll give you a call in the next couple of days. I am sorry, we need to forego the drink tonight. I'm just not up to it."

He apologised and stood up, still looking extremely pale. Caryle looked concerned.

Simon and Rose also stood up, and for the first time, Caryle realised just how tall and willowy Rose was. Even allowing for her 3" stiletto heels, Rose towered above her and must be about 6'0 tall in her stockings, she thought, with long limbs and a certain grace that had an elegance all of its own. Simon and Rose certainly made a striking couple.

They left the restaurant, and drove up to a quiet spot in Golden Grove, where they had a discussion that had been long overdue.

Kevin told Caryle all about Jindivik Winery, the money, his phone calls to "someone in the Police" to tell them anything he had found, and his suspicions about the shell companies. She realised that tonight was not perhaps the night, after all, to tell Kevin that she worked for the Australian Intelligence Service, and she was going to have to declare their relationship as part of her ongoing vetting responsibilities.

So she kept her silence and simply offered him a friendly shoulder to cry on.

She couldn't help wondering if this had anything to do with the missing Sea Wolf plans and that guy who had come over from the UK, Mike McAllister. She realised she had not seen him around at the DSTO much over recent weeks, and from different things crossing her boss's desk, she knew that an awful lot was going on under the surface.

The missile trials were due to start next week, and nerves were becoming somewhat frayed, such was the political and reputational pressure being applied for the tests to be a success. Not least because the Royal Navy was hoping to have the new systems in service the following Spring.

She sighed and made a note to speak to Terri Wilson when she got the chance.

Two days later, Kevin picked up the phone and called the number on Simon Hurdle-Jenkins' card. He felt he owed the guy some sort of an apology after the way things had gone on Wednesday evening. He heard some clicking on the line, followed by a hollowness, but paid no attention. The phones in the office were playing up all of the time. A female voice answered; he asked to speak to Simon. "I'll put you through," she said in a business-like voice.

Simon came on the line quite quickly.

"Hello there, Kevin. How are you? Bit concerned about you the other evening. Is all well?"

"Just ringing to apologise, really, Simon. It had been a long day, and it all just got a bit too much, to be honest. I really am sorry - please pass my apologies on to your new wife. And many congratulations on your marriage." And so the quite innocuous telephone call continued, with the two men agreeing to meet for a sandwich early next week to catch up in more detail. Just as they said goodbye, Kevin again heard the hollow clicking. He really hoped that the phones weren't going to go down: that really would be the last straw at the moment.

In an entirely different office in downtown Adelaide later on that evening, Special Agent Jim Brock listened to the recording of the call Kevin had made earlier.

An interesting connection.

He smiled quietly to himself.

Chapter 37

They raced along the smooth but unpaved track as fast as they could, dust swirling behind them in the early morning light. Banjo was again driving and was aware that they had basically an hour's driving to do before they were back where they started last night, and he was anxious to get through the Birdsville junction as soon as possible. There were a few early risers showing, and as they scurried south towards Marree, nearly 400 miles away, Banjo knew that they would reach a difficult potential choke point later on that day. They would need to get through it in order to turn off the Birdsville Track and join the Oodnadatta Track. But they would need to make a decision at that point because the Track forked. Either way, this was going to be a long dash, and he just hoped that his reservations were totally misplaced.

Some days, your luck is in.

Some days, it isn't.

And it often isn't when you need it to be the most.

Two hours south of Birdsville, with the expanse of the Simpson Desert stretching away on their right-hand side, they hit a large rut in the road. It was clear almost immediately that there was a problem with the ute.

"Sounds as though we may have a tyre problem," said McAllister.

They pulled over and inspected the damage. Sure enough, the rear off-side tyre was completely flat, and the wheel rim itself looked dented. They set about getting the necessary tools from the back of the vehicle. In the end, it took them the best part of an hour to change the tyre as they had been beset by missing bits of kit and damage to the wheel rim itself, forcing them to improvise.

"As long as it holds so that we can try and get a better repair" said a somewhat agitated Banjo. McAllister took over the driving. Something was up; that much was clear. Banjo was definitely not himself.

They nursed the ute over the border into northern South Australia and came to the entrance to Simpson Hills Station, one of the largest cattle ranches on the Track. The next township was a long way away, and they decided that they had no choice but to try their chances here. They went up the drive, which proved to be nearly 10 miles long, but there they found some help, albeit it was going to take a while.

So we will have to cool our heels here.

One of the hands brought out some coffee, and Banjo and McAllister sat down on a couple of tree trunks outside one of the outbuildings and settled in for what could be a long wait. They were left alone, as this was self-evidently a busy cattle station, and the hands had enough to do without nurse maiding them.

That suited McAllister just fine.

After a gentle prompting, Banjo told McAllister his fears for later on in the journey – the fact that there was, in effect, a perfect ambush point just after Marree. McAllister had pointed out that they didn't know if Lurch had spotted them or was following them or if anyone else was following them or even that whoever it was was aware they were heading for Woomera, so why would there be an ambush anywhere along the journey?

Banjo was adamant and he finally admitted that he neither liked nor, more importantly bearing in mind their line of work, trusted Lurch. If "they" had "lost" McAllister and Banjo but knew or guessed that their eventual destination was Woomera, then there were only so many ways to reach that location – especially by road, and by now, it was almost a certainty that Lurch would know that they had not left Queensland by air or rail.

And Banjo was worried that "they" may have all approaches covered. Lurch clearly couldn't do it on his own, but it was obvious that this was some sort of an organisational setup and they had to presume that manpower was not a problem.

They talked it through and made their plans as best they could. Unless things got particularly difficult, their instinct was not to try and make for Woomera tonight but to lay up somewhere of their choosing and then try and get in to the Base as early as possible the following day. They pored over the map, and Banjo identified a possible gap about 75 miles north of Marree, where it looked as though they could pull off the road safely and wait until morning. At least this wouldn't be an obvious official rest stop place either, so hopefully, if there were eyes out there, they might miss them.

McAllister asked to use the radio in the homestead, explaining to Banjo that he was just letting Wally know they were ok. That was true, but he also needed to make some contingency plans in case things went awry.

They eventually got back on the road just after lunchtime and were conscious that they were massively behind schedule. It was going to be a push to reach the layup before dark, and so they kept going with only short comfort breaks until early evening when they found the roadside pull-in that Banjo had identified on their map, and they set up for the night. They had agreed that they would take it in turns to keep watch, just to be on the safe side.

McAllister took the first watch, and he turned the situation they were in over in his mind.

We are now about 75 miles north of Marree, and Banjo is right again: we are completely isolated out here. If an ambush is waiting for us, then we are going to have our work cut out by beating them off or giving them the slip.

He was pleased when it was time to hand over the watch to Banjo. Normally, night watch didn't bother him. Gave him time to think. But tonight, he realised he needed rest because he sensed that tomorrow they would need their wits about them. He laid down on the back seat of the ute, closed his eyes and went straight to sleep.

They were up with the dawn and on the road quickly afterwards. They headed steadily towards Marree; both Banjo and McAllister had weapons on their laps, ready to be used if needed.

As they approached Marree township, there was more traffic and more people around. Already. It was only just after 0600, but as in most country places, these local folk were about their business early.

They realised that they had picked up unwanted company as soon as they reached the northern outskirts of the town. A black Land Rover with darkened windows had been sitting at the side of the road with a clear line of sight in both directions. As McAllister and Banjo passed this vehicle, they saw that there were two men in the front – one of whom was speaking into a radio. As if in confirmation, the vehicle pulled out after them and kept a safe distance, ready to react to any change in direction that might be attempted.

As they passed the main railhead, another two vehicles pulled in behind the black Land Rover.

The crossroads that was the choke point was right in the middle of town. Either they turned left onto the Oodnadatta Track leading south down to Lyndhurst, Leigh Creek and Parachilna, and would then have to try and double back towards Woomera at some stage; or they took the right-hand fork of that Track, continued to head west and then south, past Andamooka, Roxby Downs and into Woomera from the northeast. It looked as though either option would probably have a welcome committee.

"What's your bet?" asked Banjo.

"Right-hand fork," McAllister replied without hesitation.

The chase was clearly going to be on.

The two vehicles that had been parked up at various points down the left hand fork clearly had a call over the radio telling them that it was going to be the other leg that was going to be the chase and fight arena. All of the men crewing them, who had been lounging around, having a cigarette and chatting, got back into position and quickly turned the vehicles from their original positions and hit the main road, heading towards the fleeing ute.

McAllister and Banjo saw all of this in the rear and side mirrors and knew they were committed now.

Banjo floored the ute, and they shot past several flatbed vehicles parked at various locations on the right hand fork. All of them had men in the back, most of whom seemed to be waving guns or weapons of some description. Banjo's concerns about an ambush had been well founded, and McAllister was grateful that they used some time to consider their options.

However much they had planned. However, the inescapable reality was that they were now on their own, with a trail of clearly hostile vehicles following, some of which were starting to get brave and test them. One of the flatbeds started to get closer and the passenger hung out of the window and opened fire with what looked to McAllister like some sort of a shotgun. He missed wildly, but nevertheless, it was the signal for a complete free-for-all to unfold and a number of his excitable colleagues took the opportunity to let rip. The wing mirror next to Banjo was shattered early on, which meant that the following rag-tag were starting to get their eye in.

McAllister decided to bide his time to return fire: it was going to get more hairy than this, and he needed to preserve as much ammo as possible.

Banjo concentrated on the Track.

The firing was coming thick and fast now, and McAllister just had time to shout a warning as a bloke stood up on the back of the flatbed two vehicles behind; his colleague suddenly pulled out of the way, and McAllister could see he was pointing a shoulder-held RPG. The grenade left the cylinder and headed straight for them. Banjo swung a sharp right, and the vision of the grenade speeding past his window was one that would not leave McAllister for a long time. It eventually crashed into a bank of earth by the side of a curve in the Track, and clods of sand and mud rained down on the ute as it detonated.

The whole procession kept racing along.

The firing was intensifying, and still, McAllister had not returned the compliment. They had also maintained radio silence up to this point. They looked at each other, and both recognised that they could not outrun everything forever.

McAllister picked up the radio and sent out a call: "Waltzing Matilda; Waltzing Matilda; repeat Waltzing Matilda, Waltzing Matilda ."

Banjo looked at him in disbelief.

"What the hell are you doing?" he shouted over the din.

"We just need a bit of backup, matey. Keep your eyes peeled." He grinned wickedly.

Banjo shook his head.

What had this nutcase been up to now?

With that, McAllister climbed into the back of the ute, kicked out the rear window, and brought up the GPMG that he had ready and waiting sitting on the back seat. He opened fire and immediately scored a direct hit on the vehicle following; it catapulted over itself and burst into flames. Bits of body and vehicle wreckage flew off in all directions. The following vehicles had to veer wildly to avoid the carnage, but they kept on coming.

McAllister picked his next target and fired again. This time, the driver, was more wary, but McAllister still managed to pepper the front grill of the Land Rover. That vehicle also blew up.

Having seen the chaos being caused, the next two vehicles changed tactics and came off the main track. This had its own potential hazards because of the uneven terrain, even for 4WDs, as one of the chasing vehicles discovered as it disappeared nose-first into an old disused mine shaft that had remained undisturbed at the side of the road for many years.

That still left a number of vehicles in pursuit.

Everyone seemed to be firing now, and Banjo was having a hell of a job keeping ahead of the following pack. Amidst the swirl of dust and the noise of the ongoing gunfight, he saw up ahead what appeared to be a blockade comprised of all sorts of vehicles and his eyebrows raised of their own accord in shocked disbelief.

Christ: trucks, utes, artics, is that a full cattle train in there as well? All shapes and sizes of 4WDS. They are all in there – side by side across the Track. They must stand about four deep. And they all are flying the Australian flag. What's that: RAAF, Army – Desert Rats?, Royal Navy – HMS Victorious: are you kiddin' me?

What the hell?

At first sight of the oncoming barrage, the centre of the blockade moved – with the two vehicles in the middle of each row moving ahead of the others to open a gap in the road for McAllister and Banjo to pass through. A man in an Akubra standing on the back of a flatbed with binoculars was waving Banjo through and seemed to be generally orchestrating the response from the gathered group. Banjo was shouting to McAllister to look at what was ahead, and McAllister turned to see the sight before him.

It was breathtaking.

McAllister grinned.

Banjo coaxed the ute forward at an even faster rate and shot through the gap in the waiting vehicles. As they went through, the whole entourage started to move as one towards the oncoming pursuers, closing the centre gap as they did so, ensuring that Banjo and McAllister's vehicle was safely gathered in behind the group. For a wild moment, McAllister thought that this was their very own version of the gunfight at the OK Corral. Everyone on the trucks opened fire as one, and the sound was accompanied by the squeal of tyres and brakes as the pursuing vehicles realised that the odds had suddenly changed drastically against them.

Just as the pursuing pack fell into disorganised chaos, trying to find a way to avoid the oncoming onslaught, another sound rent the air above the din. McAllister could also feel the air pressure change, and he looked up to see two Bell UH-1 Iroquis helicopters coming in low above their heads with side doors open and heavy machine guns in place. They cleared the advancing group of trucks and opened fire on the group of pursuers. There was clearly going to be no escape, and they gave up the fight there and then, stopping their vehicles and getting out – making a show of placing their weapons on the ground and holding their hands up. One of the aircraft set down on the Track behind the last of what had been the pursuing group, and a number of people got out of the body of the helicopter, including, McAllister was pleased to see, Alison Fielding.

The other helicopter remained airborne and on station to ensure that there were no last-minute problems.

McAllister and Banjo had pulled over on the side of the track to watch all of this unfold in front of them.

The guys on the helicopters had secured their prisoners in handcuffs, who were now being held face down in the dust. From behind them, McAllister heard the wail of sirens and the RAAF provosts units, together with civilian Police support, came down the track and swept past them.

It was breathless stuff.

Alison Fielding walked over to them, a look of concern on her face. When she realised that they were in one piece, her face broke into a wide grin. "Wouldn't have missed that for anything," she said. "Well, you two certainly don't do things by halves, do you?"

The three of them walked amiably back towards the now crowding group of people to whom he felt he owed so much. He was met by none other than Crazy Pete: it had been clear to McAllister that he had been the one in the Akubra with the binoculars, giving the directions to the rest of the group and he was grateful to this tough guy for having come through when they had really needed some help.

"Knew yew waz trouble, McAllister, the minute I set eyes on ya in my pub," he said with a lop-sided grin. "Glad we could help. Most of the lads here have served at one time or another and were up for a bit of a fight. They were all happy to help: that's the way with us Outback folk. Even when it relates to you, Poms." His grin reappeared. "I think that the beers are on you, eh?"

McAllister and Banjo laughed and shook hands with him and many of the others who had crowded around. McAllister saw his uncle Geraint and his uncle Huw amidst the laughing, jostling throng, and he pushed his way through to them. They hugged him, and everyone seemed to be talking and laughing at once.

Gradually, the group cleared and in an unspoken agreement, everyone headed off in a gigantic trail of vehicles towards Andamooka and eventually Crazy Pete's.

It was quite a party.

Chapter 38

The phone rang on his desk.

Jan de Klerk simply lifted the receiver and said nothing.

The voice at the other end relayed his information.

De Klerk went pale and still said nothing but replaced the receiver.

He took his spectacles off and wiped them with the special cloth that he kept for the purpose in his inside pocket.

This is going to be difficult. It is not a message that I particularly wish to relay, but there is no choice.

He replaced his spectacles, took a deep breath and picked up the receiver, dialling the number of his boss.

Having heard the message, his orders were clear.

McAllister and Paterson were to be killed – quickly and efficiently. "No more mistakes."

De Klerk replaced the receiver.

He knew exactly what that meant.

It was them or him.

Chapter 39

Whilst Jan de Klerk was receiving his orders, FBI Special Agent Jim Brock was in Adelaide, waiting for Kevin Tapping, who was presumably making his way towards him through the lunchtime throng. He knew that Tapping had set up a lunch meeting with his old University pal, Simon Hurdle-Jenkins. At Brock's own suggestion, Hurdle-Jenkins had proposed the little café in Adelaide Zoo just off of North Terrace, where they could sit outside in comparative peace. Brock took up position at a corner table with a copy of The Australian and, to the rest of the world, looked like a guy out to enjoy the sunshine in lovely surroundings during his lunch break. He waited for Hurdle-Jenkins and Tapping to arrive.

This was an interesting link-up from Brock's point of view. He was a specialist in tracing companies himself and had been enticed from private accountancy practice back in the States by the lure of working on some of the most complex and sensitive cases that the FBI had to handle.

Hurdle-Jenkins was one of the best forensic accountants he had ever met and was currently on unofficial secondment engaged in another complex investigation assisting the Australian Security Services and the FBI. So he hadn't officially changed horses, but he was certainly heavily involved. It was probably only a matter of time.

So where does Tapping fit into this and does he know what Hurdle-Jenkins is currently doing?

Just at that moment, Hurdle-Jenkins appeared, his unmistakeable tall frame towering above other people in the café. He was carrying a tray with some sandwiches and a drink, and he sat down at the table for two right next to Brock.

Brock took no notice.

About five minutes later, Kevin Tapping arrived, similarly carrying some lunch on a tray. Tapping and Hurdle-Jenkins saw each other almost at the same time, waved, and Tapping made his way over to join his friend.

Brock continued with his own lunch.

After the usual pleasantries over the first ten minutes or so about wives, girlfriends, and life in general, the talk at the Tapping table turned to work.

Brock listened even more intently.

"I see you are at Delaney & Harris, then," he said, referring to one of the largest Accountancy firms in Australia.

"Yes, luckily got in there almost straight from University. Currently dealing with shell companies, fraud, that sort of stuff. Yourself?"

Tapping hesitated and looked at his hands.

"I am with the Australian Intercontinental Bank. Deputy Security Manager. One of my deployments on their new Graduate Accelerated Promotion Scheme. I will serve two years here and then hopefully get a promotion and get posted to another branch."

Hurdle-Jenkins watched him quietly through the thick lenses of his glasses.

"Enjoying it?" he asked.

"Usually."

Tapping seemed to make up his mind.

"Look, Simon, I would really appreciate your advice if you don't mind."

"Well, ask away, and I will let you know if I can help," he replied.

And so it was that Kevin Tapping, without naming the companies involved, outlined the bones of the Pineapples'R'Us, Jindivik Winery, and Simply Bottles conundrum to his friend, who unbeknownst to him was working with the man at the next table and with Terri Wilson's team.

Tapping laid out that he "felt" it was wrong and that there were other things going on here, but he couldn't find the right thread to pull. He stressed it was important, again without saying why.

"Do any of the Directors of any of the Companies have holdings or office in any other company?" asked Simon.

"It looks as though there may be a connection between two of the companies which would seem to be legit because they are in the same field, and it makes sense. Otherwise, I don't know. I am still awaiting the results of the Company searches."

"Any whiff of somewhere like the British Virgin Islands, the Caymans, or Panama?" he asked.

"Not as yet," said Kevin.

"Ok. Well that's something. Then I think you may well find that the Searches will give you the next step. If this is indeed a complex web of shell companies and central holdings, then you will find that some of your Directors will have shares or be on the Board of other companies who, at first blush, don't appear to be connected with your central concern. You really do have to just peel back the layers of the onion, Kevin. I know it is a slow process, but unfortunately, that is how it is. You may need to call in some favours from the Bank's overseas branches as well if the trail starts to lead there."

"You don't happen to have any connections who could hurry the results up, do you?" asked Kevin. "Sorry to ask, but I just have this terrible feeling that something is dreadfully wrong and I am anxious to try and get to the bottom of it. It is probably nothing, but you know what it's like," Kevin ended almost apologetically.

"Tell you what," said Simon. "Why don't you and Caryle come over to our place for dinner on Saturday night, and I will see what I can do to speed those searches up for you in the meantime. Hopefully, I might have some information for you then."

Kevin looked at him gratefully.

"That would be fab, thanks," said Kevin. "We'll look forward to seeing you."

"I will need the name of the Companies," laughed Simon, "if I am going to stand any chance of chasing up your information."

Kevin hesitated again before confirming the names to Simon.

"Don't worry," said Simon. "Hopefully, it will be nothing, but I will look forward to seeing you on Saturday."

After some further small talk, they parted company and Kevin returned to his office, feeling happier than he had done since this whole thing started.

That was until he got back to his desk and found that some mail had arrived whilst he had been at lunch. It was an amendment to the Company Search results previously sent over, and attached to it was a note from the Registrar of Companies apologising for the error on the previous results supplied.

Simply Bottles was indeed registered in Queensland, but in addition to the three officers already confirmed, it had an additional Director called Hendrik Cronje, who gave an address in the British Virgin Islands.

Kevin felt as if his heart had stopped.

Chapter 40

McAllister and Banjo somehow got back to The Shack in Woomera in the early hours of the morning after the Oodnadatta Gun Fight as it was now being called colloquially, very much the worse for wear.

But they had had a terrific time.

As they got through the door, the phone was ringing. McAllister answered, and a very business-like voice apologised for troubling him so late, but he and Banjo were required to attend a high-level briefing in the special ops room at Woomera Base the following morning at 0800 sharp. McAllister grunted and hung up.

Blast.

They reported as ordered for the briefing later that morning and went through the same procedure with the RAAF provosts, the doors, and the lift as before.

They were shown to the same Briefing Room, and the same personnel were present. Head Shed was again in command, and he tersely indicated that they should sit down at the table in the same places they had occupied on the previous occasion.

"Good morning everyone. Thank you for convening at such short notice. There have been some developments, and I wanted you to be briefed straight away," and with that, he turned towards Norman Reynolds and indicated he should proceed.

Reynolds outlined that they had now completed all of the

toxicology tests on the bodies of Zoe Schuster and Lucy Andrews. The samples had been sent to the specialist research facility at Porton Down in England for assistance, because of how little was actually known about Abrin. The specialists there had determined that Lucy Andrews had, after all, been administered Abrin, but her cause of death was actually blood loss from a severe wound on the inside of her right thigh where her femoral artery had been severed. Had she not, in effect, bled out, the latest results from Porton Down now indicated that she would have died from the Abrin poisoning anyway.

The original view that she had been administered strychnine before her death had proven to be erroneous. Quite why or how the injury to the artery had not been mentioned on the autopsy report was not known, but further enquiries into that would now be undertaken.

Zoe Schuster, on the other hand, had definitely been murdered through the administration of a significant dose of Abrin, probably through two separate methods – food and drink, and through shower or bath water or toiletries, particularly shampoo, as they had found traces of it on her scalp and in her hair.

The investigation had not made any real progress in terms of where she had been imprisoned, but due to the discovery of some papers at the Schuster home following the Doctor's death, it was now clear that he had been blackmailed to steal the blueprints to the Sea Wolf missile and possibly to also provide other sensitive information.

Due to the number cypher found by McAllister and Banjo, they were also now reasonably sure that this was not a lone wolf scenario and that they were dealing with some sort of Organised Crime gang, but as yet, were not clear on how large or how extensively they had infiltrated Government and security bodies. The fact that Dr Schuster was being blackmailed and that Chips McInerney had been in the car with Hendrik Cronje when it exploded was clear evidence that this group had reach and were using it.

When Reynolds had finished his summary, he turned back to Head Shed who took up the narrative.

"At this point, I would like to introduce you to three other people who have been assisting us with a different strand of enquiries," and with that, he pushed a button under the desk. Several seconds later, the doors opened and two men walked in: Kevin Tapping, Simon-Hurdle Jenkins and FBI Special Agent Jim Brock.

At Head Shed's indication, both sat down at the table next to McAllister and Banjo, and they were then invited to brief the gathered group as to the results of their investigations.

Listening to the outline given initially by the FBI man, and then by Simon Hurdle-Jenkins, it seemed as though the apparently innocent appearance of Jindivik Wineries, Pineapples'R'Us and Simply Bottles was an incorrect one.

What emerged from the briefing was a complex web of companies that seemed to be interconnected, each with shares in the others and/or shared officers, and which led to some key main holding companies, registered in either the British Virgin Islands, the Cayman Islands or Panama.

This web of companies included Big Byte R&D Holdings, who were registered in California, USA and which, of course, had been the initial focus for the FBI and where Chips McInerney had been showing an interest. It seemed that all of them were part of the five-strong conglomerate umbrella.

They confirmed that Hendrik Cronje had been a Director of Pineapples'R'Us, with an address registered in the British Virgin Islands.

They handed out a pack of information relating to each of the companies that they had uncovered:

- Jindivik Wineries

- Simply Bottles

- Pineapples'R'Us

- E.Lements Inc,

- Big Byte R&D Holdings

- Southern Star Mining

- Southern Star Fuels

- Direct Logistics

The main umbrella companies were:

- Fundamentals Inc, Cayman Islands,

- Plonk Inc, British Virgin Islands

- Gough Holdings, Panama

- Dig Dig Limited, Cayman Islands.

They, in turn, were owned and operated by one mother company, which appeared to be pulling the strings from the centre of the web: Gough Gifblaar Holdings, registered in the British Virgin Islands.

So far, they had been unable to get behind the veil of secrecy that had shrouded most of these incorporations. Gough Gifblaar Holdings, in particular, was proving problematic, so they were still unsure as to exactly who was orchestrating some of the events.

Tapping and Brock confirmed that they had followed some of the money transfers as far as they had been able, but it was a long, slow process and it was unlikely that they would have concrete results any time soon despite their best efforts.

"Any questions?" asked Head Shed.

"Yes," said McAllister. "What does Gifblaar mean or what is it?"

"Reynolds!" barked Head Shed, at which Norman Reynolds again took the floor.

"Dichapetalum cymosum is a small, fairly unremarkable shrub, commonly found in northern South Africa. In Afrikaans, it's common name is Gifblaar. English translation is: Poison Leaf. It is a common cause of cattle fatality in South Africa, and if ingested and then the dead carcass is eaten by another predator, that predator is also poisoned – so it passes down the chain. It is toxic to humans but not usually fatal, although it can be in the event of sufficient quantities being ingested."

Silence reigned in the room as everyone considered all of this.

McAllister picked up the conversation again.

"So, bearing in mind the theft of the plans, the involvement of Hendrik Cronje, and now the appearance of this Gough Gifblaar Holdings, do we take it that there is a South African strand to this? They are still under an arms embargo, aren't they? So presumably getting hold of the Sea Wolf specifications would be like gold dust irrespective of anything else that they might be up to."

Head Shed looked at him and cleared his throat before speaking.

"We don't know is the honest answer, McAllister. They – whoever "they" are – certainly seem to have gone to a lot of trouble and expense over a long period of time to set up such a complicated organisation, and to get involved in blackmail and murder. This certainly was not set up on a whim – it has taken years in the planning.

And the events of the past couple of days culminating in your Escape from Dodge City escapade only underlines that they are extremely serious and I am not sure that we have yet worked out exactly what their main objective actually is. What is the point of all this? To get the Sea Wolf plans? Possibly – they would certainly be useful to the South African cause."

At this, Jim Brock spoke up.

"From the US side, we don't know anything about this Gough Gifblaar Holdings at present, but I would agree with your assessment as to the time and extent of the planning that would have been required to get this far. The use of the Abrin is also not a sudden idea – that was cleverly thought out, and again, we have a horticultural connection because Gifblaar is also a plant. So my guess is that we have someone who has a keen interest in flora and fauna, turning that to their

241

own murderous purpose. But as you say, the ultimate objective is still very unclear. I am waiting for some further results to come in from the States and will update everyone when I have something to report."

Head Shed nodded and indicated how grateful HM Government and the Government of Australia were for the amount of assistance that the FBI was giving to the investigation.

Again, the group fell silent for a few minutes before Banjo asked

"What about the people arrested as a result of the Oodnadatta Gun Fight or the Escape from Dodge City, as you put it, sir? Have they not been able to provide any further information on any of this?"

"Unfortunately not, Paterson, although the interrogations are continuing. Everyone seems to be keeping extremely tight-lipped at the moment, but you never know. Right, if that is everything," said Head Shed, clearly keen to bring the discussion to a close.

"We proceed with caution. McAllister: you will remain with us on secondment, as I previously indicated; you will stay here at Woomera with Paterson for the missile trials but on a very short NTM so that we can move you both to wherever we need you quickly. So please do not go walkabout. We will have some VIP visitors coming for the trials, so security will have to be tight. We will regroup in three days in the event that we have some further results to discuss.

Incidentally, thank you, Mr. Tapping and Mr. Hurdle-Jenkins, for your invaluable assistance: we are grateful to you both for your efforts so far and will look forward to your next report with interest.."

Both men nodded and smiled self-consciously.

With that, the meeting concluded.

When they reached the open air, Paterson and McAllister made for the same tree in the car park that they had done on the previous occasion and broke out their fags.

"What do you make of that lot?" asked Banjo after enjoying his first deep puff.

"Well, we certainly have a hornet's nest on our hands," said McAllister, "and I must confess that I don't like this South African link that seems to be appearing now. But I am completely at a loss to see where it's all going. Only time will tell, I guess, but even so."

With that, they both lapsed back into thoughtful silence.

Chapter 41

The trials at Woomera started on time, and as Head Shed had indicated, a number of VIPs descended on the Base amidst tightened security. The days were busy, and McAllister and Paterson threw themselves into the various strands of the ongoing investigation, determined to try and find some answers.

Alison was at the epicentre of trying to keep everything on an even keel whilst accommodating the needs of the high-ranking visitors, and so they saw very little of her either.

Terri Wilson was at Woomera, but again, she was also very heavily tied up with the mechanics of the visits and seemed to have little time to spare for them.

Almost as if she is avoiding us.

McAllister grinned ruefully.

There was still no news from the prisoners arrested after the Oodnadatta affair – too scared to start talking it seemed; no further update from Kevin Tapping or Jim Brock on the incorporation and accounting issues either.

In fact, still a big fat zilch all round.

And then there was the problem of Lurch.

Banjo and McAllister had discussed this on several occasions and could not decide on how best to get to the bottom of it. He had not been seen at Woomera since the blockade had gone so wrong, and so they could not even approach him directly to get his explanation.

After all, he could have a perfectly reasonable and honest reason for having visited Simply Bottles just at that time.

But even as he thought it, McAllister realised just how thin that sounded. Even the timing of the visit was unfortunate, at best; suspicious, at worst.

Not getting along with someone was one thing; thinking that a serving Provost Officer was actually in cahoots with what was rapidly being seen as a seriously dangerous, organised crime gang was quite another.

He sighed and rubbed his eyes. He was feeling tired. Perhaps a walk would do him some good. Banjo was over at the other side of the room talking to one of the SAPOL officers who was assisting with the investigation, and McAllister mimed to him that he was going outside for a smoke and a walk. Banjo nodded and continued his conversation.

He set off at a brisk pace, leaving the boundaries of the Base behind him fairly quickly. He headed into the town centre, and went towards Burt and Vera's general store on the main road. He suddenly realised that as it was Wednesday afternoon, the pool would be available for use, so he changed direction and went back to The Shack for his trunks and a towel.

It was clear that RAAF afternoon had been in full swing as he saw a number of colleagues leaving, and he realised how late it must be. He quickly changed and dived in so that he could at least enjoy the luxury of a few lengths before the pool closed.

Even this late in the afternoon, it is still warm.

He glided along, enjoying the feel of the water against his

skin. He started to relax and kicked on to really feel the pull on his body. His mind started to clear as he swam, and he was completely oblivious to everything around him other than the warmth of the late afternoon sun, the water and the number of problems that seemed to be facing him in terms of the investigation.

The shock of the grab around his legs was huge, and he was pulled downwards quickly and expertly without the chance of taking a large breath before his head was well beneath the water's surface.

A strong arm suddenly grabbed him around his neck, holding him down, and squeezing his airway. He was being held down towards the bottom of the deep end, and he fought. He could not see his attacker but could sense the size and power of the man. The knife came towards him quickly and forcefully. He did his best to defend against the oncoming blow, and he saw rather than felt the knife enter his side. He grabbed the man's wrist and saw a bracelet, the same as those worn by so many different people involved in the periphery of this case and pushed the thumb backwards as hard as he could, hoping he had broken it.

At the same time, McAllister pushed off from the bottom of the pool with all of his strength, racing for the surface. He managed to grab a fast, urgent breath before his attacker pulled him back under. No slouch himself, McAllister was surprised at how long his assailant could hold his breath. He elbowed backwards, and caught the man under the chin. McAllister saw a small rebreather fall slowly through the churning water, and realised that he had answered his own question. He rammed upwards with the heel of his hand, and caught his opponent again on the side of the head.

Both men knew that McAllister was injured. There was now blood in the water, and it seemed to galvanise the fight even further. McAllister realised he probably did not have long to maintain this level of intensity before his strength started to fail.

He could see the edge of a float board that someone had left on the side of the pool from earlier swimming lessons and grabbed at it, bringing the hard plastic edge down with as much force as he could summon onto the head of his attacker. It was a good blow, and the man pulled back slightly to reposition for the next attack. It was now his turn to start considering options, as his own head wound had opened, and more blood was starting to ooze into the water.

McAllister managed to get his hands onto his attacker's face and found the eye sockets. He wrapped his legs around the man in a fearsome death embrace, forcing him down towards the bottom of the pool. He worked his thumbs into the man's eyes and pressed his head against the tiled floor.

The man opened his mouth as the pain in his eyes became intense, and he scrabbled at McAllister to find a release of the pressure. The water rushed into his mouth, and McAllister hung on, sensing that this was his moment to finish this fight. His lungs were bursting, and he was desperate to take a breath, but he knew he could not until his attacker had gone limp. There was now a considerable amount of blood and eye goo floating in the water, but McAllister closed his mind to it and tried to hold on.

When his opponent offered no further resistance, McAllister pushed up to the surface and gasped great lungfuls of air. He felt dizzy, but whether from the lack of oxygen or loss of blood, he could not be sure.

Either way, he realised he was not in good shape and needed help. He moved himself to a position where he could stand on the pool floor and hold on to the side before attempting to walk to the shallow end.

With a huge effort, he climbed up the ladder. He struggled to stand up to get to the emergency call unit that was on the wall by the side of the pool. He pushed the red button and heard the crackle of a voice but then felt the world go dark as he slipped into unconsciousness.

As he opened his eyes, he saw the concerned features of Banjo and Terri Wilson peering down at him. It seemed very foggy and blurry. He could not work out where he was. It was only after a few moments that the fight in the pool came back to him, and he automatically moved his hand to his side. He found that even that small movement was difficult. Terri Wilson was saying something to him, and he concentrated really hard to try and understand.

"McAllister: you are safe in the medical unit. You need a bit of a rest, and then you can go back to The Shack," she said.

Still in Woomera then, on Base. Can't be that serious.

Banjo was standing quietly at the bedside, looking at him.

"Can't let you out anywhere, matey. You just attract 'em, don't you?"

And he smiled his kindly, crooked grin.

Terri Wilson continued. "When you are feeling brighter, I will bring you up to speed. But right now, you need to rest.

We will see you tomorrow."

And with that, she signalled to Banjo and they walked away.

McAllister looked around and saw that he was the only occupant in a small white painted room with no windows, one door and the usual medical paraphernalia of a hospital dotted around the room. An IV drip was plugged into his arm, the bag standing guard by the bedside.

He rested back on the pillows.

Just need to think all of this through.

And with that, he was asleep.

Chapter 42

The following day, McAllister walked back into the main office at the Base – bruised, stitched, but otherwise back in operation. He spotted Terri Wilson over in the corner, and he went over to her.

"Time for a catch-up, I think," he said, without preamble.

She smiled, and indicated towards a small meeting room at the end of the main office. She also beckoned Banjo over, and the three of them made their way into the comparative calm of the separate enclave.

"Let's bring you up to speed, then," she said briskly.

"There will be a full security briefing at 1500 this afternoon, as planned. You are expected to attend. Until then, you are not to go anywhere unaccompanied. Banjo here will be with you at all times, even if you just want to pop out for a couple of minutes for a breath of air. The people we are dealing with seem to have taken a particular dislike to you and you have had yet another narrow escape, so we can't be too careful."

"Who was the bloke in the pool?" he asked. "Did you notice that he was wearing one of those bracelets?"

Wilson went quiet for a moment.

"Can't tell you that right now: it will have to wait for the full briefing later on. Did you see him, though, when you got to the pool? Can you remember?"

McAllister shook his head. "I didn't see anyone at all – not in or around the pool. When I got there, most people seemed to be leaving and I was just going to have a quick swim before closing time. When I dived in, I didn't think that anyone else was there and I certainly didn't see anyone in the water."

He shuddered involuntarily as he recalled the shock as his legs were suddenly grabbed from underneath him.

Terri Wilson watched him closely.

"Ok, don't worry about that now, then," she said. "The trials up here are finished – successfully, I might add, so that is a huge relief. We have got rid of all the VIPs and dignitaries, so we are back to normal: whatever that might be. You will be pleased to know that the Royal Navy will be receiving the Sea Wolf missile probably earlier than expected, with the first consignment going on board in January of next year. So, everyone seems much happier on that front. Any other questions ahead of this afternoon's briefing?"

McAllister shook his head, and they all got up and moved back into the main office. There seemed to be a lot of paperwork around, and McAllister wandered past the various whiteboards with their notes, arrows and photographs. Chips was still in pride of place on one, as was Lucy Andrews on another.

So many gone, and for what?

As on the last two occasions of the specialist briefings, Head Shed was in the main chair and the cast was the same as previously, including Simon Hurdle-Jenkins and FBI Special Agent Jim Brock, who were present this time from the start.

McAllister noted that Kevin Tapping was not present. Brock nodded to McAllister as he entered, smiled and said he heard that McAllister had been getting in touch with his American roots, "What with the Gunfight on the Oodnadatta Track an' all."

McAllister nodded and smiled in return and suddenly thought how long ago all of that seemed.

Must try and get back up to Coober Pedy or Andamooka to see the uncles: need to say thanks if nothing else – and see Crazy Pete.

He smiled to himself.

The meeting got underway.

It quickly transpired that the Australian Secret Service, the British Secret Intelligence Service (MI6) and the FBI were all actively working on the financial strands of the problem, and the web that had emerged at the last briefing was gradually being filled in.

Gough Gifblaar Holdings was still at the centre, and proving extremely difficult to pierce, but work was continuing apace. The links between all of the companies outlined at the previous briefing had been confirmed, and enquiries were now underway in relation to the variously named Directors. At this point, Head Shed nodded towards Jim Brock.

"Perhaps you could take up the story, Special Agent?"

Brock cleared his throat. "Yup. We have done some digging into the Southern Star Fuels company, and the sister organisation Southern Star Mining. We have put together a slide to show the interaction between all of the companies," at which point he pressed the button on his desk, and the slide projector whirred into action. Everyone turned to the large white screen on the wall at the side of the room as Brock continued.

"You will see from this slide the inter-connection between the various companies, but it is the two Southern Stars that have really caught our attention. We expected that both would have considerable holdings here in Australia, and perhaps in the US, the Middle East, etc. But interestingly they have a significant foot print in South Africa – *almost* to the exclusion of other parts of the globe where you would expect these sorts of interests to be part of a wide ranging portfolio." He paused.

"So, another South African link?" said McAllister.

"Looks like it," nodded Brock, "but we are still no further ahead with who is actually behind it. We have some friends making enquiries."

Head Shed took back control of the meeting.

"That brings us to the next area of concern: the fact that the RAAF Provost Wing may have been compromised by this group." This time, he nodded towards Norman Reynolds, who took up the conversation.

"It seems clear that the man leading the chase of McAllister and Paterson across Queensland and down the Birdsville Track was one of our own Provosts: RAAF Sergeant Peter Addams."

At this, Reynolds pressed a button on his desk and a large-sized photograph of Lurch popped up on the projector screen. McAllister and Banjo looked at each other, and Reynolds then set out the sequence of events that had led to the Oodnadatta Track events.

Reynolds continued the narrative:

"There was no apparent reason for Addams to go to Simply Bottles: in fact, we would have preferred it that no official approach was made at all at the present time. Further enquiries have revealed that his brother-in-law, a dual South African/Australian national, is one of the Directors. Matters are slightly complicated in that we cannot ask Sergeant Addams directly, as he is currently missing – AWOL in fact, and he has not reported for duty since the Oodnadatta events."

Again, the South Africa link.

When Reynolds finished his outline, there was a short silence before anyone spoke.

McAllister cleared his throat. "So, who was the bloke in the pool who tried to kill me, then?" he asked. "And have you had a chance to examine his bracelet? Those keep appearing, so they must mean something."

"They do keep appearing, McAllister – you are quite right on that. We have had a chance to examine this one, and it is certainly made from the plant pods that we discussed at the last meeting. Our best guess at this stage is that although it is a basic link with others in the same group, it also has a practical application in that it could be used as a means of suicide if the wearer got the chance and the circumstances warranted it. Although death would not be instantaneous, it would be certain - along the perameters, we have also previously discussed.

We have done some digging into the provenance of the cross that is attached to the bracelet and whether that has any particular significance. It would appear to link the wearer to a little-known sect of the Dutch Reformed Church – largely based in South Africa, but not exclusively so. We are making further enquiries into that aspect."

He continued "With regard to the man in the pool – at the moment, we have not been able to identify him. Our international colleagues are working on that, but from initial enquiries, the chap does not appear to have been an Australian – or even a Brit for that matter. We will keep you updated when we know more."

McAllister nodded his thanks, and at that point, Head Shed took up the lead again:

"To say that the link with Sergeant Addams is unfortunate is an understatement. However, it does give us a warning. As we do not know how far any infiltration has seeped into our organisations, there is to be no discussion of any of the material covered today with anyone outside of this room. Is that clear? And I mean, anyone," barked Head Shed.

Everyone nodded.

Simon Hurdle-Jenkins was then invited to give a brief overview of the financial investigations and money transfers. Nothing of any real note other than that already outlined by Special Agent Brock had emerged during the three days since their last briefing.

The meeting seemed to be winding up.

"We will reconvene again in three days unless we have anything more positive before then. And one last thing, everyone, on a slightly lighter note" said Head Shed. "Just to let you all know that we have this morning been informed by our colleagues in London that there will be a visit to Australia in the Spring by HM Queen Elizabeth II and HRH Duke of Edinburgh as part of the Silver Jubilee celebrations. The precise itinerary has not yet been released, but I have every reason to believe that she will be coming to South Australia at some stage of that visit. I understand that there will be a public announcement in the press tomorrow." he paused, and then added, "But don't forget that you heard it here first."

His thin lips moved into what McAllister assumed Head Shed thought was a smile at his own non-joke.

No one laughed, but everyone got up and made their way to the door.

Gordon Bennett – a spook who tries to make jokes. Not funny, not funny at all.

Banjo and McAllister followed their normal ritual, and made their way out to the car park for a smoke and a chat.

"Cryin'out loud, matey – Lurch in with the bad guys. I don't like the bloke, but never thought he would do something like that. What the hell is going on?" asked Banjo, rhetorically.

"Beats me," said McAllister, dragging thoughtfully on his cigarette. "I just don't like this connection with South Africa that keeps coming up. What do you think lies behind that?" he asked.

Banjo shrugged. "Don't know, matey. I only know that my granddad, Louis, who was born in the UK, was over there in the Boer War. Quite a mess, I think, but he never really spoke about it. The only thing I remember him saying was that the Boers were ferocious fighters, and his Regiment wore tartan trousers which played havoc with his legs in the heat. The horses didn't like it much either, apparently. I wasn't really old enough to ask anything else. By the time I started taking an interest in stuff like that, he had passed on. Not sure that takes your quest for knowledge of South Africa much further," Banjo said, smiling at his friend.

McAllister's mind was turning, and he wasn't really listening.

There is something about this whole thing that seems to reach back to the past. What was it his Dad used to say: Old foes cast long shadows. The Boer War – I hadn't even thought about that. Perhaps there are some long shadows here after all.

"Fancy a quick trip up to Andamooka, Banjo?" he asked.

Banjo looked at him quietly for a minute. "Sure, but why?"

"Time we renewed our acquaintance with Uncle Geraint, and if we are lucky, Uncle Huw as well. I haven't really spoken to them since Oodnadatta, and they may be able to help us. I'll give them a shout and set it up. And by the way, is there a South African history specialist at Adelaide University, do you know?"

"Don't know, but we can find that out very easily." They stubbed out their cigarettes and moved quickly back into the main building to start putting the wheels in motion.

The trip up to Beltana Station was straightforward, and Banjo and McAllister arrived slightly crumpled but otherwise in one piece. As directed, they had turned off the main track from Andamooka at the white sign announcing Beltana Station with an arrow to the left. They drove across a fairly flat and obviously arid landscape, with grazing sheep dotted here and there. The tough, barren majesty of this land never failed to impress him. Over to the east, the dramatic backdrop of the Flinders Ranges was evident, their bluish-purple escarpments rising towards the clear blue summer sky.

Another place to visit before going back.

After about half an hour of bouncing along the single-lane track, they rounded a bend and saw the homestead in front of them. Typically Colonial Australian, it had a corrugated roof, wide wrap-around verandahs that were coolly inviting against the growing heat, and beautiful filigree ironwork, which was in complete contrast with the harshness of the landscape.

As with Wally's place up in Birdsville, the bore windmill took pride of place next to the water tank right between the homestead and what appeared to be one of the main sheds.

Turn of the century, I should think. A tough and quite isolated life.

They were welcomed by Geraint McAllister, who introduced his wife, Shirley, and two daughters, Ffion and Heledd, who were about the same age as McAllister himself. Huw arrived shortly after McAllister and Banjo, and after the men had enjoyed a few beers out on the verandah, largely reminiscing over Oodnadatta, they were called in for dinner.

Banjo seemed to fit right in, and the meal was a good humoured and entertaining affair during which McAllister learned quite a bit about his own family history.

Geraint explained that he and Huw had decided to leave the

UK after the War and had emigrated to Australia in 1950. They thought that South Australia was the place to go, with the lure of the opal fields and possibly gold further over to the West. Huw had eventually decided to settle in Coober Pedy, had never married and enjoyed his life "doing his own thing," as he put it. Geraint moved out to Beltana when he met and married Shirley. They had open opal fields over to the West, where they picked up opals ranging in quality and size from the face of their fields rather than actively mining. These were the items that Geraint had been taking over to the merchant in Coober Pedy the day McAllister had first arrived up there.

The family were clearly very close and very happy. The chatter swirled about until they were shooed back out to the verandah by Shirley so that she and the girls could clear up.

The men started on the Bushmills Whisky.

The talk turned to the family back home, and for the first time, McAllister got a real insight into his own family history.

It quickly transpired that Uncle Geraint liked to tell a good yarn when he got the chance – which McAllister suspected wasn't that often – and explained that McAllister's father (and brother to Geraint and Huw) had married his mother, Hannah Taylor, in 1949. Rhys McAllister was born in Pembrokeshire in 1926 to McAllister's grandparents, Gareth and Anika.

"Yup: that's why Huw and I thought coming to Australia was a good idea back in the day," continued Geraint.

"What do you mean?" asked McAllister.

"Well, Dad served with the 1/4th Battalion of the South Wales Brigade and was in Gallipoli in 1915 alongside the Anzacs. He always admired them. He was badly injured during the fighting and shipped back to the Old Country, where our Mum nursed him back to health. She was attached to one of the Voluntary Aid Detachments that were set up to support the professional nurses. They fell in love and married in 1918. He wanted to come out here and start a new life, but that just wasn't possible with the extent of his injuries. He wanted to escape all the fuss, so as Australia or New Zealand was out of the question, they opted for a quiet life in the UK and eventually moved back to a small village in Pembrokeshire just outside of Haverfordwest called Freystrop. There were five of us originally, David who was born in 1919 but who died of Spanish flu, Huw (1920) (at this, he nodded at his brother, who was sitting quietly looking at his whisky), then Angharad, who died in 1930 of TB, then me and then your Dad, Rhys."

Geraint paused at this point and took a slug from his glass. Everyone was thoughtful.

"Anika – that's not a Welsh name, is it?" asked McAllister. "And what was "all the fuss" then? A bit of fun history coming up," he added, smiling, trying to lighten the mood.

Huw looked up from his glass and took up the story.

"The "fuss" was that her family did not approve of her relationship with Dad. She was South African, and her father was Hansie De Vries, one of the big mine owners in the Kimberley and Witwatersrand area of South Africa. He fought against the British in the Boer War and was vehemently anti-British. He was all for the South African

Republic and, if memory serves me correctly, was a good friend of Kruger and Maritz, who were key protagonists of the time.

The thought that his only daughter could then go and fall in love and marry someone from the hated enemy drove him completely nuts and from the day Mum and Dad married to the day the Old Man died, they never spoke again. She was completely ostracized by her family. I think she had a twin brother, Jan, but I don't know much more than that."

McAllister and Banjo had stopped drinking and were looking intently at Huw, who raised his eyebrows and his hands in mock comic fashion.

"What? What have I said now, you pair of galahs?"

"Nothing. It's just really interesting to hear about an aspect of the family that I never knew at all. And South Africa? Never even heard it mentioned." McAllister looked back at his uncles, who in turn looked at each other, clearly not really convinced by his explanation.

Banjo said nothing.

"So when was your Mum born, then?" asked McAllister. "And where?"

Geraint answered him.

"She was born in 1896, in Johannesburg. I think that her mother's name was Hannah."

Another silence.

"Is everything ok?" Geraint asked.

"Yes, it's fine. Really. I will have to put all of this on some sort of a chart - it might make things easier for me to remember!" McAllister said with a wry smile. No one looked very convinced, and very shortly after, the conversation wound up and McAllister and Banjo bid goodnight, saying that they would have to be going after breakfast in the morning.

The two brothers sat on in companionable silence.

"Something's going on then" said Huw, reflectively into the quiet.

"Yep. Christ knows what he has got himself into now. Better keep our eyes and ears open. We could be needed again," said Geraint.

"He's a one, that Mike," said Huw.

They both smiled and drained their glasses.

Chapter 43

Sergeant Barker from the SAPOL took the call himself. He was covering the enquiries desk at Woomera until the end of the following week, and he couldn't wait to get home. He missed his wife and family, and he hated it when it was his turn on the rota to cover Woomera.

He was bored.

As he listened almost absentmindedly to the caller and made some pencilled notes, he became increasingly focused on what was actually being said to him.

At the end, he rushed upstairs to the main office to find Terri Wilson. Dismembered body parts had been found out near the salt flats of Lake Eyre. The caller had rung Woomera, thinking that the military would be able to recover the body, and would be able to tell the necessary authorities.

But they had to move fast so that the dingoes didn't get at the rest of the remains.

Chapter 44

When McAllister and Banjo got back to the Base, they found that Terri Wilson and most of the team were out – apparently body-hunting over at Lake Eyre.

"Big place," commented Banjo. "Hope they've got more to go on than that."

McAllister rifled through the paper and messages on his desk, and found a note asking that he call Dr Liz Grant at Adelaide University.

Hopefully, the South African history buff.

His call went through quickly, and a cheery academic voice spoke, announcing herself as Dr Grant. After a brief discussion, arrangements were made for Banjo and McAllister to return to Adelaide and meet with her in person early the following week.

Apparently, there was a lot of history to cover, at which McAllister had inwardly groaned. After a quick discussion, they decided to make a quick trip down to the local library to see what basic information they could find on the Boer War ahead of the meeting with Dr Grant.

The library was in a small, brick building in the centre of the town but off of the main road. They walked through the main doors and were met with a counter upon which a brass bell was placed, with a note encouraging callers to please press for attention. Banjo duly obliged.

A lady appeared shortly afterwards, who rather reminded McAllister of Gwen up in Buderim. She was middle-aged, extremely thin and wore glasses. She introduced herself as Ellen. Banjo explained what they were after. She pulled out a drawer in a card file next to the desk and examined the contents closely. Yes, she informed them, they did have some material on the Boer War and South Africa: if they would like to take a seat in the reading room, she would bring the titles out to them. They moved through the indicated partially glazed door and sat down on the utilitarian seats provided at an old, fairly battered desk to await the arrivals.

They did not have long to wait.

Ellen arrived carrying five books, which she placed on the table in front of them and said that if they had any other requests, just ring the bell. She was happy to help. With that, she left them to it.

McAllister picked up the first title – which was a World Atlas. Smiling to himself with the thought that he knew where South Africa actually was, he nevertheless started flicking through the pages.

It wouldn't hurt just to refresh my knowledge.

He looked at the map of South Africa, and noted the Witwatersrand and Kimberley areas, thinking of the de Vries mining connection that his Uncles had mentioned. He looked westwards from Cape Town and the expanse of the South Atlantic that spread out towards South America, as always amazed at the sheer size of the Oceans that cover the planet. His eyes alighted on a small speck in the Ocean; he looked more closely and his heart almost stopped.

"Banjo, look at this" he said, turning the page towards his friend.

Banjo duly peered down at the map.

"What are you looking at?" he asked.

"The small writing there," at which McAllister pointed his finger.

"It says 'Gough Island'. Gough Holdings – - Gough Gifblaar Holdings - Gough Island. Coincidence?"

"No idea, matey. We need to find out more one way or the other," and with that, he got back up and went out to the reception desk. McAllister heard the bell on the counter ding, followed by muffled voices and Banjo returning.

"I've asked Ellen, and she is going to look and see what she can find."

When Ellen returned, she apologised and said that there was only one reference on Gough Island that she could find in their records. She placed the book on the desk and opened it at a place she had marked with a cardboard tag. McAllister looked down, with Banjo having come round the desk peering over his shoulder, and he saw the one paragraph that she had found. He looked back up at Ellen, and thanked her and said that they would let her know if there was anything else. Ellen duly left.

McAllister and Banjo read with interest:

"Gough Island.

One of the most remote islands in the world, it is named after the British mariner, Captain Charles Gough, who sighted the island in 1732. It was not formally claimed for Britain until 1938 and, is a dependency of Tristan da Cunha, and is part of the British overseas territory of St.Helena, Ascension and Tristan da Cunha.

Covering an area of 35 square miles, it sits in the Southern Atlantic Ocean, approximately 1700 miles west of Cape Town, and 1500 miles northeast of South Georgia Island in the British Falkland Islands.

It is uninhabited save for a small team of personnel based at the weather station which, with British permission, is maintained by the South African National Antarctic Programme. The site has been in place since 1956, and the teams rotate on an annual basis. Its highest peak is Edinburgh Peak at 2986 feet, and it has an Oceanic climate."

McAllister and Banjo looked at each other.

South Africa – again.

"Ask Ellen if we can take these books out on loan," said McAllister, "and then I think we need to get back to the Base. We need to speak to Terri Wilson and Jim Brock urgently."

Chapter 45

When they got back to the Base, they rushed straight up to the office to see if Terri Wilson was back. She was, and they found her uncharacteristically slumped in her chair with her head in her hands at her desk. They were reluctant to intrude on her thoughts, but clearly, they needed her urgent input.

Without looking up, a weary voice emerged from the cathedral of fingers. "Yes, boys, what is it?"

She looked up at them then, and they saw how desperately tired she looked.

"Is everything ok?" asked McAllister.

"We got a call that human body parts had been found near Lake Eyre. We got out there quickly in the hope that we could collect them before the dingoes got stuck in." She looked very sad. "Sorry to tell you, but it looks as though the parts belong to Sgt. Addams. So no, McAllister. Unfortunately, everything is not ok."

Banjo and McAllister looked at her in silence.

Taking a deep breath, she continued, "We will obviously conduct an investigation and I will keep you updated. However, you didn't come over for that: what are you up to now?"

"Might be something; might be nothing," replied McAllister, and he succinctly outlined their discoveries at the library. As he spoke, he could see the light of her old enthusiasm start to kindle in Terri Wilson's eyes, and he felt an odd gladness at that. As soon as he had finished, she picked up the phone to Special Agent Jim Brock. A call on the secure line was arranged for 15 minutes time, and they promptly adjourned down to the secure meeting room in the basement.

The call on the secure spider phone connected exactly on time, and McAllister again outlined their morning's work. Brock confirmed that they had connections through one of their "other Agencies" with the South Africans, and he would try and get some more information both about the Island and, more importantly, the people who had served at the Weather Station just in case there was a link there that could help. He would ring Terri Wilson as soon as there was any news, but in the meantime, a provisional meeting was set up for 1000 the following morning when they would re-group.

Banjo and McAllister went to their usual post-meeting place under the trees in the car park.

"So Lurch has bought it then" McAllister said. "I know you should never speak ill of the dead, but he was clearly swimming in extremely murky waters, to put it politely."

"Mmm. Bit of a shocker that. I am just wondering whether he had a hand in Lucy's disappearance. She would have trusted him, obviously, so it would have made her very vulnerable. If he picked her up after the barbie at our place, she would not have thought there was anything suspicious. It could also explain the fact that she was tortured: he would have told them that you had arrived from the UK, so they would have wanted to know about you, why you are here, and whether you presented any threat. If that assessment is right, then it's a good job for him that they got to him first," Banjo said flatly. He pulled on his cigarette, his face looking pinched and pale.

McAllister said nothing but thought it over.

Makes sense. At least it is a possible explanation – which is a step forward from where we have been all this time.

He sighed.

"Come on," he said. "I think that's enough for one day. Let's pay Crazy Pete a visit. I feel like letting my hair down."

There was no argument from Banjo.

They reported to the office the following morning slightly worse for wear. The trip to Crazy Pete's had turned into exactly that – a crazy time, but it had been fun. Coffee and aspirin were working their magic, and they walked into the secure briefing room five minutes ahead of time, slowly starting to get their brains working again.

They were met with Terri Wilson already in position and Head Shed at the top of the table, looking even more sombre than usual. The Base Commander was also there, but no one else.

Head Shed waved them to seats, and they opted to sit down next to Terri Wilson.

The doors opened again, and in walked a tired-looking Jim Brock.

This whole thing is really starting to take its toll. Everyone is starting to look quite frayed.

Brock briskly nodded to Head Shed and all present and sat down.

"Right. Let's get underway," pronounced Head Shed, and

with that, he briefly outlined the events of yesterday both in relation to the discovery of the dismembered body parts and the investigation at the library.

"Special Agent Brock. Over to you."

"Thanks. We have had some discussions with the South Africans and have secured a complete list of all of their personnel who have served at the Weather Station on Gough Island since the first base was set up there in 1956." Brock pressed the button on the desk, and as on the previous occasion, the screen on the side wall illuminated and a slide appeared showing a list of names and the year(s) that they had been posted to the Island.

Everyone present scanned them quickly, and it was immediately clear that there were several that had been posted there on more than one occasion.

"We are currently in the process of tracing everyone on the list," continued Brock. "It seems that some of those who have been posted there more than once have specialist knowledge, and they were either furthering experiments started by other teams or undertaking fresh research in their specialist areas as part of a larger specific project. At this stage, it would appear that everyone on the list is a South African national and from a quick check, we understand that none of them have any previous criminal convictions or suspicious history of any kind – that is part of the initial vetting undertaken by the South Africans prior to a posting being offered, and anything - however minor, even a parking ticket – usually counts against being selected for this posting. Special permission may be given in exceptional circumstances, but it seems on first inspection that they run a fairly tight ship. Notwithstanding the extremely harsh environment and the length of the posting, it seems that this is an extremely prestigious appointment in scientific circles and competition for selection is extremely high."

Brock paused.

"We have not yet been able to establish an evidential link between anyone serving on the Island and Gough Gifblaar Holdings, but I am awaiting an update on that as we speak."

He paused again.

McAllister was staring at the screen. One name in particular had caught his attention, and for a moment he did not hear the question being addressed to him as his mind was completely occupied elsewhere.

Is that a coincidence, or is de Vries a really common South African or Dutch name – like Smith or Jones back home?

Brock almost shouted at him.

"McAllister. Are you listening?"

Coming back to the present, McAllister nodded and mumbled an apology.

Perhaps the trip to Crazy Pete's had not been such a good idea after all. A foggy brain is not helpful this morning. Perhaps I am seeing things that aren't there as a result. More coffee is needed.

The discussion then turned to Lurch and his demise at Lake Eyre.

The details, albeit rather gruesome, were read out by Terri Wilson in some detail and were accompanied by some photographs of the scene and which were equally gruesome. One thing was clear: this had not been a quick death, and he had obviously upset some serious players.

The investigation had uncovered the fact that his sister was married to a South African national, who was a Director in Simply Bottles. Quite why that had not been unearthed as part of his vetting when he joined the RAAF or updated in the years since, no-one could really say, but that was the fact of the matter. So a possible route in to whatever organisation was behind this was becoming clearer. Investigations were now underway into that Director in particular.

"But just because he is South African doesn't mean he is linked into whoever is behind all of this, surely?" asked McAllister.

"That is true, McAllister," replied Head Shed tetchily. "However, it is an unwelcome coincidence and I don't like coincidences of any kind, and particularly not in what is turning into a particularly nasty series of events. So we will continue to approach that part of the investigation with extreme caution, planning for the worst but hoping for the best."

He turned away from McAllister, effectively ending that part of the conversation.

The meeting wrapped up fairly shortly afterwards.

Banjo and McAllister made their usual visit to the smoking tree.

"Bit of a coincidence, that," said Banjo after the first few satisfying drags.

"What is?" said McAllister.

"That bloke de Vries appearing on the team list for Gough Island."

"Yup. But then we don't know how common that name is, but it is certainly a bit of a coincidence – and we both know what the Head Shed thinks about coincidences and I tend to agree with him."

McAllister looked down at his shoes and took his own drag on his cigarette.

McAllister ground what remained of his cigarette into the dust and said, "I'll ask Terri Wilson to make some enquiries about my grandmother and see where that takes us," and he turned and walked purposefully back towards the office.

As he walked through the main doors, he headed upstairs towards Alison's office – he needed to find out what options there were to trace relatives through official Australian avenues before speaking with Terri. He entered the office and found Alison on a step ladder, putting up Christmas decorations.

"What on earth are you doing?" he asked her.

"Getting ready for Christmas, of course," she replied, laughing. "It is only a couple of weeks away. Are you going to the pageant down in Adelaide? It will provide a bit of relief from all of the political drama going on at the moment."

"What pageant is that then?" he asked, smiling.

"Well, Johnnie Martin's Christmas Pageant. It's a great procession that goes through the main streets of the City. It is supported by the departmental store in Rundle Mall, Johnnie Martin's, and lots of local community interests and businesses. Lots of people take part, and an awful lot of work goes into the floats. It's great fun and raises a huge amount of money for charity every year. You really should give it a go if you are going to be back in Adelaide then." She grinned at him again.

"I hear you have an appointment at Adelaide University later on in the week, so you might want to stay down and go to the Pageant."

He laughed, shaking his head in wonderment that she clearly knew more about his diary than he did.

"Okay, I'll think about it. Which brings me to why I wanted to have a quick word."

She looked at him with mock suspicion, which turned into a thoughtful look as he outlined what he wanted to know.

"I can probably get some information for you quite quickly – we have some back channels, obviously," she said.

"Obviously. Thanks, Alison. Can you let me know as soon as possible?"

"Sure. It might take a couple of days so please let me know if you leave for Adelaide before then, but I'll do my best. I take it this sudden interest in family history is under the radar?." He nodded.

"Yes it is. Will do," and he waved goodbye as he turned to go.

Chapter 46

Two days later, McAllister and Banjo were on their way back down to Adelaide. They had eschewed the red-eye flight from the Base in favour of driving down, as McAllister realised he had never done the journey by road and they had time. The radio was burbling away, and the news was all agog with the announcement of the forthcoming Royal Jubilee visit which, it seemed, would be taking place in March of the following year.

"Sounds as though Queenie will be visiting everywhere whilst she is on the tour" commented Banjo. "I also heard a rumour that it looks as though she is going to be in Adelaide right at the end of March. Another headache."

Banjo wasn't happy, and McAllister realised that this whole business with Lurch and Lucy was really getting to him. He had really hit the booze hard at Crazy Pete's earlier in the week, and although McAllister himself was no slouch when it came to partying, he had wondered even then if Banjo was struggling to come to terms with all that had happened and had thrown himself in at the deep end in an effort to forget. McAllister also realised that there had been no mention of Trixi for a while, and Banjo had made no attempt to call her - or at least, not whilst McAllister was within ear shot.

Another problem.

The journey down to Salisbury East took them nearly seven hours in the end – there had been an accident on the highway which caused a delay. McAllister found he was very relieved when he walked through the door of the Weemala house: it was calm, ordered and comfortable. As much as he had enjoyed making a good friend in Banjo, he was pleased to have a bit of time to himself.

Hot bath and a Bushmills.

Whilst waiting for the bath to fill, he turned on the television. All of the main news channels – ABC, and Channels 7, 9 and 10 – were giving details of the Silver Jubilee visit. McAllister turned the set off. He needed time to think.

The bath, the Bushmills and a good night's sleep left McAllister feeling much brighter and more optimistic than he had done for several days. He picked up Banjo as agreed, and they headed into the City to meet with Dr Grant. Banjo, unfortunately, was not brighter or happier. In fact, if anything, he seemed even more unhappy than he had done the day before.

"What's up, mate?" he asked Banjo.

Banjo sighed deeply and looked out of the window.

"Trixi isn't happy. She wants me to leave the RAAF and set up a business – probably a pub. Where the hell did that one come from? No chance. I enjoy my job. If she wants to go out to work, that's fine and it's up to her. We had a massive row. Things were said that shouldn't have been – or at least, not in the way that they were. She accused me of having an affair with "someone." She has essentially given me an ultimatum: her or the RAAF. Quite frankly, mate, the way I feel at the moment there is no contest, and it is the service all the way. I just don't want to live my life like this." Banjo sighed again.

McAllister was quiet for a while.

"Really sorry to hear that, Banjo. I take it there is nothing I can do?"

"No, but thanks. I've just got to work it out. I've been dreading coming back to Salisbury East, and that says everything. I should have been really excited, bearing in mind how long we have been away up in Woomera and Queensland, but not a bit of it. She didn't seem that thrilled to see me either. Just do me a favour?" he turned to look at McAllister.

"Sure – just ask."

"Keep an eye on me in case I miss something. There is so much going on with this investigation. I am really concerned that with my mind elsewhere at times, there could be something that I just don't "see" as it were. I don't want to cause any problem." Banjo looked really concerned.

"Of course – we watch each other's backs, always," replied McAllister. "Do you want to come and stay up at the Weemala house for a while – give yourselves some space?"

"That might be a good idea, matey: thanks," replied Banjo. "Really appreciate it."

With that, the conversation lapsed, and the rest of the trip into Adelaide was made in silence, each man wrestling with their own thoughts.

They found the Napier Building of Adelaide University without difficulty and asked at the reception desk for Dr Liz Grant. After a very short wait, a tall, somewhat gangly lady in her early 40's approached them. She had dark hair, dark eyes and an animated manner about her that suggested to McAllister that a frightening level of intellect lay behind her

278

demeanour. She introduced herself and led them upstairs to her office.

McAllister gave her the agreed outline as to their interest in the Boer War and South African history generally, and she duly launched into a potted history. Most of it, McAllister did not know and despite himself, he found it interesting. He had not realised, for example, that the Australian Government had sent over 16,000 troops to fight in the Boer War, over 600 of whom were killed and five Victoria Crosses were awarded for bravery. He also did not know that New Zealand had also volunteered men, totalling approximately 6,500 in all, supplying continuous support in tranches of troops between 1899 -1902. Or that so many countries had sent troops to fight on one side or another: sometimes compatriots from the same country fighting on opposing sides.

"For a diary-style analysis of the conflict, I can do no better than refer you to the publication of Arthur Conan Doyle - yes, *that* Arthur Conan Doyle -The Great Boer War. He had served as a volunteer physician at a field hospital near Bloemfontein in 1900, and he wrote the original version of the book later that year. He subsequently revised the text as the War ground on and indeed made subsequent alterations to reflect changes in outcomes and events, but the main part was obviously written during the conflict and is delivered very much from the British viewpoint of the time. You may then want to contrast that view with some of the others that have been published in more recent times and I can give you a list of those if you are interested in further reading."

Dr Grant paused. Realising that they did not have any

questions as such at that point, she pushed on and gave an outline of the key players on the Boer side, including Kruger, Maritz, Smuts, and Botha. She also highlighted the role of General Cronje and the lead-up to the battle of Bloemfontein. McAllister and Banjo looked at each other.

Cronje again.

Dr Grant was clearly an enthusiast. She had prepared slides, photographs and documents to support her commentary. McAllister thought his head was about to explode.

"What about the big industrialists and mine owners at the time: did they play a part in all of this?" he asked.

"Absolutely. One in particular, Hansie de Vries, was a key adviser to Smuts and Maritz and is believed to have been instrumental in the development of the strategy of the war, particularly in the early years. De Vries owned large mining interests in the Witwatersrand and Kimberley areas of the Transvaal and was extremely influential in terms of contacts, being able to command support and funding for the War from other countries. He was a passionate Boer and really led the way in terms of the strategic fight."

McAllister and Banjo sat quietly, mulling all of this over.

"Did he have a family?" asked Banjo, "and if so, what happened to them?"

Dr Grant smiled, nodded, and continued:

"You really are testing my memory now, Mr Paterson. As far as I can remember off hand, Hansie de Vries was born in Johannesburg in about 1855 or so. He was busy setting up the Plek Van Rykdon (or, in English, the Place of Riches)

Mining Company in his earlier years and had turned it into one of the largest mines in South Africa at the time. He was principally interested in gold but had also hit a rich diamond pipe in the Kimberley so he was rapidly becoming both extremely wealthy and influential in political circles. He was strategically astute, as I have already said, and he was one of the first people to realise the potential propaganda power of newspapers. He became a silent partner in the Central News Agency, which had been started by two entrepreneurs in Johannesburg in 1896 and which started with several publications, including, I think, The Star, The Standard and Diggers News. He saw the potential in being able to get "messaging" out to ordinary people in the street, and he was instrumental in supporting the two owners, Davis and Lindbergh, in expanding the business and promoting the Boer cause but in a very subtle but effective way. As far as family is concerned, he became concerned with establishing a dynasty to pass on his growing wealth and business interests. He met and married Hannah in the mid-1880s, but they were childless until the mid 1890s – in fact, not that long before the outbreak of the Boer War – when she finally bore him twins: a boy and a girl. I cannot remember their names off hand, but I can certainly research that for you if you feel it is important. They were the only two offspring. If memory serves me correctly, I think the son eventually married the youngest daughter of Christiaan Maritz, the leader of the Rebellion – but again, I would need to check that for you. The key point here is that de Vries was a devout Boer, as I have said, and he undoubtedly would have brought his children up in the same belief system."

Dr Grant paused and looked at them expectantly.

"So, what happened to the daughter?" asked McAllister.

"Ah, well, there's the rub," said Dr Grant, pushing her thick spectacles up to the bridge of her nose. "Not that much is known about her other than, for whatever reason, it appears that she did not agree with her father's views. She was only a child at the end of the Boer War, of course, but by 1914, she had got her own views about things and by all accounts was taking a keen interest in the emerging suffragette movement, for example. It seems that she was very independently minded and perhaps rather more like her father than he was comfortable with. She left South Africa and travelled to the United Kingdom, where, during the First World War, she volunteered to work as a nursing aid. Her father was furious and initially put it down to her finding her own feet. That was until she met a British soldier injured at Gallipoli in 1915, nursed him and they fell in love. They subsequently married. Hansie de Vries never forgave her, and, so the story goes, she was completely ostracised by her family. She was completely erased from the family history from that point on."

McAllister couldn't breathe. His brain was trying to work out what this actually meant. The inescapable conclusion was that his Uncles had been right, and Hansie de Vries was his great-grandfather. That also meant that there was now a serious possibility that someone involved in current events was a distant cousin of his. After all, a de Vries has been on the list of scientists who had been stationed on Gough Island.

Gordon Bennett. There's a turn-up for the books. Even so, de Vries is a very common South African name. That is probably just a coincidence, but unfortunate in the circumstances.

They bade farewell to Dr Grant at the end of the discussion, feeling both slightly overwhelmed at the amount of knowledge she had managed to impart in a comparatively small amount of time and anxious as to the result that seemed to have emerged unbidden from the detail. They walked back to their car and sat in silence for a few moments.

"What are you going to do?" asked Banjo.

"Nothing tonight," replied McAllister. "I will think it over, stay down here this weekend, and then go back to Woomera on Monday, by which stage I will hopefully have settled in my own mind what I am going to tell Terri."

"Sounds like a plan," replied his friend.

"Want to go to the pageant tomorrow? I understand it is on another tick off the list of local events," said McAllister.

Banjo half laughed. "Yeah, whatever you want. Could be a bit of a wheeze," and with that, they headed back to Weemala Road.

The Johnnie Martin's Christmas Pageant was everything a child could wish for big floats, lots of colour, noise, fancy costumes, waving flags, bands, marching girls' teams, balloons, and ice cream – loads of ice cream. It was immediately clear to McAllister why this was such a popular local event, and in some ways, he wished he was a child again just so that he could really enjoy this very special moment. He struggled slightly with the fact that he was standing amongst the crowds anticipating Christmas in soaring summer temperatures, and as Father Christmas took pride of place near the end of the procession, resplendent in his bright red outfit trimmed with white faux fur, it hit McAllister for the first time that he would be away from home for Christmas – again. Since joining the RAF Police, he had only had one Christmas in the UK – and even then, he had been stationed at RAF Aldergrove in Northern Ireland so not exactly local to home or very festive.

At least the weather here is better.

After the procession had wended its way through the streets, past the point where McAllister and Banjo were standing watching, they turned away to the park where the Pageant Funfair was set up and awaiting eager customers. As they approached one of the big dipper rides, they passed a large tent with a trestle table outside with a sign encouraging people to come and try the new all-Australian product – Cham-Pine.

Jindivik again. They certainly get around.

Banjo nudged him and they both looked on as the unforgettably statuesque figure of Anika de Klerk took centre stage at the tables, doing the whole saleswoman bit. It seemed that she was very good at her job, as business was brisk. McAllister and Banjo moved over towards the hovering crowd and decided to buy a dozen bottles.

"Christmas is only just around the corner," said Banjo. "God knows what we will be embroiled in by then, so let's have a bit of backup in the fridge, eh?"

McAllister laughed.

Armed with their purchase, they found their way back to the car and set off back to Weemala Road. As they opened the front door, the phone was ringing, demanding their immediate attention.

McAllister picked up the receiver.

"Yup"

"Need you back up here as soon as possible, McAllister," said Terri Wilson in a brisk, businesslike tone. "We have a special briefing tomorrow at 1200. You are both expected to be there. A flight will be leaving the Base near you at 0700 – be on it."

"Right. Will do." Responded McAllister, his heart sinking. This clearly was not going to be any party piece, and something else was obviously going on. He replaced the receiver and turned to Banjo.

"We fly out in the morning. Called back to the Base. Special briefing at 1200, and we are expected to be there."

Banjo looked down at his feet, shrugged and said, "No problem. Better get this lot in the fridge, get something to eat, and some kip. Sounds as though we will need our wits about us tomorrow."

McAllister sighed.

Here we go again.

Chapter 47

The aircraft landed in Woomera on time, and McAllister and Banjo went straight from the reception area on the military base over to the administration block. They found Alison in her office. She looked up, smiled and said that she had heard a rumour that bacon butties were on offer in the canteen if they were interested. That got a thumbs-up from Banjo.

Alison went on to say that Terri Wilson and "the others" were all congregating around the main office, ready for the briefing at 1200. She looked around on her desk for a short moment or two before finding a handwritten note, which she promptly passed over to McAllister.

"I think that is what you wanted," she said.

He looked quickly at the detail inside and nodded at her.

"Thanks, Alison," and promptly left her office. He pulled Banjo to one side and showed him the note. It read:

"Anika Hannah de Vries

Born 3ʳᵈ October 1896, Johannesburg, South Africa.

Father: Hansie de Vries, Industrialist and Mine Owner;

Mother: Hannah de Vries, housewife.

Address: Mieke Homestead, Klerksdorp, Transvaal.

Record of marriage to Gareth Huw McAllister, of Ffynnon Cottage, Rosemarket, Pembrokeshire, farmer, 20ᵗʰ July 1918."

"It's for real then" said Banjo, looking directly at McAllister.

286

"Seems so." He read on as Alison had then added an additional note:

"Mike: we also found the following entry which may be of interest:

Jan Hansie de Vries

Born 3rd October 1896 Johannesburg, South Africa.

Father: Hansie de Vries, Industrialist and Mine Owner;

Mother: Hannah de Vries, housewife;

Address: Mieke Homestead, Klerksdorp, Transvaal.

Record of marriage to Imka Mia Maritz, of Golden Hill, Klerksdorp, Transvaal; spinster, 21st January 1921.

It seems that they were twins. Anticipating your next question, we are trying to trace whether Jan and Imka de Vries had any offspring. Hope this helps in the meantime. A"

McAllister and Banjo looked at each other.

"We are going to have to tell the briefing all of this. Could have a material relevance" said McAllister.

Banjo said nothing, but nodded his agreement.

McAllister sighed deeply.

This just keeps getting better and better.

The briefing followed the same pattern as before, with Kevin Tapping present time this, sitting next to Simon Hurdle-Jenkins and Jim Brock.

Head Shed was in quite an ugly mood.

McAllister's heart sank.

287

Special Agent Jim Brock was tersely invited to open the discussion.

"Thanks for coming, everyone. We have an update in relation to Southern Star Fuels, which has a controlling interest in Big Byte R&D Holdings and Direct Logistics. You will remember from an earlier briefing that both of these firms are linked, albeit loosely, to Pineapples R Us, Simply Bottles and Jindivik Wineries. You may also remember that in spite of many links in the chain, all of these companies actually come back to Gough Gifblaar Holdings, registered in the British Virgin Islands. We have managed to obtain some information – albeit limited – in relation to that parent company and it would appear that there are three directors. Two are still unidentified, although, as you would expect, we are continuing our investigations on that. The third, however, is Jan de Klerk, who you will remember is also on the Boards of Jindivik, Simply Bottles, and Pineapples R Us. In light of that, we have looked into Mr de Klerk a little deeper. Thanks to the work of Kevin Tapping and Simon Hurdle-Jenkins (at this point, Brock nodded towards the two men), we have been tracing some of the financial transactions that Gough Gifblaar Holdings has been undertaking. That in itself is extremely complex, reinforcing the view expressed at the previous briefing that we have some serious players at the centre of all this. They are covering their tracks well, and it is taking a huge amount of time and effort to peel back the layers. De Klerk has received several huge payments from Gough Gifblaar Holdings, in addition to any remuneration he has from the other business interests, totalling over US$5,000,000. "

There was an involuntary murmur from several at the table

at this point in view of the size of the payments.

Brock continued:

"It looks as though he also has significant shareholding interests in other firms in the US, including some up-and-coming technology companies, and on top of all that, he is a large shareholder in the North Sea oil exploration fields in the UK and Norway, which are currently coming on stream and will certainly be a key factor in the UK's energy development and therefore industrial and economic productivity in the future. In fact, he is one of the largest investors in that sector after the institutional shareholders such as BP, Shell and the pension funds. He is a seriously wealthy individual with a wide-ranging and very lucrative portfolio of interests."

Head Shed interjected at this point.

"So, apart from the fact that he is seriously wealthy with perhaps dubious contacts, what do we actually know about this man?"

Brock continued, unhurried:

"He was born in Ladysmith, Natal, South Africa, in 1920 and was the fifth of seven siblings born to Boer parents who were at the forefront of the second Boer War 1899 – 1902. He was educated entirely in South Africa and was due to study at Stellenbosch University until the War broke out in 1939. Instead – and somewhat interestingly – he enlisted at the start of the Second World War in the 2nd South African Infantry Brigade, which was under British command. He saw active service both in East Africa and in the Desert Campaign in North Africa/Egypt until he was injured at El Alamein in

1942. During his convalescence, he was transferred to an intelligence posting in Cairo, where his particular skills could be best exploited for the Allied cause. It seems that his special talent was in relation to interrogations, and he is credited – if that is the right word – with several new innovative methods of extracting information from prisoners. He was apparently an admirer of Heinrich Himmler and his methods and seems to have tried to emulate some of those. That may – or may not – have a direct link to some of the events that have occurred here, not least the particularly gruesome deaths of Lucy Andrews, Zoe Schuster and Sgt Addams. He married a former Miss South Africa runner-up – Anika Cronje – eight years ago, and she is many years his junior. They do not have any children."

Brock paused and looked around the table to see if there were any questions, but everyone remained silent.

"The old adage "follow the money" applies here. We have tracked some of the money into a Swiss Bank Account, which was interesting in itself, and we have no chance of getting behind that to see exactly what he has stashed away. We have also discovered that he has a safety deposit box in one of the largest banks in London, and he has held that for a long time. That raises the suspicion that the box is keeping secrets rather than anything of hard worth, such as gold, money, or jewels. We could be wrong, of course, but that seems to be the "feel" of this. We have asked our British counterparts in MI5 to apply for a warrant to get into the deposit box, and that is currently going through the system. Apparently, the application will go before the local Magistrate tomorrow.

And I think that really leaves us with a number of questions to try and answer:

1. What is he doing here in South Australia as the managing director of a small winery, albeit with interests in other related businesses? No disrespect, guys, but he would appear to be a very big fish in a small, rural pond.

2. Why would a guy with his background *volunteer* to serve with the military for one of his family's most hated enemies – the British? Did he have some sort of a long ball game in mind, even in those early days, to "get back" at the Empire?

3. What is it that he is providing to Gough Gifblaar Holdings that is worth such huge amounts of money?

4. What is it that Gough Gifblaar Holdings is actually doing? The nature of their business seems very murky, and we are finding the veil of confusion that they have created around themselves almost impenetrable, and last but not least,

5. What role, if any, has he played in the deaths of our people and to what end?"

Brock finished and sat back in his chair. Silence reigned in the room.

Terri Wilson broke the silence.

"Do we know, Jim, whether Anika de Klerk, nee Cronje, was related in any way to Hendrik Cronje – the guy who chose to lock himself in the Datsun Cherry that night out on the highway?"

"Yes, and yes, she is," replied the American. "They were/are second cousins. Hendrik and Anika are both great-grandchildren of the South African Boer General Pieter Cronje. He died in 1911 before either of them were born, of course, but the link is definitely there albeit through different strands of the family."

McAllister cleared his throat, and it sounded extremely loud in the silence in the room.

"Do we know anything more about the people who have been stationed on Gough Island and is there any link with any of the people we have come across so far?" he asked.

"That is slow going, I'm afraid," replied Brock. "We are trawling through what we can, but to be frank, the South Africans are not being particularly helpful. Is there anyone in particular you think might be of interest so that we can narrow the field a bit? That would be really helpful if so.."

He looked expectantly back at McAllister, as did Terri Wilson and Head Shed.

Now or never.

"I think that one of the names on the list was Pieter de Vries. I have recently learned that I may have a familial link with a family called de Vries, but I have no idea at all whether this is the same de Vries family or a completely separate group and whether either or neither of them have any links with this investigation."

Terri Wilson looked as if she was about to explode, and if Head Shed's demeanour could have got any colder, he would have frozen solid where he sat. Brock, Tapping, and Hurdle-Jenkins sat looking at him, almost with their mouths open.

McAllister carried on.

"It seems that my grandmother was from South Africa, a Boer family, and her father was a major industrialist in the Transvaal called Hansie de Vries. When she left South Africa shortly before WW1, came to the UK and eventually married my grandfather, her family were very unhappy and basically ostracised her. It could all be a terrible coincidence, but nevertheless, I thought I should say something now in case it has a material bearing on the investigation."

McAllister stopped.

No one said anything for a few moments.

Brock broke the silence.

"OK. Thanks bud. We will look into that. De Vries is a very common Dutch/South African name, though, so I wouldn't worry too much. Still, we will investigate and let you know. Anything else we should know?"

McAllister took another deep breath.

"She had a twin brother, Jan de Vries. He apparently married the youngest daughter of Manie Maritz, who led the Maritz Rebellion in the lead-up to the Second Boer War. I don't know any more than that, and I don't know if they had any offspring. All of my grandmother's children are either in Wales in the UK or here in South Australia – at Coober Pedy and Andamooka – and have been for many years."

Head Shed could contain himself no further.

"For the love of God, McAllister, when in hell's name did you think you were going to impart all of this? As Brock has said, it might be nothing, but it *could* be something, *and* if it is, *you* will be directly linked to it albeit completely unintentionally. You bloody idiot."

He was clearly furious.

McAllister said nothing.

Head Shed resumed.

"Right, Special Agent Brock. As soon as you get any information on the de Vries side of the investigation, you are to please report *to me* immediately. With regard to the rest of it, we will await the outcome of your further investigations into the money and the de Klerks. In the meantime, our British MI6 colleagues will assist with our enquiries into events at this end. Your rhetorical question as to what is de Klerk doing here in a rural village in South Australia is well placed, and I suggest (and at this point, he turned to Terri Wilson) we make that question one of our most pressing lines of enquiry."

Brock and Wilson both nodded.

Head Shed turned back to McAllister.

"And as for you, McAllister, you will continue to support this investigation until we have some concrete evidence one way or the other. However, should the investigation turn up anything that links your family – however remotely – with any of the participants in these events, then you will be off the case and returned to the UK immediately. Do you understand?"

McAllister nodded.

Head Shed continued. "Right. We will call the meeting to a close. I will not set a new briefing date as it seems we are largely in the hands of the investigations that are now afoot. We will, therefore, re-convene when we have something definite to impart. Thank you all."

With that, he stood up, gathered his papers and almost stormed out of the briefing room.

McAllister let out a sigh. He hadn't even realised he had been holding his breath.

Terri Wilson wouldn't look at him and also left swiftly.

Jim Brock came over and clapped his hand on McAllister's shoulder.

"Don't worry about him," he said, nodding his head in the direction of Head Shed's departure.

"That's rough, but we will do what we can. Just don't expect fast results. As I say, we are running into some particularly heavy weather with the South Africans at the moment – not least as a result of the arms embargo – so this will take some patience. I'll let you know if we get anything of interest." He smiled his slow Southern smile, and turned to leave accompanied by Hurdle-Jenkins and Tapping, both of whom had kept their distance whilst the exchange with Brock had taken place.

You've made another good impression, then, Mikey, my boy. Another great career move.

He looked up at Banjo, and without a word, they both got up, left the room and headed for their favourite smoking tree.

Chapter 48

McAllister and Paterson returned to Salisbury East the following day and tried to resume some semblance of normality in the weeks that followed. McAllister pottered about the DSTO, most of the pretence of his original posting having been lost as the various events had unfolded. No one on his team really knew what to make of him now, and he spent his time supporting them where and when he could but also helping out with general security issues as they arose.

As such, he found a new friend in Toby "Jugs" in the security office. His first impression of Jugs all those weeks ago, soon after his arrival at the DSTO, that he seemed largely to be a bloke after his own heart, had proven accurate as he had got to know him better.

Apart from some of the better drinking holes in the area, Jugs also introduced him to Aussie Rules, and McAllister found himself enjoying this very physical sport which he realised was a cross between rugby, football, and on occasion, from what he could see, all out strong arm wrestling.

Despite himself, he had become a keen Port Adelaide, or Magpies as they were colloquially known, supporter. He had even taken part in a few training sessions at the Base at RAAF Edinburgh, where there was a keen hard core contingent who regularly supplied players to the wider RAAF Aussie Rules team for inter-service competitions, and had really enjoyed himself.

Banjo's home life went into free fall, and he was more or less living at the Weemala Road house with McAllister permanently now. It seemed to McAllister that his friend was basically waiting for divorce papers any day.

Worst of all, there was no news on any aspects of the investigations. Terri Wilson had been noticeable by her absence, and there had been no re-convened briefing. Nothing had been seen or heard of Jim Brock, and McAllister had to admit to himself that he was starting to feel extremely twitchy.

If I was paranoid, I'd think that they were purposely cutting me out of the information loop.

McAllister, Banjo and Jugs ended up spending Christmas Day together – they took two large eskies down to the beach and enjoyed a day people-watching, swimming, surfing and getting slightly drunk. On reflection, McAllister couldn't remember a day he had enjoyed more – certainly not a Christmas Day.

"Well," said Jugs, leaning back on the sand with his nose covered in sun cream, "I wonder what 1977 will bring. Got any New Year resolutions or requests, boys?"

Banjo wriggled his toes in the sand and drank deeply from his bottle of beer. "Nope, as long as we don't have any more of the political uproar that we have had this year. I am completely sick to death of politicians."

McAllister didn't know what to say. The last six months since he had left Cornwall seemed to have flown past, and he reflected that he had travelled across some fantastic parts of the country – and yet he had not even scratched the surface, such as the size and diversity of this extraordinary continent. He found that, if he was honest with himself, he did not really want to return to RAF St Mawgan. He was enjoying his life here, he had made a couple of really good mates, had found some long-lost family that he had never known he had, and he had settled in far more easily than he would ever have considered possible. He realised with a bit of a shock that going back to the UK was going to be a real wrench.

Banjo piped up, seemingly realising that McAllister was struggling.

"Well, at least we have the forthcoming visit of Queenie to look forward to in the Spring. That should keep us busy for a while!" and he laughed.

Jugs laughed and raised what was left of his beer.

They fell back into companionable silence, watched the sun starting to get lower in the sky and broke open some more beers.

Chapter 49

It was in fact, nearly the end of February 1977 before the call came for McAllister and Paterson to join a reconvened security briefing. The wait had seemed endless, and McAllister had come to terms with the fact that the authorities – from all sides – had apparently decided that he was not to be included in any further investigation or information discussions.

And yet.

They had not yet sent him home, and he kept that thought close to him on days he found himself particularly frustrated by the lack of news and the lack of action.

When the phone finally rang one evening, McAllister was relieved to hear Terri Wilson at the other end asking them to attend a briefing that was to be held at RAAF Edinburgh that coming Friday at 11:00.

Until then.

Another day, another briefing.

The same personnel, different location. Head Shed was in a slightly less hostile mood than on the last occasion, but it was still scarcely a party. Terri Wilson and Jim Brock both looked tired to McAllister's eye and seemed to be feeling the pressure.

As on the last occasion, Jim Brock was invited to open the discussion.

"I am pleased to report that we have progressed since our last meeting. You will all have realised that in view of the time it has taken us to be able to reconvene, the pace of progress has been glacially slow. However, looking at the positives, we are at least further forward.

We have managed to establish the Directors of Gough Gifblaar Holdings. In addition to Jan de Klerk, there is Carmen Cronje and Pieter de Vries.

Taking Cronje first.

She appears to be part of the Cronje dynasty which includes Anika de Klerk and Hendrik Cronje, so again has long-established links back to the Boers. She was born in Johannesburg in April 1937; she is an only child, her two older siblings (Hannah and Christian) having both died in childhood of scarlet fever and in a mine accident, respectively. There seem to have been family links with both the de Klerk and de Vries families throughout her life. Her current address is in an extremely affluent part of New York, where she appears to live alone, and we are now watching her extremely closely. She seems never to have married or had children.

She has worked for a world-famous jeweller for many years, based in New York but travelling extensively, and is now their chief buyer – which says everything in terms of her knowledge and connections.

Other than that, very little is known about her.

Pieter de Vries is also something of an enigma. He was born in Johannesburg in November 1935. His grandfather was Hansie de Vries, who founded the Plek Van Rykdon Mining Company in Witwatersrand in 1885. He was extremely wealthy, having both significant gold and diamond finds to his credit. Hansie de Vries actively supported the Boers during the 1899 – 1902 War; he took part in the Maritz Rebellion, which was an armed insurrection in 1914 and opposed South African support for Britain in WW1. He was keenly pro-German but first and foremost, he was desperate to see the re-establishment of the South African Republic in the Transvaal. He was also instrumental in developing the use of newspapers as a means of propaganda distribution.

Hansie de Vries had twin children born in 1896: Hannah – who we heard from McAllister on the last occasion, made her own choices and was ostracised for them. We have traced the lineage, and it is confirmed that Hansie de Vries *is* McAllister's great-grandfather.

The other twin was a boy, Jan. By the sound of things, he was also a very independently-minded individual but much more "on message" in terms of Hansie's own beliefs and views.

Jan de Vries married Imka Mia Maritz on 21st January 1921. She was the daughter of Manie Maritz, who you will remember was a close friend of Hansie de Vries and who had led the earlier rebellion. Jan joined the family business and was groomed from the outset as Hansie's successor. The mining interests continued to flourish, and in due course, Jan diversified into some other interests, including oil (both exploration and extraction).

Imka Maritz was also very independently minded, and she had a keen interest in jewellery – principally diamonds. She had completed an apprenticeship learning her trade with the largest diamond house in the world which was a significant achievement in itself – as far as we know, the only woman to ever have been offered – let alone completed – such an apprenticeship. She then became freelance in order to buy and sell stones, and work her own designs when she wished. She established a very profitable boutique high-end jewellery line of her own, called Simply Imka.

If I can pause there for just a moment, there is an obvious alignment here with the Simply Bottles company name. We don't know at the moment if that is a coincidence or whether this was a direct nod to Imka de Vries.

The couple seem to have been very happy, and eventually had three children – two daughters and a son, Pieter, who was the youngest.

Which brings us neatly to the third Director of Gough Gifblaar Holdings, Pieter de Vries.

He was born in Klerksdorp, South Africa, in November 1935. His mother, Imka, died suddenly in 1948 and Jan de Vries struggled both with the loss of his wife and with bringing up the three children on his own. The older daughters were still at home, but it seems fair to say that apart from trying to find suitable husbands for them, he largely ignored them and any career aspirations that they may have had, notwithstanding Imka's own successful path, and focussed almost exclusively on his son.

When Pieter turned 14 in 1949, he was sent to his Uncle, who owned a vineyard in Nuriootpa, in the Barossa Valley of South Australia, ostensibly to widen his horizons and learn a bit about the world. He stayed there for five years, learning about wine, vineyards and the business generally, and which had the additional benefit from his point of view of enabling his love of plants to flourish. He was a keen amateur botanist and, to all accounts, found that side of the wine business fascinating.

He returned to South Africa in 1955, where he attended Stellenbosch University in the Western Cape, reading for a BSc in Metallurgical Engineering and then taking a Masters in plant pathology and virology. He was one of the first students in this speciality within the Faculty of Agriculture at Stellenbosch and completed his Doctorate in 1961.

He then returned to his father's mining business, immediately taking a seat on the board and sitting at his father's right hand in terms of all business decisions and was the clear heir apparent.

Jan de Vries died in 1963, and Pieter inherited extensive mining rights (particularly gold and Uranium mines in the Transvaal and diamond pipes in the Kimberley area). He adopted a progressive policy with the business and built on the wealth that his father and grandfather had previously established.

In 1967, his uncle in the Barossa died and left the whole of his vineyard and winery interest to – you guessed it – Pieter de Vries, who then became the sole owner of what at that time was called Maritz Vineyard. It was de Vries who changed the name to Jindivik Winery when he transferred the ownership from himself in his personal capacity through the web of companies, finally to Gough Gifblaar Holdings.

McAllister was correct when he suggested that we look closely at the names of the teams who have been posted to Gough Island with the South African Weather Service. Pieter de Vries *did* spend a year stationed on Gough Island as part of the small team there in the 1958/59 cohort. He was there in his capacity as a botanist, specialising in plant virology and tropical plant adaptability and indeed seems to have used some of the research that he conducted whilst stationed on the Island as part of his Doctoral thesis.

As far as we know, de Vries has never married and has never had children."

Brock paused to take a drink of water, looking around the table whilst he did so to see if there were any questions. He realised that he had the undivided attention of everyone present, and so took that as an indication to carry on.

"As far as some of the questions that were posed at our last meeting, we are starting to piece together some of the information which may enable us to answer these before too much longer. We have still not been able to obtain a copy of what you guys would probably call the Memorandum and Articles of Association of Gough Gifblaar Holdings, so we do not yet know the precise objectives or purpose of the company.

We have been able to obtain partial financial records, and it is clear that the company is in robust financial health and has significant income – the source of which remains somewhat unclear at this time.

The payments to Jan de Klerk that I mentioned earlier are definitely from this company, and I am sorry to say that we are still none the wiser as to what those payments are actually for.

So, to summarise, we now have three Directors of Gough Holdings: one with pro-Nazi sympathies and who actively admires the torture methodology of Heinrich Himmler, and who, despite his own significant personal wealth, has chosen to live and work in a small corner of a rural area in South Australia; a female with extensive connections to the key gold and jewellery buyers around the world, who appears to also have significant personal wealth enabling her to live in one of the most expensive areas of New York and whose job could be said to provide the perfect cover for undertaking less above board work; whether it is or not remains to be seen, but there is the potential there for that to happen. And finally, we have someone who is fabulously wealthy with extensive business interests across the world and who has a keen interest in – and professional knowledge of – botany generally and viticulture in particular.

All three have known each other for many years, their families having been close comrades in the Boer fraternity and they have all pursued careers or businesses within similar fields. Now, that particular fact is not unusual, given the background of these guys. Those who are less generous may feel that this cartel has been in play for some years, and the links between them indicate a level of ideological closeness that surpasses the veneer of business convenience."

Brock paused again.

Terri Wilson piped up at this point.

"Do we have any photographs of either Carmen Cronje or Pieter de Vries?"

Brock sighed.

"Unfortunately not. Jan de Klerk is not a problem – if you look at the screen, we have a photograph of him – admittedly taken from fairly long range, but it is clear enough – and of his wife, Anika."

Everyone turned to look at the photographs that flashed up on the projector screen.

"Both Carmen Cronje and Pieter de Vries seem to be particularly adept at spotting any cameras and avoiding photographers. They rarely, if ever, appear at major public events, such as awards ceremonies or charity dinners, and until we know more about their circle of friends and business acquaintances, it is very difficult for us to put a plan for greater surveillance in place. We are, of course, continuing our efforts in that regard."

At this point, Head Shed interjected.

"So where does this leave us in relation to the Sea Wolf missile plans, which, of course, started this whole mess off?"

"The suggestion at this stage is that there is some sort of an arms embargo-busting plan afoot. That would fit with the multiplicity of businesses that seem to obscure the objective, as I have already said, and with the ability to move around the world in various business circles without raising any suspicion at all. However, our evidence for that – certainly at this stage – is not strong. There are whispers in arms dealers' circles that the plans are up for auction, so even if the trio themselves - or as a front for the South African government - are not currently in possession of the plans and selling to the highest bidder, they will almost certainly be interested in the bidding themselves *if* their motives are indeed questionable."

Again, a thoughtful silence descended.

Head Shed again.

"Right, so we at least know who is behind Gough Gifblaar Holdings, even if we don't know what they look like or what their objectives are. That is something anyway." He turned to McAllister and Paterson. "You two will remain on the team, notwithstanding your ancestral connections to de Vries, McAllister. I entirely accept that these are both remote and, until this recent turn of events, completely outside of your knowledge. You will remain down here and will continue to support Miss Wilson with her enquiries. Perhaps that is an extremely convenient moment for you to update us on those enquiries?" he said, turning towards Terri.

She took a deep breath and said that as her team's investigations had largely been centred upon the financial trails, Simon Hurdle-Jenkins and Kevin Tapping would lead the discussion at this stage.

The two moneymen deftly outlined a series of transactions that they had been able to identify between Gough Gifblaar Holdings and two of the three Directors. It appeared that only Jan de Klerk was fronting another business directly under the umbrella of Gough Gifblaar Holdings - Carmen Cronje's business seemed to be entirely separate, and payments to her were presumed to be some sort of personal dividend. They had only managed to uncover one payment from Gough Gifblaar Holdings to Pieter De Vries, and that was for a small amount – nothing like the size of the transfer that had been sent to Jan de Klerk, for example.

Their investigations were continuing.

The only other point that Kevin Tapping wanted to bring to the meeting was that there seemed to be an increased frequency in the number of transactions now taking place. It seemed to be building towards some sort of a critical point but there was no indication that they could see as yet as to what that point might be.

"Thank you for that update," said Head Shed. "We are at least starting to get a feel for these three people and their organisation. Unless anyone has anything else that they wish to raise at this stage, then I would like to move to the final item of this briefing."

Everyone remained silent, so Head Shed pushed on.

"We have now received the itinerary for the Jubilee visit for HM The Queen and HRH Duke of Edinburgh. They will be visiting all states in Australia during March, arriving in Canberra, then travelling up to Brisbane, then down to Sydney by HMY Britannia. They will then fly via RAAF transport Queen's Flight down to Hobart, and after a couple of days in Tasmania, they will fly back to Melbourne. They will then re-board HMY Britannia, where they will be based, to complete their itinerary in Melbourne before sailing for Adelaide. They are due to arrive here on Sunday 20th March, and will remain in State until Wednesday, 23rd, when they will fly to Papua New Guinea for several days. After that, they will fly back to Darwin and then finally head down to Perth and rejoin the Royal Yacht for the final stage of the visit. They will finally depart Australia on 30th March. As far as the South Australian specifics are concerned, I am authorised to confirm to you that, after a day of events and visits specifically requested by HM The Queen on Monday 21st, there will be a Gala lunch in Nuriootpa hosted by the South Australian Wine Industry Association the following day on Tuesday 22nd March. HM The Queen will be making a formal speech at that event. On the final day of the visit here, there will be a Royal walkabout in the centre of Adelaide, in Rundle Mall, before the Royal couple leaves on the next leg of their journey."

At this point, Head Shed looked directly at McAllister and Paterson. "Both of you should keep yourselves readily available to assist with any security provision that we will need to put in place in relation to the visit. Although the main arrangements are obviously being handled by London and Canberra, we are nevertheless working closely together, as you can imagine, and we may need all available serving personnel to help support this wide-ranging visit. As soon as those arrangements have been confirmed, we will be in touch with you."

McAllister and Paterson nodded.

"Will Jindivik Winery be part of that gala lunch?" asked McAllister.

Everyone looked at Head Shed.

"As far as we know, yes because they are members of the Association. They are of course one of the smaller wineries, and the event has been arranged by some of the big players in the sector."

McAllister pressed on. "What about Jan de Klerk? Does he not present a particular threat bearing in mind his background?"

"I agree it is far from desirable, McAllister, but unless we have some concrete evidence to the contrary, we are stuck with the position that they are entitled to attend the event as members of their own trade association. There is nothing we can do about that – certainly not at this stage. If something – and by something, I mean cold, hard, irrefutable evidence - emerges that would change that risk assessment, then that is a different situation. At the moment, however, there is nothing to say that there is any appreciably increased risk here."

McAllister was about to say, "But…" when Head Shed gathered his papers together, saying, "Right then, everyone, well done so far. My feeling is we still have a lot to do, and we will reconvene when necessary. Dismissed."

Everyone stood up, and after some quick side discussions around the table, the participants started to drift away. McAllister looked at his watch and was surprised at how much time had passed. He and Banjo made their way up to the fresh air and got to the car. They headed back to Weemala Road and the journey was conducted in silence as each of them digested the huge amount of information that they had now received.

But where does that leave us overall?

McAllister's little voices were chirping big time, and he didn't like that one little bit.

Chapter 50

Jan de Klerk sat working alone in his office when the telephone on his desk rang.

He looked at it for a couple of seconds before lifting the receiver. He did not say anything but just waited for the person at the other end to speak.

The metallic, heavily doctored voice from the other end of the line gave him the instructions that he had been waiting for.

He said nothing in response but gently replaced the receiver.

His glasses glinted.

His thin mouth grimaced into his impression of a smile.

Anika would give him great pleasure this evening.

But his greatest pleasure, his one true love – indeed obsession, was now within his grasp.

He did not have much longer to wait.

He picked up the telephone receiver and placed a call to his Bank in Switzerland. They needed to be aware that a much larger than usual transfer would be arriving in his account shortly.

He then made a call to his private pilot. He kept him on standby – a strictly confidential arrangement that even Anika did not know about. His "arrangement" facilitated his personal trips for his own pleasure and he reasoned she had absolutely no need to know about those, any more than she knew about his Swiss account or the safety deposit box in

London.

He smirked to himself.

De Klerk gave instructions that he would require his private aircraft to be fully fuelled and prepared for take-off, possibly at short notice, for a long-distance flight out of Australian air territory. Destination details will be supplied at the time.

In response to the pilot's enquiry, he confirmed that there would probably be only one passenger.

He replaced the receiver, leaned back in his chair, and formed a steeple with his fingers.

Unfortunately, he would have to make a trip to Adelaide to the Bank in order to retrieve the contents of the safety deposit box he held there. That could be risky, not that he thought Anika would be snooping around, but she was a woman and you never knew with them. They took the most idiotic ideas into their heads at the most inappropriate times, invariably causing trouble for everyone.

Yes, he would have to be careful.

Otherwise, things were working out in an extremely neat and satisfactory manner.

And he liked things to be neatly concluded.

Yes, that settled it.

Definitely only one passenger on the final flight.

Chapter 51

McAllister and Banjo were in the office in Adelaide, deep in paperwork. They were still trying to piece together some of the information that had been unearthed through what now felt like an extremely long-running investigation.

"Let's get a cuppa," said Banjo. "My brain is fried."

McAllister nodded. As he stood rubbing his eyes with tiredness, he couldn't agree more. Perhaps a short walk in the Mall might do the trick – a breath of fresh air and all that. He suggested it to Banjo, who agreed.

He turned back to the desk and picked up his jacket from the back of the chair. As he did so, the phone on the desk started ringing. McAllister wavered as to whether he would pick it up. He really needed a break. On the other hand, you just never knew who or what was going to be at the other end.

Putting a hand up to Banjo, asking him to wait, he leaned over and picked up the receiver.

"Hi. Mr McAllister? It's Kevin Tapping from the Bank" came a slightly nervous sounding voice.

"Hi, Kevin. How are you? What's up?" replied McAllister, sensing that perhaps it was a good thing he *had* picked up the phone after all.

"Sorry. I don't have long but I thought you ought to know, and I can't get hold of Terri Wilson. Jan de Klerk is coming into the Bank in a few minutes' time to gain access to his safety deposit box."

"Is he indeed?" replied McAllister. "When did he make the

appointment, Kevin?"

"Literally 20 minutes ago. He said he was down here in Adelaide on business, and wanted to pop in. Obviously the Bank cannot say no, but he has to be escorted to the box and he is then left alone with it until he rings the buzzer to let us know that he is finished. We then go in and resecure the box."

"Ok – we'll be there in 5."

With that, McAllister hung up, and with adrenalin suddenly pumping in his veins, he signalled to Banjo that they needed to shift – and fast.

They set off at pace through the remainder of the building, down the stairs as there was a queue for the lift, and out of the front door into the warm Autumn sunshine. They raced down King William Street and around the corner into Rundle Mall. They slowed to a walk as they got within 200 yards of the Bank and discussed how to approach the situation. They couldn't tail de Klerk, as they didn't have a vehicle readily available. Their best option was to observe and follow as best they could. With any luck, he might be on foot for at least a short way down through the Mall before picking up his car, probably somewhere along North Terrace or Curry Street.

Banjo remained outside in the Mall, taking up position on a bench and he picked up a discarded copy of the newspaper whose headlines blared, "Royal Visit details inside – get your free Jubilee flag." He sighed.

He would keep watch on the front door of the Bank.

McAllister entered the Bank to see if he could see Kevin

Tapping before de Klerk arrived.

He walked through the doors, and as he did so, he noticed Kevin Tapping standing to one side – obviously waiting for someone: whether that was him or de Klerk, McAllister wasn't sure. Either way, it made his life simpler.

"Where are the safety deposit boxes kept?" asked McAllister.

"Downstairs as the first part of the vault," replied Kevin.

"Ok – have you ever met de Klerk before?" asked McAllister.

"No," said Kevin.

"Quickly then: show me the way to the vault," and with that, they set off at a quick pace towards the rear of the main customer reception hall. They went through several sets of double doors and then down two flights of stairs. They reached a large metal door, which was typical of most Bank vaults: multi-levered with a large spoked wheel that served as the handle in the middle. Unusually, however, there was an electronic pass code pad at the side. The correct pass code had to be entered for the security levers to release before the handle could be turned.

"The easiest thing will be for me to accompany you both down here," said McAllister.

"Tell him that the Bank has been receiving threats to its customers, and I now accompany all visits to the security vault, just to be on the safe side. "Kevin gulped.

"Ok."

"Just behave entirely normally; don't show any nerves;

otherwise, he will smell a rat. Get me some sort of badge that just says security or something, and that will hopefully get us all down here."

"Ok," said Kevin again, and they scurried away up to the back offices away from the main trading floor. They made their way up to the security office, and Kevin picked up one of the security badges, which McAllister promptly put on to his lapel, and introduced him briefly as "Mike who will be helping us out today."

The two guys in the security office simply nodded, as Kevin was deputy Head of Security after all, and turned back to the screens in front of them.

"I need to go and see the Chairman," said Kevin, nodding towards the screens, "but you stay here and look at the CCTV – we have only recently had it installed, but it shows you in real-time who is entering the Bank. That should at least forewarn you when the customer arrives. I will come back and collect you from here." McAllister nodded.

When Kevin had left, he looked at the various screens in front of him and realised that the Bank vault had its own camera focused on the vault door. He kicked himself, as he hadn't noticed it when they had gone down a few minutes before. Perhaps he wasn't meant to and it was camouflaged. Either way, he realised he should have thought about that.

The minutes ticked past.

That 20 minutes is taking a stretch; perhaps he is out there just checking to see whether anyone is watching. Hope Banjo has got his eyes on it.

Another 10 minutes went by.

Definitely late. He is up to something, that's for sure.

Kevin returned and simply nodded at McAllister. They stood together in front of the screens, watching the entrances to the building.

In the meantime, Banjo had been sitting outside in The Mall on his bench with the newspaper, to all intents and purposes, appearing to be simply taking a break in the sunshine. He was satisfied that he had a good view of the front entrance of the Bank, and because it was a pedestrianised area, he knew that de Klerk would have to arrive on foot. There were quite a few people in The Mall, going about their business, but there was nothing untoward. He saw the old tramp sitting on the floor two doors down from the Bank, with his cardboard sign out saying "Thanks," and watching him nod as kindly passers-by put coins into the old bush hat that he had laid on the path next to him. He smiled sadly to himself, wondering what turns life takes that leads a man to that situation.

Shaking himself, Banjo looked at his watch.

Mmm. 30 minutes gone. Where is this geezer?

Just at that moment, a man of medium height with thin wire-framed glasses walked past his bench. He was dressed immaculately, and from it's cut and the cloth used, the suit he was wearing was clearly extremely expensive, and his shoes were highly polished leather – probably hand made. They had that sort of "look." He was carrying a leather attache case. Banjo had the feeling that although the man appeared not to be taking much notice of his surroundings, he did, in fact, have eyes everywhere.

Bingo. De Klerk. Better move before he comes out. Not

317

collecting anything heavy then, if that case is all he has brought with him. Over to you now, Mikey. Just keep your wits about you.

Banjo watched de Klerk enter the Bank through the front doors, and after a minute or so had passed, he calmly folded his newspaper up, put it under his arm as he stood up, lit a cigarette, and wandered off – apparently aimlessly – down The Mall. As soon as he got to King William Street, he turned a sharp left and, stepping up the pace, turned left again in effect doubling back on himself. He raced on towards Curry Street, before turning left again to appear at the other end of The Mall. He approached the Bank from the other direction, and found an unused doorway, where he had an unhindered view of the front of the Bank building.

He leaned against the doorway wall, lit another cigarette and waited.

Business obviously wasn't that good for the tramp, as Banjo saw that he was slowly pulling himself up to a semi-standing position, holding onto the wall as he did so to steady himself. The old man bent down and picked up his hat, looked carefully at the coins that rested there, and took them out, slowly putting them into the pocket of his great coat. He put the hat on his head, the card board sign going into the other pocket, before crossing over to Banjo's side of the Mall, and finally wandering somewhat unsteadily towards Curry Street.

Banjo hoped that he would never be in that position, and switched his attention back to the Bank.

The tramp approached Banjo's surveillance point, and just as he reached the doorway, Banjo's eyes flicked to the old man in front of him. Their eyes met, and suddenly Banjo realised that the eyes that peered back at him were not the rheumy tired eyes of a tramp, but the bright highly focussed eyes of someone much younger and fitter. With a shock, Banjo realised he was suddenly in great danger and without conscious thought, he hit out at the tramp just as the blade of the knife glinted in the sun. They fell into a tussle, Banjo hemmed in now by the doorway that he had considered to be his safety. The man was strong, and Banjo was having problems keeping the blade away from his vital parts. The fight was vicious as they traded blow for blow to their bodies, but they were contained in the doorway.

Banjo found himself pinned down on the floor, and he reached up and pulled off the old grey wig that the man had been wearing. He had tightly cropped blonde hair underneath, and the facial disguise that he had been wearing was starting to come away from his face. The man got his arm across Banjo's throat, preventing him from calling out and restricting his breathing. He raised his other arm, positioning the knife for maximum thrust and impact into Banjo's exposed windpipe.

Frantically, Banjo tried to get his thumbs up towards the man's eyes and realised that he was fast running out of options. He was starting to black out as his airway was compressed further under the weight of the man.

How could I not have seen him?

"You see, officer, I told you that there was something wrong with this tramp – now he is fighting this other man." The female voice rang out stridently behind the man holding the knife.

Almost at the same time, arms reached forward and grabbed the man's arm, deftly removing the knife. The Police Officer who stood behind the man was enormous, and he quickly wrestled Banjo's assailant out of the lock on the ground and pinioned him, arm tightly behind his back, against the wall. He got the handcuffs on, before calling in for support.

Gasping for air and holding his throat, Banjo managed to get his head up from the doorway floor and looked at the lady who, in effect, had saved him. She was all of 5'3, grey hair, mid-60s, black handbag clutched tightly in one hand and her stick in the other. She was peering at him with concern.

"Are you alright?" she asked.

Banjo could do no more than croak a response and nod. He gave her a weak thumbs up.

"Really. In the middle of Adelaide. It's terrible what goes on these days. You need a nice cup of tea, lad," she said. "Nothing like it. Johnnie Martin's does a nice afternoon tea with scones, not the same as the Lyons Corner House in London, mind, but nevertheless extremely good. But I'm sure the Police will know what to do."

With that, she smiled and turned away as the air was filled with Police sirens and the sound of running feet as uniformed officers appeared from every direction.

"Er, not so fast, lady," said the large Police Officer. "We need to have a bit of a chat."

"Very well, officer." She replied. "I will sit down here on the bench and wait until you are ready, but I need to catch my bus, so I would be grateful if you could please be as quick as you can. Even though I can see that you clearly have your hands full," and with that, she gingerly sat down and held her stick and her handbag in front of her.

Suddenly, there were Police officers everywhere. An ambulance had arrived and the crew was already tending to Banjo. The prisoner had been quickly and efficiently removed from the scene and put in the back of a Police van, which had driven off from the site. The area was taped off, and a large, rather evil-looking knife with a razor-sharp blade had been secured and placed in an exhibit bag.

The large Police Officer was speaking to the lady who had raised the alarm and who gave her name as Vera Waterman. It was arranged that she would not have to get the bus at all, but a Police car would take her home. It was the least they could do.

Banjo tried to speak to the arresting officer, but his voice came out as a croak. He was bundled off into the ambulance and driven away from the scene. He tried to tell the ambulance crew about McAllister, but they had given him a sedative and before he knew it, his eyes had closed apparently of their own accord and he had drifted away.

Chapter 52

Oblivious to Banjo's difficulties outside, McAllister and Kevin Tapping awaited the arrival of Jan de Klerk with a mix of anticipation and concern. McAllister knew that this was one mean guy, and given the slightest hint that all was not what it seemed, he could easily turn into quite a handful.

From the upstairs security office CCTV, they saw him arrive and report to the customer reception. A tannoy clicked on almost immediately afterwards, and a message for Mr. Tapping to please report to customer reception was sent out.

Bit like Woolworths on a Saturday morning.

McAllister studied the picture of the man they had been hunting and he noted, as had Banjo, the cut of his suit and the overall impression of expensive taste covering what appeared to be a fairly tough frame.

They made their way down to the trading floor, and Kevin introduced himself and nodded to McAllister as a member of security, giving the agreed line about additional security for customers of the Bank.

De Klerk seemed to hesitate for a split second, and McAllister felt the eyes behind the steel-rimmed glasses boring into him, weighing him up, assessing what sort of threat – or prey – he might be. Notwithstanding the fact that McAllister had met some dangerous individuals in his time and didn't frighten easily, he felt the intensity of de Klerk's scrutiny and his spine went cold. He could sense that this man enjoyed taking time over, causing extreme pain to those who got in his way, and unbidden, the image of Lucy

Andrews hanging in the mangroves sprang to his mind.

Very dangerous! Screamed his little voice.

Seemingly unaware of the mutual psychological appraisal and unspoken challenge which appeared to be taking place between the two other men, Kevin Tapping was standing to one side inviting de Klerk to follow him down to the safety deposit area. There was a nasty little silence after Kevin had finished speaking whilst de Klerk and McAllister finished their mutual sniff test.

Neither liked what they saw or felt about the other, and Kevin looked anxiously from one to the other.

"After you," said McAllister suddenly with a smile, and he lifted his arm towards Kevin, indicating the way.

Almost reluctantly, de Klerk broke eye contact and moved away towards Kevin.

"Let us get this done as quickly as possible. I am a very busy man," he said abruptly.

McAllister fell in behind and made sure to memorise the shape of de Klerk's head, neck and shoulder area. He was certain that he would be seeing them again. And next time they were unprotected in front of him, he vowed that he would not be so obliging as to simply follow along behind. He was certain in his own mind that this was the man responsible for Lucy's horrible death.

The tense little group wound down the stairs to the vault area, and as they did so, McAllister's eyes fell down to De Klerk's left hand. And there it was.

The wooden bracelet.

The same as the others that kept cropping up in this case, and never for the best.

Had there been any doubt in McAllister's mind, there was none now. De Klerk need expect no quarter next time they met, just as he had not given any to a poor girl simply doing her duty.

McAllister would ensure that de Klerk paid for what he had done.

And pay heavily.

When they reached the vault door, McAllister asked De Klerk to turn towards him whilst Kevin entered the electronic code. De Klerk's face tightened with anger, and his already thin mouth disappeared into a line in his face. His eyes were blazing.

Putting on his most charming persona, McAllister smiled again and explained it was simply to ensure the integrity of the code – which he was sure Mr De Klerk would appreciate.

Of course, McAllister had calculated that the CCTV camera was somewhere behind him, in the corner of the vestibule. If so, then it also meant that the CCTV operators in the security office had a good clear view of De Klerk and if, as he also guessed, the CCTV footage was being filmed, then it would provide some very current intelligence as to what De Klerk actually looked like – how he held himself, his mannerisms, his walk – so that they could study it closely back at the office.

The cold hostility in De Klerk's eyes was frightening, but McAllister stood his ground and stared back.

As soon as Kevin had entered the code – which only took a matter of seconds but for some reason seemed to take forever – he swung the vault door lock, there was a satisfying clunk as the levers disengaged and the heavy door swung open.

McAllister raised his hand and arm and gestured to De Klerk that he was free to enter the vault. No words were exchanged, and De Klerk simply turned away and walked into the vault, closely followed by Kevin Tapping.

McAllister stood by the door and watched as Kevin went through the procedure for access. He noticed that each of the boxes had a double lock system: the Bank held one key, the box owner the other.

Kevin moved over to box number 135, placed his own key in the tumbler, turned once to the right, and then moved away.

De Klerk reached into his pocket, took out a leather note folder and removed his key, which he held in his hand whilst McAllister looked on.

"Thank you both," said De Klerk. "That will be all. I will press the buzzer when I am ready to leave."

Kevin nodded and looked at McAllister. With a wry smile, McAllister slowly turned and followed Kevin Tapping out of the vault. Kevin stepped over the threshold of the door, and McAllister followed him. Before Kevin could say or do anything, McAllister reached for the vault door and slammed it shut, spinning the door wheel mechanism into a locked position before Kevin could say anything.

"Well," said McAllister, looking at the shocked face of Kevin Tapping. "He can't say he wasn't given free access to his box, but he sure as hell isn't going anywhere. And frankly, that's the way I like it."

Kevin was speechless and numbly followed McAllister back up the security stairs to be met by one of the security guards from the CCTV room.

"Don't know what's going on, boss," he said to Kevin, " but all hell seems to have broken loose outside. There are Police everywhere and an ambulance. We have locked the Bank doors as a safety precaution."

McAllister raced over to the front windows of the Bank and sure enough, what had been a busy and orderly pedestrian shopping zone had turned into an almost apocalyptic scene. As the guard had said, there were Police cars and officers everywhere. An ambulance was leaving as McAllister watched, and the whole area was being cordoned off with Police tape. There were groups of people gawping at the unfolding drama whilst others scurried out of the way so as not to get caught up in whatever was happening.

Banjo.

"You need to let me out of the Bank, urgently," said McAllister to the security guard, who then looked uncertainly at Kevin Tapping. Kevin nodded, and the guard quickly unlocked one side of the access doors to allow McAllister to slip through, and then resecured the doors behind him.

McAllister stepped out into the melee, De Klerk and the Bank forgotten, and quickly scanned the crowd and the officers at the scene. He couldn't see Banjo anywhere, and he could feel his anxiety rise. He made his way over to an enormous Police officer who was speaking with a lady – who presumably was a witness – and interrupted, saying he was looking for his colleague.

"Wait over there, please, sir," came the gruff reply. The officer finished his conversation with the lady, brought over a female officer and said that this officer would drive her home. He thanked the lady for her bravery, for helping the Police and they would be in touch again very shortly. As the lady stood up and walked off with the female officer towards one of the waiting Police cars, he then turned to McAllister.

"Now then, sir: what bee is in your bonnet?" He peered down at McAllister.

Must be a good 6 feet 8 or 9 tall. Talk about the long arm of the law.

McAllister explained who he was and asked about his friend.

The officer did not answer immediately and looked at McAllister thoughtfully.

"I know you," said the officer, after a short pause. "You were involved in the car bombing we had here a few months back. Involved with the Secret Squirrel mob, if memory serves me right. Trouble certainly follows you doesn't it?" he asked rhetorically, with a grin.

His face turned serious.

"Your friend was attacked by a man we now have in custody," said the officer, "and he has been taken to the Royal Adelaide Hospital for observation. He will be ok but if it hadn't been for the brave and timely intervention of the lady I was just speaking to, I am not so sure it would have been such a good outcome."

McAllister nodded his thanks, and said "Please make sure that if the man you have in custody is wearing a wooden bracelet, it is taken off him and secured."

The officer looked at him quizzickly.

"We think that the bracelets are not only a signifier of membership to a particularly nasty organisation, we think that they may also be made of something that can be used as a poison."

The officer suddenly looked extremely concerned.

"Righto: thanks for the heads up. I'll get on to that right away," and with that, he turned promptly on his heel and headed off towards the nearest Police car, immediately reaching into the dash board for the radio set, where he started speaking urgently.

McAllister set off for the King William Street office. He needed to find Terri Wilson, or at the very least get a message to her. Things seemed to be getting a momentum of their own, and he didn't like the direction that momentum was carrying them.

Chapter 53

Inside the Bank vault, Jan De Klerk was fuming. He had heard the door clang shut behind that idiot security guard, and before he could move to the doorway, he saw the spoke mechanism spin into locked position. It dawned on him that he would not be able to get out of the vault without assistance from outside.

He told himself to think rationally. This would not be a problem, because he had the buzzer and the usual procedure for when he had completed his private business.

So the best thing was to behave exactly as they would expect him to behave. That would also enable him to complete the task that he had come here to do.

He double checked that there were no obvious cameras or other surveillance equipment in the vault, and when satisfied that he was not being viewed, he took some deep breaths as much to calm his rising eagerness as much as any panic.

He was not given to panic under any circumstances.

He turned his attention back to his security deposit box. He unlocked it, taking out a black velvet pouch which appeared to be covering an object approximately eight inches or so long, and about four inches high, by eight inches deep. He placed it gingerly onto the only item of furniture in the room, which was a steel table bolted to the vault floor.

He unwrapped the velvet pouch, almost reverentially, and stared at the golden box that was contained within it. The Nazi swastika engraved on the top of the casket was clearly visible.

His eyes glittered, and despite himself, he smiled at his recollections.

The box itself was of course solid gold. He recalled that his father had had it cast from the gold teeth of Jews brought to the concentration camp at Dachau, where, despite having been born in South Africa albeit of German parents, he had been appointed Camp Commandant. Between the Wars, his father had wholeheartedly embraced the increasingly Nationalistic fervour of a Germany struggling with the legacies of WW1, and he actively supported the rise of the Fuhrer, enlisting in the Wehrmacht back in the early 1930s when Hitler had first risen to power. He had been instrumental in formulating the strategy for what evolved into Kristallnacht in 1938, and his career had progressed quickly after that.

How they had laughed when Jan De Klerk had agreed to enlist in the *British* Army when the Second World War had started, as his father thought that he would be far more useful to the Fuhrer's cause there than in the German forces. The stupid Britishers had actually thought that he was working for them – when all the while he was actually a double agent. The plan had worked stupendously well, and by a miraculous stroke of luck, when he had recovered from his injuries sustained at El Alamein in 1942, they had put him into an intelligence posting in Cairo.

It had been absolutely brilliant from the Nazi viewpoint, and it had enabled him to feed a lot of current intelligence directly to Rommel's forces in North Africa. The Nazis had had an extensive spy network operating throughout the area, so getting the information out had been relatively easy. The British had never known that his father was actively engaged in implementing Hitler's Final Solution, and De Klerk had enjoyed his double life.

He was psychologically made for it.

He was sent to Malta in 1943 in order to "convalesce," after the German siege had been repulsed by the Island. His father had arranged everything from that point. De Klerk had been taken as a passenger on a fishing boat from Valletta, and met his father in Sicily. They spent a wonderful two weeks there, relaxing in the sun and letting the cares of the War drift away. They enjoyed catching up with all the news and ensuring that De Klerk received his next set of orders to implement on his return to Cairo. Malta was in a state of confusion, and was urgently attempting to rebuild following the devastation of the Seige, with the resultant benefit to De Klerk that one minor recuperating Army officer was not missed.

Whilst in Sicily, he had been particularly delighted to meet his hero, Heinrich Himmler, who had been the special guest at dinner one evening. He laughed out loud at that. Such a shame that he had never had the chance to meet Josef Mengele as well: now that could have really been educational!

De Klerk had been sorry when the War had ended, and he was particularly bitter that the Allies had succeeded. His father had died some years after the end of the War, having escaped from Europe before he was captured. He had lived out the last years of his life happily, and in financial comfort, in Argentina.

On his death, he had left the casket, together with considerable wealth, to De Klerk. The casket was probably De Klerk's most prized possession, and no-one knew of it's existence.

No-one.

He opened the box and checked the content, nodding in satisfaction as his eyes took in the separate box containing three vials, the faded photograph of his father in full Nazi uniform, the small velvet bag containing 25 diamonds of the highest quality, and finally, two small spools of film.

Closing the casket, he placed it back in it's protective velvet covering and then put the whole thing into a small cardboard sleeve that he had brought with him for the purpose, and put the entire package into the attache case.

He then reached back into the safety deposit box and removed the last remaining items: an Argentinian passport in the name of Alejandro Herrera, a bundle of various currencies including Argentinian Pesos, Swiss Francs, US Dollars and GB Pounds Sterling which together amounted to a considerable sum in hard currency, and his personal Sig Sauer pistol together with the ammunition he stored with it.

He double checked the safety deposit box to ensure he had not left anything behind, and then closed the door, re-locking it and removing the key.

Almost without conscious thought, he touched his tie to ensure it was in the correct position, re-buttoned his jacket and pulled the sleeves down to the correct length above his cuffs.

Satisfied that he had completed his usual rituals, he cast his eyes once more around the safety deposit box vault to ensure that he had not missed anything, picked up the attache case and then pressed the buzzer.

He exhaled.

At last.

The final stages of the plan were about to be put into action and he would be free to leave this place. And he would ensure that he was free of Anika.

Very neat.

And he liked things to be neat.

Chapter 54

The main Adelaide Police Station in the heart of the City was abuzz. Officers were rushing about, phones ringing, paperwork – masses of the stuff – was being created by the minute it seemed.

In the centre of the throng, in a private office towards the back of the main building, sat Terri Wilson. She had just come off the phone from Mike McAllister. After thinking quickly for a moment or two, she picked the receiver back up and called Head Shed.

After a particularly terse conversation, she sighed deeply after replacing the receiver in it's cradle.

She took a slug of very cold tea from the cup which, up until now, had sat untouched on her desk. Having collected herself, she picked up the receiver and called Mike McAllister.

"You've got to let him go, Mike" she said.

"What?" came the explosion down the line. "But we've got him here in the safety deposit vault. He ain't goin' anywhere. We need to nab him now." The frustration, anger and almost shock at her orders were clear to hear from the strained tone of his voice down the line.

"Sorry, but those are the orders," she replied coldly. "We just don't have enough evidence to arrest and then hold him. Can you imagine what the publicity on that would be like, bearing in mind that he is extremely wealthy and can afford the best lawyers? He would make no bones about making

334

our life hell. And we simply can't allow that to happen. No, McAllister, we bide our time. Although we have to let him go, there is no reason why you and Banjo couldn't follow him and see what he is up to."

It suddenly dawned on McAllister that Terri Wilson was, as yet, completely unaware of the attack on Banjo. Quickly, he filled her in and her shock was clear to hear.

"Thanks for explaining. I will go to the hospital then and check that he is ok, but we need eyes on De Klerk now for as long as possible. You stick with him. I will see if Jim Brock is available to go with you straight away – he knows a lot of the background, and if De Klerk happened to meet with any of the big – but not central – players, then he may be able to identify them, whereas you may not. I'll ring him now and come straight back. Wait one," and with that, she was gone.

During the space of the next few minutes, McAllister collected a few items and put them in his jacket pockets so that he was ready to go as soon as the orders came through. He briefed Kevin Tapping as far as he could, and Tapping told him that De Klerk had just pressed the buzzer down in the vault indicating that he was ready to leave. Time had therefore run out.

Just at that moment, the phone rang on the desk in the Bank's security office. Terri Wilson confirmed that Jim Brock would be outside, waiting to follow De Klerk, and whom, McAllister decided, he would personally escort off the Bank's premises.

He set off down the stairs with Kevin Tapping in tow. They reached the vault, and Tapping entered the pass code. The door swung open and an immaculate Jan De Klerk smiled, picked up his attache case, and walked straight out of the door. As he passed McAllister he turned his head and – just for a moment – they were virtually eye ball to eye ball. De Klerk's look clearly told McAllister that he had made a dangerous enemy here; McAllister's look told De Klerk that he had better be on his mettle, because this was one mean dude who would not be giving up very easily: he was dangerous to The Cause, and dangerous to De Klerk personally.

Another loose end to be tidied up thought De Klerk.

I'm going to get you for what you did to Lucy, and there won't be any rock big enough for you to crawl under. I will find you and you will pay, thought McAllister.

Kevin Tapping sensed the tension, and indicated to De Klerk that he should follow him up the stairs. The small procession duly wound their way up to the main trading floor, where De Klerk continued to march on towards the main glass doors. Without a backward glance or a word to Kevin Tapping, De Klerk walked through the doors and was quickly out into the sunshine of Rundle Mall.

Interestingly, once outside, he paused very temporarily and appeared to be casting around to spot someone. He did not seem to find what – or who – he was looking for, and he turned right and set off at a brisk pace.

McAllister could see Jim Brock sitting on the bench opposite the Bank – almost the exact same spot where Banjo had sat earlier.

Brock left the bench and started to follow De Klerk at what

he trusted was a safe distance. He was under no illusion that this guy was surveillance trained, and he – Brock – was going to have to have his wits about him. He could see De Klerk looking in the shop windows as they passed, not to look at the wares displayed there, but to check behind him in the reflection to see if he was being followed.

In the meantime, McAllister also left the Bank but raced in the other direction, back towards the main City Police Station, where he collected Englebert. Terri Wilson had confirmed the RV point with Brock as the corner of Rundle Mall and Curry Street. There was a main public car park near there, and they had to guess that De Klerk was going to park there – suitably inconspicuously – and then move on when he was ready. It also gave several different routes out of the City, and if he were De Klerk, Brock would like it like that – options: and this game was all about options.

One big problem was that they did not know if De Klerk was being chauffeured, or whether he was driving himself. If he wanted to keep the visit to the Bank totally under the radar, then it was likely it was the self-drive option so the Curry Street car park made sense. Otherwise, it was probably the former and that would be difficult to keep tabs on especially if the driver/car were ready and waiting at a pre-set location. He would just have to hope that McAllister got the timing on this one right – and that was absolutely in the lap of the Gods.

Brock saw De Klerk cross Curry Street, and enter the pedestrian footway to the side of the exit barriers.

Excellent. Self drive then.

He found a less conspicuous place to stand, but where he could still see the exit from the car park, and waited for

McAllister. He saw the automated car park arm lift, and the sleek snub-nose of a Mercedes Benz ease through the barrier.

The car definitely fits this guy's style.

Brock saw that it was indeed De Klerk driving and he was alone in the vehicle. De Klerk checked the one way traffic coming from his left, and turned into the near side lane moving steadily with the flow. Just at that moment, Brock spotted the Austin Freeway also moving with the flow about five cars behind the Mercedes.

Brock broke cover, and made his way through the traffic to get into the vehicle which McAllister had slowed enough to allow him to complete the manouvre, but not actually stopped to cause any sort of jam or disturbance that could attract De Klerk's attention.

They saw the Mercedes change lanes, and it was clear that he was heading north out of the City. Chances were that he was going back up to Nuriootpa.

They followed at a discreet distance, and sure enough, the various inner Adelaide suburbs slipped by and gradually they made their way out on to the Main North Road. The speed picked up, and McAllister knew that he would now have to be extremely careful – especially as the traffic was starting to thin out.

They made good time, and it seemed as though De Klerk was indeed going for Nuriootpa. Fortunately, McAllister managed to wedge himself behind a large artic which gave some cover but which still enabled him to have a clear view of the Mercedes.

McAllister readied to watch the Mercedes peel off down the

track towards Jindivik Winery as they reached the outskirts of Nuriootpa, but it didn't and the little convoy just kept on going. Brock and McAllister looked at each other. This was definitely new ground – or they had been spotted and they were now on a wild goose chase.

Time will tell.

The main A20 Sturt Highway stretched out in front of them, and De Klerk suddenly decided to floor the Mercedes. McAllister couldn't tell whether that was because he had spotted Englebert, or whether he had just got bored with the fairly pedestrian pace of the journey. Either way, McAllister knew he was going to be hard pressed to keep up with his quarry: not least because he would need to get around the artic, and that wouldn't be easy.

As the signposts flashed past, it seemed to Brock and McAllister that the next main town would be a place called Waikerie, which was about 65 miles ahead, and if this road was fairly straight – and it appeared from the map that Brock was desperately trying to follow that it was – then they were heading straight for Murray River country, and the next place that would have a telephone to call in any support would probably be Waikerie itself.

McAllister overtook the artic, and could see the Mercedes some way ahead in the distance. He floored the Austin, which responded majestically, but was no match for the Merc. They flew along, and Brock realised that McAllister was driving with a grim determination that belied how badly he wanted to catch this guy.

The Merc started to slow as it approached the town environs – De Klerk was clearly not taking any chances in catching the attention of any bored country copper who might be sitting quietly in some lay by just waiting for a speeding City slicker in a posh car.

McAllister did likewise, and followed the Mercedes as it turned off the highway and entered a tree lined side street. The river was on the right, and it was much larger than McAllister had expected. The road that they were on wound round to the right and sloped quickly downwards, appearing to be heading directly for the Murray River itself.

McAllister pulled over in a lay by at the highest point and he looked through the window, whilst Brock got out of the car with his binoculars, leaning on the roof of the car to follow the final yards of the Mercedes.

De Klerk drove the Mercedes into an empty car parking space next to what appeared to be a new, lowline office building. He got out of the Mercedes – carefully locking it – and after casting about to see if anyone was watching, he carried his attache case into the silver coloured building in front of him.

Brock and McAllister looked at each other.

"This is new then" said the American. "What do we know about this place?"

"As far as I am aware, absolutely nothing" replied McAllister. "We need to call this in, so that we can get someone on to this pronto."

"Yup, guess you are right, but why don't we sit tight for a little bit and see what – if anything – happens? You never know who or what else might just turn up," said Brock.

McAllister nodded.

It made sense.

Just at that moment, a stunning silver Ford Landau, with black leather hard top, cruised elegantly down the drive past the stationary Englebert and made it's way towards the parked Mercedes.

Neither Brock nor McAllister could breathe with excitement.

They watched silently as the car parked, and after several minutes, a pair of very shapely legs wearing needle thin stilettos emerged from the driver's side of the car. The legs were followed by a very slim female torso, dressed in what – even from this distance – was expensive couture. It was impossible to put an age on the woman, save that she was somewhere between 25 and 50: she appeared to be approximately 5'6 or so tall and she had dark, bobbed hair. She wore thick framed very dark sunglasses which completely hid her eyes and the top part of her face. Her lips were exposed, and those were painted a vibrant, bloody red. She also wore gloves – which were a bright canary yellow, and which threw the black of the rest of her outfit into sharp relief.

Brock let out a slow whistle.

"Wow. That is one hell of a broad. Do you reckon that could be the Cronje woman?"

"No idea" replied McAllister, "but I reckon there's a good chance it is. She certainly has both the attitude and the money. How the hell does she drive a car like that though in those heels?"

Brock let out a laugh.

"Of all the things I expected you to say, Limey, it wasn't that! But you are right – what the hell. So – do we have two ducks in the nest then? Are we going to be lucky enough to get the final one? Or is she just some floozy as you Brits call hookers and he is out for a bit of a good time and she is nothing to do with the investigation at all?"

Before McAllister could answer, they saw movement down on the quayside in front of the office building, but their view was partially obscured by the building itself.

"We need to move" said McAllister, and with that, he got out of Englebert and started running down the roadway towards the office.

If they have surveillance on the place, then I have just blown our cover.

But he kept on going, reaching the corner of the building just in time to see the woman and De Klerk stepping into a sleek, white hulled motor cruiser. It had what appeared to be a main covered saloon on the central deck, and then a higher area covered by a sun shade that doubled as a drinks/relaxation area and the actual captain's cockpit. McAllister noted that she was called "Imka II" which was painted in gold sloping writing on her stern.

Brock appeared at his shoulder and also watched as the motor cruiser cast off, and started to head up stream.

"Blast, damn and blast" said Brock.

"The temptation is to nick that saucy little speedboat moored just up there" said McAllister, pointing further up the jetty to a racy, red speedster called "Spirit," "but we would show out in no time. We need to call it in now, and see if we can get some air borne surveillance on that cruiser. At least the name gives us a clear link to the whole Gough Gifblaar mess. Let's find out if they left the door open."

As he said this, his hand turned the silver knob on the door frame next to him and it clicked open.

"Haha – open sesame!" he whispered, and he pushed the door open further. A set of stairs was immediately to his right, and he looked around for any CCTV cameras. Not seeing any at all, which surprised him, he gingerly made his way up the stairs, taking care to make as little noise as possible. Brock followed behind, and had already drawn his personal firearm which he held in readiness.

At the top of the stairs, the floor opened out into an office space with desk overlooking the river, and a leather couch the colour of which almost matched the colour of the mystery woman's lipstick. It was a vibrant, blood red and it seemed out of place against the sterility of the rest of the room. There were no pictures, and nothing of any personal nature to indicate who occupied this area.

There were a number of doors leading off from this main entrance area, and Brock opened the first one. He put his head in and then found a light switch. There were no windows in here – it was completely black other than for the artificial illumination he had just found.

He saw the chains with handcuffs and manacles attached that were slung over one of the metal building supports in the middle of the room and the one table, which was the only furniture and that appeared to be firmly bolted to the floor.

There was a metal grill in the floor, an electrical plug near where he was standing, at about shoulder height in the wall, but absolutely nothing else. He had worked with the CIA in the past, and it was an experience that he was happy to forget. But he saw the room for what it was and realised that they needed to get forensics down here fast.

He motioned to McAllister to come and look at the room; he took one look and his face said everything. They moved away from the torture chamber, and went back into the office where a phone rested on the desk. Could they risk it? They looked at each other and nodded. McAllister picked up the receiver and got a dialling tone.

He immediately rang Terri Wilson and gave her as much as he sensibly could over an open line. He asked for urgent air support, and for the Imka II to be followed.

One blessing: she is on the river and not the open sea. That should make finding her slightly easier.

Terri Wilson told McAllister to wait at scene, and "they" would be with them as soon as they could scramble.

McAllister quietly updated Brock, and then indicated to move towards the next of the doors which was set down a separate hallway from the main room.

When McAllister opened the door, the room was again in darkness. He switched on the light, and the two men were met with a collection of photographs on the walls of the room. Most were in colour; some were in black and white. Some were quite old – at a guess, McAllister would put them as having been taken before and during the War: most seemed to be from concentration camps run by Nazis, as

344

most of the people in the photographs were either wearing Nazi uniform or the striped prisoner outfits he had seen in the Imperial War Museum in London.

Some of the photographs seemed to include senior Nazis of the time – McAllister could recognise Heinrich Himmler, for example, and Herman Goering, but most of the others he did not know. The rest of the photographs were more recent, and appeared to catalogue the most obscene progression of depravity that McAllister had ever seen. As they reached the end of the "display," McAllister felt the nausea rise in his throat as he looked straight into the pleading eyes of a clearly still alive, but very badly injured, Lucy Andrews hanging from what appeared to be the restraint chains in the room next door.

I will avenge you, Lucy: you can count on it.

With Brock trailing after him, McAllister got out of the room as fast as he could, raced down the stairs and went outside into the cooling early evening breeze that had picked up. The breeze and the river seemed to be the only clean things around him just at that moment, and he could feel his skin crawling as he realised the magnitude of what they had actually found.

He took out a cigarette and lit it, pulling deeply.

As Brock stood next to him, McAllister passed him the packet.

Neither man said anything, but both looked at the deceptive calm of the Murray as it flowed slowly past this ghastly place.

Chapter 55

The helicopter setting down at the Waikerie Airfield bore no markings on it's fuselage to arouse suspicion, but it quickly disgorged two, four man Special Forces teams onto the concourse. Three Land Rovers with blacked out windows were waiting next to the tarmac at the rural air strip. The teams quickly piled in, with the vehicles speeding off away from the landing strip within seconds of the helicopter having touched down.

The rotor blades did not stop, and as soon as the soldiers were out of the fuselage, the helicopter took back off, heading towards the River.

Old Doug Harrison, who owned and operated the landing strip, stood in his oily dungarees watching all of the "goings on" and scratched his head. As he would later tell most of the Bar in The Riverland Hotel, he had never seen anything like it in all his born days. At first, he had thought the call from the Police was a hoax, some sort of prank. But he quickly revised the opinion when "things" started happening, not least being that, within 20 minutes of the initial call, blacked out vehicles that were obviously very high spec arrived at the site.

No-one had got out of the Land Rovers; they had simply waited by the side of the strip. And not long after that, the helicopter had arrived. He had grinned to himself: never mind tonight, this would keep him in beer down at The Riverland Hotel for weeks. Nothing this exciting had happened in Waikerie for years – if ever. He rubbed his hands together as he thought of all the pints of amber nectar lining up on the bar, so that the story telling could continue uninterrupted.

One of the Land Rovers pulled off the main drag through Waikerie to a pre-agreed RV point. It's team disgorged from the vehicle and disappeared into the vegetation, heading downwards to the river. The Land Rover was moving again in seconds.

The second vehicle approached the lay by where Englebert was still standing, and pulled up behind. Again, all four of the team disgorged from the vehicle quickly and efficiently and made down towards the building. One of the team remained on the higher ground under vegetation cover.

The sniper, thought McAllister when he saw what was happening.

One of the soldiers came towards McAllister.

"I'm red leader. Boss said to give you this" and he promptly handed over a walkie talkie. "Have you checked the whole building?"

"No, we haven't. There didn't appear to be anyone else here, but we have not looked in the other rooms – only the first two. The one on the left from the main reception area appears to be some sort of torture chamber; the second is a photographic collection. God only knows what they have got in the others."

McAllister felt the hard eyed appraisal of red leader, and was immediately reminded of Crazy Pete.

Oodnadatta seems an awfully long time ago.

Red leader simply nodded, and made hand signals to one of

his team who was covering the corner of the building. Without further discussion, they entered through the doorway in tandem, covering each other, leaving McAllister and Brock on the parking space outside, next to the Mercedes.

Brock simply raised his eyebrows at McAllister, but said nothing.

"I just hope we have got some sort of air support looking for that cruiser" said McAllister.

"Roger that" replied the quiet American.

Both men stood quietly, lost in their own thoughts.

Chapter 56

The Murray River is the longest river in Australia, stretching through three States and covering over 1500 miles end to end. It flows from the Eastern State of New South Wales and provides the State boundaries between Victoria and then South Australia, where the river finally wends its way across the State down to the sea. As with most great rivers, it has provided life giving water, food, recreation and acted as a transport artery almost since the colonisation of that part of Australia, and it's ancient history of use by the indigenous peoples of the land goes back much further to long, long ago in the dream time.

Jurisdiction nowadays for Police matters arising on the river is usually determined by exact location, local "arrangements" and in most cases, necessary pragmatism.

Having flown from Doug Harrison's airstrip, the helicopter made straight for the Strategic Control Centre based at Renmark, which is the last major town on the South Australian side of the State Border and just a short hop in air time from Waikerie.

The main national highway passes through Renmark, and it is the centre of the Riverland country. From that location, Police and military support can reach most places in South Australia, Victoria, or New South Wales quickly either by air or water. It also gave an additional option in reaching the Australian Capital Territory, namely Canberra, quickly and from an unexpected direction should any sort of national emergency arise requiring "unexpected" responses.

As soon as the helicopter touched down on the helipad, Terri Wilson alighted and raced towards the main Control Centre building. She passed through security and went immediately to the Command Bunker, albeit she had to admit that "bunker" was probably a bit of a stretch in description. It was a secure room used for high level security briefings, not dissimilar to that in Woomera but nowhere near as sophisticated and not built below ground. However, as British and American special forces often used the location in addition to Australian Police, Intelligence services and special forces units, it had become known as "the bunker" somewhere along the line, and the name had stuck.

Head Shed met her at the door, and they entered together. There were a handful of military and Police senior figures present, and Head Shed lost no time in convening the meeting. He promptly handed over to Terri Wilson and she outlined the current situation, and the information that they had as at that moment.

Head Shed confirmed that the surveillance systems operated out of Pine Gap had been utilised, and the Murray River was currently being "swept" to find the Imka II. In addition, water borne special forces and Police units were already mobile on the river itself. An update from Red Leader on site at the office complex on the River bank was awaited, but it seemed clear from the initial report that one and possibly two of the Directors of Gough Gifblaar Holdings were present on the boat. Imka II had to be found at all costs.

After some discussion, Head Shed issued a series of instructions and the meeting broke up. Terri Wilson headed straight back out to the helipad, and they took off – heading back to Waikerie, where she arrived barely 10 minutes later.

Disembarking from the aircraft, she headed for the Land Rover that was at that moment sweeping back alongside the air strip. She got in, and the Land Rover swept back out again and they headed for the office building complex.

Old Doug Harrison was, by this time, sitting on an old oil drum in the shade of his workshop, with a mug of tea on his desk, but from where he had a bird's eye view of the comings and goings airside. Whatever was going on, it was something really big. He laughed to himself again, enjoying every moment, and awaiting the next arrival.

The Land Rover carrying Terri Wilson pulled promptly to a halt outside of the office building complex. As she got out, she nodded to McAllister and Brock who were still outside, and almost at the same moment, the swing door to the building opened and Red Leader appeared.

"Building swept, and no-one else is here" he reported. "There are some things that you should see, though." With that, he turned on his heel and Wilson, McAllister and Brock followed him in single file back into the building and up the stairs.

Red Leader paused briefly to show Terri Wilson the torture chamber and then the room containing the Nazi photographs. He then moved on to a third room, on the right hand side of the complex. He opened the door and ushered the trio in.

The first thing that grabbed McAllister's attention was the large chart on the wall. It had lines drawn on it between photographs.

Not dissimilar to the white boards that we have been using at Woomera to try and establish our own connections.

These photographs made those present gasp.

They were all Service issue, showing the subject in full military uniform. The first was of Lucy Andrews; the second of Peter Addams; the third of Banjo in full RAAF Provost uniform, and the final one was a photograph of McAllister himself.

Where the hell did they dig that one up from?

There was also a photograph of McAllister and Banjo at – *where was that? - hell's bells: that was at the shack up in Mooloolaba. We were under surveillance from this lot even then?*

As McAllister thought about it, he realised that it made sense. The fact that "they" had known that McAllister and Banjo were heading for Toowoomba and Simply Bottles, and had mobilised Lurch so quickly, spoke for itself. He may even have taken the photographs himself.

The last four were photographs of Terri Wilson, Jim Brock, Dr Schuster and Simon Hurdle-Jenkins. The photographs of Andrews, Addams and Schuster had been crossed through with a red felt tip pen.

In addition, there were fairly recent newspaper clippings particularly of the Adelaide car bombing that McAllister had been involved in, and the discovery of Lucy Andrews.

There was silence in the room as the group digested what they had found.

"You should also look in the cupboard to the left," interjected Red Leader, breaking the tension.

Brock moved over and duly opened the cupboard, which was filled with large jars. He stood back so that the others had a clear view of the contents. Each of the jars appeared to contain a quantity of clear liquid, and suspended in each, were various human body parts.

In addition, each jar was labelled.

McAllister's eyes alighted on the jar marked "Lucy Andrews" and looked with horror at the single eyeball that stared unblinkingly back at him. Involuntarily, his mind went back to the night they had found her body in the mangrove swamp and the fact that one of her eyes had been missing. He had assumed that this was because it had already been eaten by the various critters that were in the Estuary. It had not occurred to him that it had in fact been *purposely removed* as part of the torture process and kept as some sort of a sick trophy.

His gaze moved on to the "Zoe Schuster" jar, where a human toe still wearing a silver toe ring rested.

There was no mention of a removal of any part of her anatomy in the autopsy report. Who did this? Is there someone else on the "inside" that is actively collecting these trophies for this lot of weirdos?

And as for Lurch, his jar appeared to contain…...

*Surely not; that really can't be what I think it is. Christ: it **is** what I think it is. That's his dick.*

For the second time that day, McAllister felt sick.

There was total silence as the group digested the sights before them.

Again, Red Leader broke into their thoughts.

"Nice lot you are hunting. Looks like you will need to keep your wits about you."

Just at that moment, his radio crackled, and Red Leader held his earpiece firmly into place. He simply responded, "Roger that," and spoke again to the group:

"Looks like we have eyes on Imka II. She is about 15 miles south of Waikerie, and one of the Flipper units has eyes on." He turned to Terri Wilson, clearly awaiting further instruction.

"Right. McAllister and Brock – you come with me. Red Leader – request civilian Police assistance to preserve the scene, and get photographic and forensics up here urgently. We need to get this lot catalogued as quickly as possible. But no-one removes anything at all without my express permission: is that understood? Should anyone else turn up – they are to be detained immediately for further questioning, and under no circumstances are they to be given access to this building."

Red Leader nodded, and turned away, immediately talking into his radio – but for all the world from the back looking as though he was speaking into his own shoulder.

"Let's go," barked Terri Wilson, and the three of them moved quickly back towards the stairs and got back into the Land Rover that was still waiting patiently by the roadside.

They moved quickly back up the hill, through Waikerie centre and out to the air strip.

By the time they got there, the pilot had arranged and

completed a re-fuelling of the aircraft from an extremely happy Doug Harrison, and already had the rotors spinning in readiness for their arrival. They alighted from the Land Rover, moved quickly over the tarmac of the strip and got into the helicopter, Wilson in the front next to the pilot and Brock and McAllister in the two rear seats. They took off immediately, and the pilot swung a hard left to start following the river.

The Pilot's voice crackled into the headsets that had been pointed out to them.

"We are heading south west down River. The Imka II has been spotted about 15 miles away: we should be there in about five minutes. Water borne units are on their way, and a Flipper unit has eyes on."

No-one said anything, but the three occupants nodded in understanding.

The aircraft flew fairly low over the countryside, and kept crossing the Murray River as it wound it's way lazily along it's course. Huge eucalyptus, or River Gums, dotted the banks and not for the first time, McAllister marvelled at the beauty of this country.

The pilot started hovering, and with binoculars, McAllister could see a white river cruiser below them but much further ahead. A small black inflatable boat, with five black clad figures on board, appeared to be approaching the craft.

From this distance, they look almost like ants.

The inflatable moved alongside the cruiser, and he watched as they threw ropes up on to the aft hand rail of the cruiser, and almost immediately, four of them were swarming up to the deck. As soon as they were aboard, the inflatable moved off and stood astern to await further developments.

McAllister could only assume that these were men from the Flipper Unit that everyone had been referring to, and therefore probably special forces – or more probably, Royal Marines Commandos.

Or whatever the Australian equivalent is.

Almost as if reading his mind, Terri Wilson piped up through the crackling communications system:

"Those are British Royal Marines Commandos; they were over here on a training exercise as part of an exchange visit – and it was too good an opportunity to miss. We have been given special clearance by the Australians for them to undertake this "live" operation. The skipper of the inflatable is an Australian special forces operative, just to ensure that this is truly a joint operation."

Brock and McAllister looked at each other, and nodded.

As the group in the helicopter looked on, one of the black clad figures returned to the aft rail and started waving his arms, which those on the helicopter assumed meant "no go – nothing doing – no one on board." Their sense of frustration was palpable.

"We need to find a landing space to set down" Terri Wilson said to the pilot, who nodded in understanding and immediately started looking at the landscape beneath them to find a suitable site.

Deep in the vegetation at the side of the river, but slightly further upstream from the Imka II, two people sat completely camouflaged, silent and still, watching the approach of the inflatable and the boarding of the cruiser by the four men. They looked at each other, and then looked back at the cruiser. One of the men had returned to the aft rail and was signalling with his arms – presumably that there was no-one on board.

And presumably that also meant that there was a helicopter that was presently out of sight and earshot that was watching everything that was going on.

Well, they are going to enjoy watching this then....

One of the people hiding by the river bank was holding a small rectangular shaped device. The antennae on the top was pulled up to maximum, and with one blood red, immaculately manicured finger, the large button in the middle of the device was carefully pressed.

A split second later, the Imka II erupted into a massive fire ball.

The flames lit the river bank, and showed the huge smile of wicked satisfaction on the face of one of the people hiding there. The other seemed to show no emotion whatsoever.

They quietly moved from their position whilst they presumed that all eyes were on the shards of debris that were now falling from the sky, having been catapulted in all directions by the blast, and on the flaming inferno on the water itself as the fuel tanks on the cruiser – plus the three incendiary devices that had been planted there on purpose – exploded. Huge flames and plumes of smoke covered the scene, and for a minute or so, it was impossible to even see the floating debris of what had once been the beautiful cruiser.

The team in the helicopter looked on, appalled at the devastation that had been wrought below them. They could see no sign of any of the men who had been on board, nor of the inflatable with the additional member of the team – that too had seemingly disappeared completely in an instant.

Another five good men gone.

Christ, De Klerk, you and your little gang are going to pay for this.

The radio broke into a multitude of chatter wanting a sit.rep, wanting to know how many casualties, whether any of the bombers had been detained – the list was endless.

The pilot of the helicopter ignored them all, controlled the aircraft through the pressure wave from the explosion, and found as safe a place as any to set down. It was in the middle of a stretch of scrub land, and was about 500 yards from the trees lining the river bank. McAllister, Brock and Wilson alighted from the helicopter and crouching down to avoid the still whirring rotors, ran forward in cramped position to reach the tree line as quickly as possible. They disappeared through the large old River Gums, to try and get to the scene. They found pieces of debris along the way, and McAllister heard a muffled "For fuck's sake" from Brock, who grabbed his shoulder and pointed into the foliage. There they saw a dismembered arm still clad in black, hanging limply from the lower branches of a tree – almost in an obscene "hello there" gesture.

McAllister gritted his teeth, and they raced on towards the water's edge where they found a litany of debris and rubbish that had been washed up already following the blast. What they did not find, see or hear were any survivors. One of the oars from the inflatable bobbed past them, together with pieces of burned wood, a life jacket, and, bizarrely, what appeared to be a half empty bottle of Dom Perignon Champagne.

Wilson was on the radio, and it was clear that the cavalry was on it's way. Indeed, McAllister could hear the faint wailing of the first of the emergency services vehicles presumably coming towards them.

This really has turned into a major cluster fuck.

Pound to a penny that detonation was remote controlled. Bet they are still here somewhere. No chance to really get away as yet.

He turned to Brock.

"I don't think the bombers have got away yet. Bet this was remote controlled, and they are waiting their moment. Let's scan the water line – they can't be far. Stay in radio contact."

Wilson interrupted.

"I don't want any heroics from you two. You stick together. We have lost enough people on this blasted job already."

McAllister was about to object, but he took one look at Terri Wilson's face and decided against it. Something was better than nothing after all.

"Reckon they would have been closer than this, but this side because it's easier to hide. Let's go this way," said Brock, setting off down towards the point where the burning carcass of the Imka II was settling down low in the water.

Brock and McAllister gingerly picked their way through the undergrowth, trying to keep as quiet as possible but with their eyes everywhere. Both had drawn their sidearms.

They approached a smallish clearing in time to see a Land Rover, with blacked out windows, driving calmly away from the scene. McAllister could see the registration plate: black with white lettering. It looked as though there was something – AMF?- at the top and then the registration number: 192 – 446.

Is that them? Surely couldn't be anyone else.

Having directed Brock's attention to the vehicle, McAllister immediately opened fire, aiming at the tyres. Brock joined in, and they issued a barrage of bullets towards the vehicle which quickly disappeared out of sight. He called Terri Wilson on the radio and told her what they had seen, and why they had fired.

"AMF means Australian Military Forces," she replied. "But we haven't used that since 1972 as the registration system changed from 1973 onwards, so it must be on the register of military transport vehicles somewhere. I will call it in, and we can see what we can find out. Did you hit them?"

"Dunno," interjected Brock. "They were already moving and we were a fair distance away. I wouldn't say it was impossible."

"Right. Stay where you are. I will be with you shortly," and with that, the signal went dead.

Up ahead, the Land Rover carried on it's journey. It had not been hit, and the two occupants were laughing at their success and what they considered to be a puny response from those idiots who had got to the clearing faster than expected.

"That was definitely a blast," said the one who had pushed the button. "If you will excuse the very poor pun."

Her companion said nothing, but nodded and in extremely good humour, they went on their way. As they turned on to the main highway, they noted the number of official vehicles – Police, fire, ambulance and military – that appeared to be heading from the centre of town down towards the river. They turned south, away from Waikerie, and several other emergency vehicles headed past them in the opposite direction – sirens wailing. The vehicle headed back towards the Barossa Valley, it's occupants extremely satisfied with what they considered to be a very good day's work.

"That should keep them busy for a while," said the driver.

His companion smiled and settled down further into the passenger seat.

They quickly reached the small township of Blanchetown, and drove into the transport yard at the back of an old disused warehouse. There, they got out of the Land Rover, took off their camouflage/combat gear, revealing their civilian clothes underneath. They were satisfied that the vehicle was clean, as they had both worn gloves when anywhere near the Land Rover, and to set it on fire would only draw attention to it: especially in a small township like this one. That was the last thing they needed. They simply closed it up, locked it, tossed the keys away amongst the rubbish that was in the warehouse, and moved over towards two waiting cars. The transfer took less than two minutes.

The cars left separately, but both headed towards Nuriootpa

initially. In due course, the first turned down the approach track of the Jindivik Winery, whilst the other sped on towards Stirling in the Adelaide Hills. It's driver owned a beautiful, and very discreet, old Colonial property (some would call it a mansion) up there that had fantastic views over the City and which caught the breeze during the hot summer months.

And that was her own, very private, bolt hole where she could do as she wished. Her "visitors" when she was in the mood were her business, and she enjoyed the understated and reclusive luxury that she was able to afford. Of all her properties dotted across the world, this was her favourite.

Apart from her occasional visitors, no-one – save for one important exception - knew of it's existence, and she intended to keep it that way.

She smiled to herself as the electronic entrance gate slid silently to one side, allowing the car to pass into the privacy of the Estate, far from any prying eyes.

*Oh yes. Champers, a hot fragrant bath and some fun tonight as Gifblaar is in town. Very convenient, and he will be particularly pleased with today's events so we should have a great evening. After all, I think I **have** earned a bit of a reward.*

Chapter 57

By the time McAllister walked in the door of the Weemala Road house, he had to confess that he was completely bushed. It had been one hell of a day. He walked into the kitchen and immediately reached for the bottle of Bushmills on the breakfast bar, and poured himself a huge slug. He just didn't have the energy to run a bath, but he definitely needed to get in the shower: the rank filth and ghastliness of some of the discoveries today seemed to be clinging to him, his clothes, his hair, and he needed to get that washed out before dropping into bed.

He walked into the bathroom, with drink in hand, and turned on the shower. He walked over to the handbasin, and caught sight of himself in the bathroom mirror.

Christ: I even look as tired as I feel!

In his peripheral vision, he saw the door handle of the bathroom turn. He was immediately looking for a weapon – the goblet containing his drink would have to do, plus the element of surprise. He did not move from the basin and waited for the attacker to come through the door.

The door opened further and in walked Banjo.

"For God's sake, mate: you had me thinking you were an attacker" said McAllister breathing out a huge sigh of relief and smiling at his friend. "Mind you, you look as though you have gone a few rounds yourself."

Banjo smiled back, but he was clearly feeling the after effects of the events in Rundle Mall. He had a nasty cut over one eye that had been expertly stitched and bandaged by the hospital staff, and a huge welt around his neck where his attacker had tried to throttle him. He looked completely done in.

"Wasn't sure if you were going to be back tonight," he said to McAllister.

"Neither was I. Are you ok – or at least as ok as can be expected?"

Banjo smiled again. "Yep. I'm good. Nothing a good night's sleep won't cure."

"All for that. Just going to have a shower and then hitting the sack. It will be another early start in the morning, and today has just been one thing after another."

McAllister grinned. "But of course, that is the way we like it, right?"

Banjo managed another smile, raised his hand in salute and turned and tottered off to bed.

McAllister's smile faded as his friend left the bathroom.

Will have to tread carefully tomorrow with the stuff we found in Waikerie – not sure he is up to knowing that we found Lucy's eyeball. Mind you, finding Lurch's dick might give him a laugh.

Despite himself, McAllister let out a soft laugh, and went to step into the shower until he realised that the water was not jetting out with it's usual efficiency and it was more of a trickle.

What the....!

Oh, forget it – I'll sort it out in the morning.

With that, he grabbed another drink and then flopped into bed.

Repeatedly assuring McAllister that he felt up to a road trip, Banjo got into Englebert the following morning, gingerly easing himself into the passenger seat. They set off just after sun up, and quickly headed out towards the Barossa Valley with McAllister giving Banjo a potted history of everything that had happened the day before.

Banjo whistled in appreciation. "No wonder you looked done in when you got back! What a shame about losing the cruiser: do we know definitely who owned it?"

"We should have more on that today," replied McAllister. He then carefully outlined what else they had found at the office unit by the river, at which Banjo went rather quiet.

The rest of the journey to Waikerie was undertaken in silence, with each man lost in his own thoughts.

"By the way, have you had any problems with the shower?" asked McAllister suddenly. "I couldn't get any water out last night or again this morning – not like it is usually."

"No. Must confess I didn't even try when I got back from the hospital. That is unusual as the plumbing has been extremely good. We will have to get one of the maintenance lads out to have a look. I'll sort it out when we get back."

McAllister nodded, and kept on driving. The miles slipped past, and before long, they were through the Barossa and heading up to Waikerie. He had toyed with the idea of paying an unannounced visit to the Jindivik Winery, but common sense got the better of him and he realised that that could be a very high risk strategy – without the level of reward to go with it.

Before reaching the office complex, they pulled in by the river to look at what was left of the scene of the previous day's blast.

Banjo let out another low whistle as he looked at the devastation that was spread for quite a way along the river bank, and the still slightly smoking charred spars which was all that was left of the cruiser, lying sadly in the middle of the river. There was a recovery team hard at work, securing the carcass of the vessel in order to tow her into the bank and then on to the transporter truck that was already waiting silently, ready to take the load away for thorough forensic investigation.

Not that they will find anything much. This lot are too clever for that.

Involuntarily, McAllister looked at the tree and was relieved that the dismembered arm had been removed. Despite himself he shuddered. It really had been gruesome.

"Come on. Let's go up to the office block. Hopefully we will hear all the latest news," and McAllister turned back towards Englebert, with Banjo following on behind.

As they approached the office complex, it was clear that representatives of a significant proportion of the Australian military and civilian law enforcement agencies were already there and were busily recovering items, searching the grounds and the scrub leading to the office block, and it also looked as though there were search teams working in a methodical fashion down each of the banks of the River looking for any item of forensic value that may have been missed or overlooked.

Just to make matters worse from McAllister's point of view, there also appeared to be a number of news teams from the main television channels swarming around the entrance to the offices, who were clearly aware that something was going on and were keen to get the latest update. McAllister couldn't blame them, but they really did not need this sort of attention right now.

Just at that moment, the door opened and a man that McAllister did not know stepped out in front of the waiting journalists. Lights popped, and microphones were hurriedly shoved in front of the newcomer. It seemed that some sort of briefing or update was being given to the press. Goodness knows what was said, but as soon as the new guy had finished speaking, there was a mad scramble as all of the reporters made for their waiting vehicles, which then roared up the hill past where McAllister had again parked Englebert, and disappeared on the road into town.

McAllister and Banjo took the opportunity that had so helpfully presented itself and drove down and parked outside the now deserted office block.

The newcomer was still at the door, and greeted them with a smile.

"Hi, I'm Tristan – press officer to the Boss. I take it that you are McAllister and Paterson. Terri asked me to expect you both. In case you are wondering, the press have all gone off to talk to Doug Harrison at the airfield. I am sure he will be delighted with the attention, and with any luck, will keep them busy for a bit."

Smiling, he turned and beckoned them into the office complex.

McAllister shook off another involuntary shudder as he thought about what lay ahead up the stairs, but they moved forward quickly and found Terri Wilson surrounded by a hubbub of activity. People in plastic coverall suits, with cameras, lights, black medical type bags containing phials and bottles: in fact, all sorts of equipment was everywhere – it seemed that this place really was being gone over with a fine tooth comb.

Seeing them, Terri beckoned them over to a corner of the main floor. Tristan made his excuses, and departed to deal with one of the telephones that was ringing. A quick de-brief followed, including the fact that the Imka II had indeed been owned by Gough Gifblaar Holdings so the link was now well and truly established.

The material that had already been recovered from this site provided conclusive evidence that people closely connected to the Company were involved in the torture and murder of Lucy Andrews, Peter Addams and Zoe Schuster – not to mention the four Royal Marine Commandos and the Australian special forces soldier killed yesterday in the boat blast. The office complex was also held in the name of Gough Gifblaar Holdings.

Something was worrying McAllister.

"This is beginning to feel a bit too easy and too staged," he said at last, looking at Terri Wilson.

"How do you mean?"

"Well, after months of chasing our tails and not being able to pick out any particular threads of the puzzle – or at least, not without a huge amount of time, work and patience – suddenly we have boats that are openly registered to the Company with a name that was almost guaranteed to grab our attention, and then leading us directly to this office complex which has thrown up a huge amount of information and evidence. It is almost as if they are taunting us. Particularly so with the trophy jars labelled as they were. Clearly De Klerk was working with someone in Rundle Mall, because of the lengths they went to in order to disguise themselves and then attack Banjo. They obviously know exactly who we are from the photographs on the board. Can we be absolutely certain that this whole thing has not been one huge set up? De Klerk knew that he was probably going to be followed from the Bank, and made sure that he led us here – and then waited to blow the boat when he knew that there would be some of our guys aboard? That was just an added bonus from his point of view, and more or less guaranteed that we would throw everything at this site. It has neatly distracted us away from Salisbury and Adelaide – and the Barossa for that matter - making this the centre of our focus and activity, at least for the present, and tying up some of our scarcest resources into the bargain." He paused.

"So the 64,000 dollar question is: why do they want us out of town?" McAllister paused again. Now he had articulated this out loud he was almost certain that he had hit the nail on the head.

Banjo and Terri Wilson looked at him in appalled silence.

"Let's be honest," continued McAllister. "We don't know

who we can trust on our side. We didn't know until it was too late that Lurch was feeding information to the bad guys; there may be others who are doing the same thing. This would have been the perfect ruse to give them – whoever they really are – a bit of breathing space to work with. But the question remains: why do they want to distract us? Are we really closer to seeing the point of all this than perhaps we realise?"

Banjo and Terri Wilson looked thoughtful.

"What about chummy from Rundle Mall? What has he had to say?" Banjo asked.

"Not a lot," replied Terri. "He has been taken to the hospital under armed guard, as he was taken ill earlier this morning." She looked downcast.

"Abrin?" asked McAllister.

She shrugged. "Don't know, but it could be: he is displaying the right symptoms. In which case he won't be speaking to anyone, as he will be dead within the day."

McAllister and Banjo looked at each other.

"Ok. So how do you want us to proceed?" asked Banjo.

"Go back to Woomera. I know that is not Salisbury, or Adelaide either for that matter, but we have immediate access to other resources there and you can be back in the City quickly by air from there if needs be. I will also feel more comfortable knowing you are with people I *can* trust – Alison Fielding for one, Kaz MacNamara for another – albeit Kaz is obviously out at Coober Pedy. And you seem to have developed a little safety network all of your own out there with Crazy Pete and your Uncles, so all in all, I think it would be best for you both to drop out of sight for a bit. As far as the investigation is concerned, putting you there will not alert the other side to the fact that we may have worked out what they are getting at either, so that could be quite convenient. When you are at Woomera, you are working on lines of investigation coming out of the events here – clear? As you rightly say, McAllister, unfortunately, we just don't know who we can trust right now, so let's play them at their own game."

Both men nodded, and said that they would be on their way then. They confirmed that they would call in when they got to Woomera.

"Just need to make a phone call before we leave," said Banjo.

"We are having a problem with the shower at the Weemala house, so if we are going up to Woomera for a while, it will give the maintenance boys a chance to sort it out."

Terri Wilson nodded, and turned away at that point to speak with one of the officers who was hovering at her shoulder, wanting her attention.

Phone call made, a wave to Terri Wilson, and they were off – back down the stairs and into Englebert.

"Woomera here we come then" said McAllister, and with that, they turned towards the main highway and headed west.

Are we finally entering the end game? McAllister wondered.

Time will tell, boyo, time will tell.

Chapter 58

It was odd, thought McAllister, but driving into the car park at Woomera almost felt like coming home and some of the events and people that he had met since his first landing here all that time ago flashed through his mind. He was pleased to see Alison's Ford Falcon in the car park and decided that they should call in to her office first, not only to let Terri Wilson know that they had arrived without mishap, but also to have a chat and find out the latest from the Woomera end.

Before they got as far as the administration building, Alison herself came down the stairs and McAllister realised that he was extremely happy to see her. Her straightforward, friendly dependability was just what he needed right now, and he smiled as they walked towards her.

"Hiya," Alison smiled in return. "Hear you two and Jim Brock have been lighting up the River Country. Don't believe in having a quiet life, do ya?" she laughed.

"Yes we have been having quite a time," he replied, and the three of them walked in companiable silence back into the building and made their way up to her office. As usual, the phones were ringing off their hooks, and she seemed to have a myriad of notes waiting for her attention sitting on the desk. She ignored them all, waved towards a couple of chairs and put the kettle on.

"Tea?" she asked.

Both Banjo and McAllister nodded gratefully. They hadn't stopped on the way from Waikerie and were definitely ready for a brew.

"So – what's the latest up here?" McAllister asked, as Alison placed the hot mugs on the desk in front of them.

"Well, apart from trying to help with following up some of the lines of enquiry from the Waikerie end of the investigation, we are now also juggling with the Royal visit arrangements and supporting our colleagues from Canberra and London with that as well. So, to say we are busy at the moment is an understatement. But it is good to have you back up here, anyway."

"When does the Royal visit start again – I have rather lost track of the days," said McAllister.

"The Royal party are currently in Melbourne, and will be leaving on the Britannia tonight. They will arrive here in Adelaide on Sunday, stay in South Australia until Wednesday when they do the Royal Walkabout in the middle of Adelaide, and then off our hands," replied Alison.

"Be warned, you may get roped in to some of that – we are very short handed at the moment, even with the influx of teams from London and the East, so two more properly cleared officers would be of great assistance – even though I know that is not what you are really here for," she replied.

McAllister nodded.

HM The Queen and The Duke of Edinburgh are arriving against this backdrop. It sure doesn't get any easier. What a headache.

"Is the Wine Industry Gala still on for Tuesday?" asked McAllister, vaguely recalling the itinerary that Head "don't forget you heard it hear first" Shed had rattled through all that time ago.

"As far as I know, yes, it is. I will double-check, though. Why?"

"Well, that might be a real help to Banjo and me. If we could wangle an invitation to that event, then we may be able to move our own investigation forward whilst still rendering some security assistance in relation to the Royal visit. Could you ask the question? They can only say no, but I really think that could kill two birds with one stone" McAllister replied.

"Sure. Sounds good," said Alison, and promptly reached over to a red coloured phone that was perched on one side of her desk. She picked up the receiver and quickly dialled a number. The phone at the other end was answered promptly, and Alison quickly entered into a conversation with a lady called Linda, who seemed very nice and who obviously knew Alison very well. It seemed that Linda had the unenviable task of trying to co-ordinate the Gala arrangements.

"Okay," Alison was saying. "And where do you want all of our security and support people?"

Listening to the reply through the receiver, Alison was making notes on the pad in front of her.

"And are there any private meetings before or after the formal Gala?" she asked.

McAllister gave her the thumbs up.

Good thought, Alison. Well done you.

"Thanks, Linda. See you soon, but no doubt speak to you again in the next couple of days." She hung up, and turned back to McAllister and Paterson.

"Yes, is the short answer. All systems are go apparently for this really swanky Gala, where HM The Queen will be making a formal speech. The Gala will be held at one of the largest and oldest Wineries in the Barossa. Do you want to go as guests or as obviously part of the security detail?"

She looked expectantly from McAllister to Banjo and back again, waiting for an answer.

"My initial reaction is to say as guests," said McAllister. "If the Jindivik bad guys are there, they are going to know us anyway, so it may give us more latitude to poke around a bit if we are not locked into the actual security detail – which could cause problems if anything kicked off. But we will need some sort of comms so that if we do discover anything, then we can call it in."

"Yeah. I agree," croaked Banjo. "But there's just one thing: do I have to wear a tie?"

Alison and McAllister both turned to look at him in astonishment before bursting out laughing.

"Glad you are feeling brighter, Banjo," said Alison. "And yes, you most certainly do have to wear a suit and tie – so you had better get down the hire shop and get one sorted out!"

Leaving Alison to the incessant demands coming at her from all directions, they went up to the main office and cleared their desks of the notes, cups, fag ends, and empty packets that had somehow migrated there during their absence. Having picked out what appeared to be still current messages and having returned a few calls, they decided to call it a day and go out to Crazy Pete's for a few beers before finally going back to The Shack to get their heads down for a few hours.

The next few days could prove to be very hectic indeed, so they would at least try and get some kip whilst the opportunity presented itself.

A few beers in fact turned into a bit of a thrash, as Crazy Pete himself was up at the Bar, as was Bull and several of the others who had been in on the Oodnadatta gunfight. So what with one thing and another, the beers flowed and it was gone midnight by the time Banjo and McAllister got back to The Shack, pretty much the worse for wear.

Oops – probably not a great idea but what the hell. Hopefully, it will have done Banjo some good anyway.

With that happy thought, McAllister drifted off.

The following morning, McAllister relished standing in the shower at The Shack and letting the steaming hot water cascade over him. He enjoyed washing his hair, and watching the soap suds flowing down the drain hole in the floor.

I must have stunk yesterday.

An image of Zoe Schuster suddenly popped into his head, unbidden. *What was it Norman Reynolds had said at the briefing: the Abrin could have been administered through food, water – even toiletries in the shower?*

McAllister's blood ran cold, and he got out of the shower unit quickly.

Wrapping a towel around him, he went into the kitchen to find a bleary-eyed Banjo sitting propped at the breakfast bar with a black coffee and a cigarette in front of him.

"Did you get hold of the maintenance guys yesterday, mate?" he asked.

"Yep. They are hopefully going to Weemala today to look at the plumbing for us." Banjo slowly took in the shocked look on McAllister's face. "Why? What's up?"

"I may be seeing things that aren't there. But we need to warn the maintenance team to be extremely careful. I'm not sure that the water tank at Weemala hasn't been compromised with the addition of Abrin."

It was Banjo's turn to look shocked. He stubbed out his cigarette and picked up the phone that was hanging on the wall next to the breakfast bar. He rang Alison's number in the hope that she was in the office early. True to form, she was there and picked up quickly.

"Hello. Alison Fielding."

"Hi, Ali. Banjo here. Can you get on to the maintenance guys down in Adelaide urgently? We think that the water tank at the Weemala house may have been tampered with – possibly with the addition of Abrin. They should go with complete HazChem suits and take all precautions, just in case. Hopefully, we are wrong but I would prefer that we work on the side of caution."

Banjo held out the receiver towards McAllister so that he could hear the conversation. After a couple of silent seconds, Alison responded:

"Ok. I will get on to that immediately. You two need to get back here urgently, then, and give me a full debrief. But I will speak to the teams down there straight away. See you shortly." And with that, she hung up.

McAllister nodded.

"Thanks, mate."

"Bloody hell. This gig just gets better and better," replied Banjo.

"I need a shower – not sure if I am brave enough now," but he got off his stool at the breakfast bar nonetheless and moved off towards the bathroom.

They were back in Alison's office within 30 minutes. She looked tense, which was unusual because ordinarily, she seemed to McAllister to be completely unflappable. Noting her half-drunk cold cup of tea standing on the desk and that she was on the phone in what was clearly a fairly lengthy conversation, McAllister walked over to the kettle and made three fresh cups, setting one down in front of her. She looked at him gratefully, and the conversation started winding up.

She put down the receiver and gave a large involuntary sigh.

"Right, I have spoken to the maintenance leader down at the Unit. He is going to go to Weemala himself straight away, together with his deputy who, in a previous life, was in the Royal Navy and well trained in HazChem procedures. No-one else will go near the site, and you are not to return to Weemala until I give you the all-clear. I have put a message out to Terri to let her know, and am waiting for her to call.

So, what makes you think that the tank has been tampered with?"

She turned to McAllister.

"I was in the shower at The Shack this morning," he replied. "And for some reason, Zoe Schuster popped into my mind, and I remembered what Norman Reynolds had said at one of the briefings: about the method of administration of the Abrin being, possibly, through something as innocuous as a shower, shampoo, or toiletries, particularly in light of the tox results on her hair. It occurred to me that she had been kept prisoner for several days beforehand, so it would be logical that if they changed the routine and moved her from where she was originally imprisoned and put her somewhere less awful on some sort of pretence – say, that they were going to be releasing her and it had all been a dreadful mistake - the first thing she would want to do would be to get in the shower, clean herself up and wash her hair. She had nothing with her, so she would automatically have used any toiletries provided. If those were laced with Abrin, she was actually administering the poison to herself.."

He stopped talking.

The silence in the room engulfed him.

The look of sadness on Alison's face was awful to see.

"I hope to God you are wrong," she said quietly. "But I have to say that there is a dreadful simplicity in what you have outlined. I will let you know as soon as I have spoken to Terri and as soon as we have any update from Adelaide. In the meantime, just take care of yourselves. I don't know who these people are, but they obviously don't care who they hurt or how. And for whatever reason, they seem to have taken a huge dislike to the pair of you. Just watch your backs."

The phone on her desk started ringing again, and McAllister and Banjo took that as the signal to leave her be for a while.

Without a word, they went back out to the car park to the smoking tree.

"When you put it like that, mate, it gives me the hooby goobies," said Banjo quietly.

McAllister said nothing, took a deep pull on his cigarette, and looked into the distance. He shivered involuntarily.

"We need to find Pieter de Vries," he eventually replied. "We need to cut the head off the snake. And fast"

And with a grim determination, he threw his stub down and ground it into the earth. With one last look at the distant horizon, McAllister walked back towards the admin building. Banjo looked at the firm set of his friend's shoulders and his deliberate stride and, glancing skywards, thought about what on earth was going to be coming at them next and how McAllister seemed to attract trouble. He sighed and then followed him into the building.

Chapter 59

Just at that moment, Terri Wilson was receiving a good news call from Alison Fielding. It was grim stuff; she couldn't deny it. She was keeping her fingers crossed that the Weemala end was a bit of a red herring – jumping at shadows, that sort of thing. The problem was, McAllister did not strike her as a "jumping at shadows" type – and his hypothesis was both simple and deadly effective.

And he hadn't been far wrong up to now.

She sighed and realised that she seemed to be doing a lot of that these days. She leaned back in her chair and turned towards the window to let her thoughts run free. The work load over the last few weeks had been significant, and she really needed to get away and unwind - perhaps with a good game of golf thrown in, which would be a bonus. But that was totally out of the question until this investigation was wound up, and the Royal Visit was over.

Without admitting it to anyone else, Terri was desperately worried about the Royal Visit itself, even though she knew that the British and Australian Secret Services, plus all of the other law enforcement agencies and units necessary, were in place, trained, briefed and ready to spring into action should the need arise. The first full day was due to get under way the following morning with a series of private visits organised at the express request of HM The Queen, which was not so much of an issue.

However, Terri realised she was not at all relaxed about the Gala in the Barossa on Tuesday or the blasted walkabout right down Rundle Mall on Wednesday morning.

When this (whatever "this" actually was) was all over, I will be quite happy never to hear the words Barossa Valley or Rundle Mall ever again.

She thought about her request to Head Shed for the Gala to be moved out of the Barossa down to Adelaide central, or preferably cancelled altogether, bearing in mind the involvement of some of the Directors in the Jindivik Winery in the other current investigation, but he had refused. He had argued that the Gala had been arranged at the express request of Her Majesty, that there was no appreciable risk to the Royal Party, and that to change the arrangements at this very late stage would just cause confusion and very public embarrassment to all concerned - not to mention the political fall out that would follow.

After the major Constitutional crisis that had been triggered by the dismissal of the then Prime Minister Gough Whitlam from office in November of the previous year by the Governor-General Sir John Kerr, there would be absolutely no appetite whatsoever to do anything that would stir the already troubled political waters of the country as a whole.

As Head Shed also pointed out, a decision had been taken at the very highest levels in Canberra and London for the Royal Visit to continue against such a turbulent and controversial backdrop anyway, and had only gone ahead because it was felt that, after the shock to the whole Australian political and constitutional system that the crisis had caused, a visit from the Monarch to celebrate Her Majesty's Silver Jubilee was exactly what the country desperately needed.

Terri had asked him to at least speak with the State Premier about the possibility of a change of venue, but he had flatly refused and said that the matter was closed unless she could produce firm, irrefutable evidence that there was an appreciable risk to the Royal party or anyone else involved in the occasion which, after all, he had argued, was a flag ship day for the Barossa particularly, and South Australia as a whole.

And, of course, she couldn't.

Not that she thought there was a risk as such – it was just that she did not like Jindivik being involved in this sort of high-profile event, given all that was going on in the background.

Another sigh.

At least McAllister and Paterson would be on site – that was something, although with those two anything could happen. Still, perhaps that was what this investigation needed – a bit of the unexpected.

She turned back to her desk, picked up the phone, and rang the armourer downstairs in the basement shooting range.

It might not be improving my golf swing, but at least I won't be rusty should I really need to fire in anger.

With that, she left her office.

When she returned a couple of hours later, she found a note on her desk from her secretary. It was headed "Urgent" and asked her to ring Mike Whitely, the leader of the maintenance team sent to Weemala Road, straight away.

Her heart sank, and she immediately picked up the phone.

"Hi – is that you, Mike? Got your note. What's up?"

She liked Mike Whitely and found his calm, Cornish tones particularly helpful at times like this. She also trusted him completely, and she knew that he was related to, and lived next door but one, to the Fielding clan. He had been a sensible head on several occasions in the past, and she as grateful he was leading the team on this one.

"Hi Terri. We have been to the Weemala Road house, and thank goodness we went with the full kit. The main water tank in the roof has definitely been tampered with – can't say just at the moment whether anything has been added to the tank itself, but we have taken water samples and those have gone down to the lab straight away for testing. It seems that whoever was busy taking off the lid for some reason also turned the main feeder tap off and forgot to turn it back on – which is why the boys did not have any water in the house, let alone the shower. Good job, too, if what we suspect to be the case proves to be right. We hope to have the lab results in the morning, but as you know, they may not be able to turn it around that fast, especially bearing in mind it has gone 9 pm now. We have asked for the tests to be done as a matter of extreme urgency, though. Hope that was ok, boss?"

"Absolutely, Mike. Thanks again. Please let me know as soon as those results come in – whatever the time."

"Will do," he replied and hung up.

Time seemed to have raced away from her. She looked at a telex that had also arrived whilst she had been down in the shooting range, confirming that the Royal Yacht had arrived in South Australian waters and was safely moored off shore, ahead of a (hopefully) triumphant arrival into Adelaide the following morning.

Time to go and get some kip.

With that, she picked up her bag and jacket and headed for the door. Together with several of the other senior field officers, she had a sleeping bunk available to her on-site whenever she needed it, and she had long ago decided that she would use it for the duration of the Visit. At least then, she was on site should anything go wrong, and she was needed urgently.

As she lay down under the rough Army-issue blankets, she tried to think of happy things before finally drifting off.

But it was a troubled sleep, as she couldn't shake off the mental picture of the jar labelled Zoe Schuster in the cupboard in Waikerie, containing a single toe complete with a toe ring.

What had they missed?

Chapter 60

Jim Brock sat at his desk in the FBI office, located in the US Embassy in Canberra, Australian Capital Territory, and was flicking through what seemed to be a mound of messages and telexes that had come through overnight. He took another slug of his coffee and fought the temptation to light up another fag. He was desperately trying to give up, but the demands of this current investigation involving Gough Gifblaar Holdings and its cast of characters were not helping much in that regard.

Although it was still early, everyone was in – as had been the case since the Royal Silver Jubilee Visit had started earlier in the month. Security was red hot, and even though the US was not directly involved in British/Australian security concerns for the trip, there was an obvious overlap and the FBI – and the CIA, for that matter – were doing all that they could to help support the Visit. And the significant time difference, with Canberra being 14 hours ahead of Washington DC, did not help matters in that regard.

Brock released his top button, pulled his tie askew to loosen the pressure and ploughed on. He was hoping that he would finally have some results from his contacts in South Africa about the whereabouts of Pieter de Vries: he reflected that it really had been like pulling teeth. He buried his head in his hands and tiredly looked at the neatly organised piles in front of him.

Yet again, nothing.

He sighed, stood up and stretched his back. He seemed to

have been at it for hours – and he realised that, indeed he had been. Time for a refill, he reflected and he wandered off to the coffee machine. As the hot liquid was pouring out of the machine, he heard raised voices in the main office and, through the glass of the office partition, saw Max from the messaging centre running about the floor plate, waving papers and asking people something.

Brock poked his head around the partition and called out.

"Hey Max, you looking for me, bud?"

Rolling his eyes skyward and waving the papers in his hands even more rapidly and with his dark curly hair bobbing frantically, Max raced over to where Brock was standing.

"I've been looking for you everywhere. This has come in for you – marked Top Secret – US Eyes only – Extremely urgent. You need to call the States now."

"What?" said Brock, taking the papers from the clearly very flustered Max. "Any idea what it's about?"

"Nope. Just that it is *really* urgent – and you need to call The Director's office pronto."

Brock looked up from the papers whilst he processed the last part of Max's message. "The *Director's* office? Are you sure?"

"Of course, I'm sure," retorted his exasperated colleague. "Why the hell do you think I have been running up and down through this damn building trying to find you? Just get a move on. The direct number is on the papers. It is URGENT, man. Move"

Coffee forgotten, Brock returned to his office straight away and closed the door. Using the secure phone rather than the usual landline, he dialled the number on the papers that Max had given him and waited. He was still not sure that this was not some sort of wind-up from one of his mates States-side. The call connected very quickly, and Brock asked for the Director's office. Confirming he was Special Agent Jim Brock calling from Canberra, Australia, he was put through immediately and suddenly found himself speaking with the Director of the FBI himself, Clarence M Kelley.

The following few minutes proved to be the most extraordinary in Jim Brock's life.

At the conclusion of the call, with the next steps having been agreed and having been assured that the Head of Station in Canberra, Steve Barnaby, was about to be fully briefed, Jim Brock quietly replaced the receiver into the cradle on the telephone and sat down – virtually dumbstruck. It took him several minutes to process the information that he had just heard and try and make sense of it. Without a second thought, he took out his cigarette packet and lit one. If ever he had needed a fag, it was now.

Without saying anything to anyone else in the office – as he had been ordered by The Director – Brock quietly collected his things and left the office. Once outside, he took his car from the car park and drove immediately to Canberra Airport, where he parked up in the long-stay car park. He took his "Go Bag" that he always kept in the boot of the car "just in case" and made his way to the ticketing desks to buy a ticket for a flight to start what could prove to be the single most important – and dangerous – assignment he had ever undertaken on behalf of his country.

Chapter 61

McAllister and Paterson were in the office in Woomera early on a Monday morning. The radio set in the office was tuned to the security services channel so that the progress of the Royal Yacht and the Royal party could be monitored as HM The Queen and His Royal Highness the Duke of Edinburgh commenced the South Australian leg of the Royal Silver Jubilee visit.

McAllister had not slept well, and he was very grumpy. He had the dreadful sense that, for some reason, time was rapidly running out for their investigation and the clues were almost like gossamer on the wind, tantalisingly within reach but never close enough to make a real difference to their progress. He was haunted by Pieter de Vries, and he had made a mental picture in his own mind of what his adversary actually looked like, or at least, what he *thought* he would look like.

Several cigarettes and cups of coffee had done nothing to improve his mood, and even Banjo had left him to his own devices. A special flight had been laid on for them for 0500 the following morning so that they could get back to Nuriootpa early and prepare for the Gala – particularly as the Weemala house was out of action until further notice. If he was honest, McAllister was dreading the toxicology results from the house. He had no real idea when those would be in, but the more he thought about it, the scenario that he had outlined to Alison was the only one that made any real sense.

The phone on his desk rang, jangling him from his thoughts. It was Jim Brock. McAllister was surprised but pleased to hear from him. They had not spoken for some time but McAllister had not had any doubt that the US end of the investigation was continuing.

"Hey Jim," replied McAllister. "Great to hear from you. How can I help?"

A tannoy sounded in the background.

Sounds like he's at a Station or an airport or something.

He was suddenly concerned. "You ok, Jim?"

"Yeah, good buddy," came the comforting Texas drawl. "Can you come and meet me – need a quiet chat. Completely off the books, if you know what I mean."

McAllister was silent for a few moments.

"Sure. No problem. Where and when?"

"Do I remember you telling me once that you have an Uncle who lives out at Andamooka?" asked Brock.

What the … …

"Yes, that's right. Beltana Station. You want to meet there?"

"Yeah, if that's ok. Shall we say 1700 tonight?"

Again, McAllister was silent for a few moments.

"I will try and get hold of him and arrange it. How can I contact you in case things don't pan out?"

"You can't. If it's a no-go, I will meet you on the road somewhere," replied the American.

"Can I bring Banjo?" McAllister asked.

Brock hesitated.

"No. Sorry, buddy, but not this time. And as I say, this is totally off the books, so you tell no one, and I mean no one, about the meet. Is that clear?"

With that, the line went dead, and McAllister sat back in his chair, completely at a loss to understand what on earth was going on. He wrestled with the idea of whether he should just turn up at Beltana and see what unfolded or whether he should ring first. He decided on the latter. He gathered his things and then left a message for Banjo saying he had gone walkabout for a bit to clear his head but would see him for the 0500 flight in the morning. That in itself would raise all sorts of problems but he would just have to deal with those in due course.

He drove back to The Shack to put a call in on the radio. Geraint himself answered the call, and the arrangements were made. McAllister simply said that he was meeting a friend. If Geraint assumed that the friend was Banjo, then there wasn't a lot he would be able to do about that any more than he could do anything about the fact that his uncle was probably in the queue behind McAllister himself wondering what it was all about.

McAllister realised he had a judgment call to make.

Do I trust Jim Brock implicitly?

If he had learned one thing in his life, it was that politics made people do weird things but you should always trust your gut. And his gut said that Jim Brock was Ok.

But you never knew.

Perhaps it would pay to have a bit of a contingency up his sleeve, just in case. As he put his sidearm in his bergen, and collected his jacket from the chair, McAllister fervently hoped that his gut was not mistaken. His life may well depend on it.

Chapter 62

When Banjo got back into the office, he saw that McAllister was not at his desk. Before he could say anything, one of the girls in the office saw him and as she rushed past, said that McAllister had asked her to tell him that he had gone walkabout to clear his head but that he would see him for the 0500 flight in the morning.

Banjo stood in the middle of the office dumbfounded.

"What? Are you sure that's what he said?" he called after her.

"Sure. Look, Banjo, can't talk – really busy just now. He was perfectly ok; he just didn't want you to worry." She backed down from the office as she was relaying this information.

To himself, Banjo wondered what the hell was going on and he walked over to the desk. He found the various notes and scribblings that McAllister had made during the course of the day, but there didn't seem to be anything there of any note. He turned to Ted, the guy at the next desk, and asked if McAllister had said anything to him or whether he knew if McAllister had seen anyone or spoken to anyone before leaving the office.

Ted could not provide much information but "thought" that McAllister had received a call, but he could not be certain about that. It was very busy, and he had not been paying that much attention.

Banjo sighed in frustration.

He turned and made his way up to Alison's office. She was

also in the midst of a number of demands, but he waited his turn and he asked her the same question. She said she had not seen McAllister all day. Looking at Banjo's pale face, she asked if everything was alright.

Banjo had to answer that he simply didn't know, and he told Alison the message. She stopped still and watched him.

"Do you think someone's got to him?" she asked in the end.

"Christ knows, Ali. Something is definitely going on, but I don't know what it is. This is not like him, though. He would usually ask me to go with him if he was off on one of his Celtic hunches. Well, can't do anything about it now – we will just have to wait for him to turn up tomorrow. At least he still intends to be on the 0500 flight; I could really do with the support before we walk into that Lion's Den tomorrow in Nuriootpa. Will keep you posted."

And with that, Banjo turned and left Alison's office.

He went out to the smoking tree, and over yet another fag, thought about what he *really* knew about Mike McAllister and whether there was more going on here than met the eye.

He might be a great bloke, but after all, he's not an Aussie, is he? If the chips were really down, what side would he choose?

Hunching his shoulders, coming to the conclusion that such lines of thought really wouldn't get him anywhere and weren't worthy of his friend, he decided to call it a day and went to get the car from the car park – to find that the Land Rover Defender was gone.

He's taken the bloody truck! Thanks, mate – really good of you. Some walkabout, that is, if you need wheels.

Grumbling to himself, Banjo walked over towards the pool dock to find Greasy and see if he could blag another set of wheels until tomorrow. The only thing still in the pool was an old Morris Minor, "Everything else is out, mate," Greasy had explained cheerily "It's that or nothing."

Banjo had taken the keys to the Morris and was now bouncing along on it's lively suspension as he drove back to The Shack.

Well, he ain't here either – no Land Rover – and some of his kit is gone too, including his best bib and tucker that he is going to be wearing tomorrow. Not coming back tonight, then. What the hell is going on?

He can't have got himself a bird – I would have known about that. Where is he likely to have gone? There are only three places I can think of: Crazy Pete's, Coober Pedy to see his Uncle Huw, or Andamooka to see his Uncle Geraint. Why he has gone to any of them in this weird manner is a different question entirely.

Immensely frustrated and with a fit of growing anger, Banjo went to the fridge to get himself a beer. As he reached in, he froze as he saw the note taped to the top of one of the cans. The note was in McAllister's hand writing.

"Andamooka. Bring Bess."

Banjo had to read the extremely short note three times before it really started to sink in. Bess was the nickname he had given to his own personal firearm: a Smith & Wesson Model 29. It was a monster, and it was licensed to Banjo privately rather than through the RAAF.

395

So, McAllister is expecting trouble as he clearly wants me to come loaded for bear.

He nodded to himself and went straight to his bedroom to throw a few items of clothing, together with his suit for tomorrow, into a bag. He took Bess out of her secure storage place in the wardrobe and checked the chambers. Satisfied she was clear, he loaded all six chambers with .44 ammunition and put the now-loaded gun into his shoulder holster.

He took another four boxes of ammunition from the storage container, together with the RAAF issue rifle and four boxes of ammunition for that as well.

Within 10 minutes, he was away from The Shack and on the road to Andamooka, bumping along in the Morris, wondering – not for the first time – what it was that his new Welsh friend had got himself into and hoping fervently that he was not too late to help him deal with whatever it was that was unfolding.

Chapter 63

McAllister pulled the Land Rover over off the track as he approached the Beltana homestead. He suddenly felt very exposed, so he moved the vehicle off into the scrub to find a quiet place to sit and watch the house for a while – just to see what, if anything, was going on. He was fortunate in finding a cluster of gum trees that afforded him some protection from prying eyes, and he settled down to see what was going to happen next.

Brock had said to meet at 1700, and it was near that now – by the time he had got his kit together and travelled up to Andamooka, McAllister was already running later than he would have preferred. He got out of the vehicle and, standing behind the large comforting trunk of a Gum with long whispering branches providing good cover, used his binoculars to carefully look at the buildings and the homestead in particular, just to check that there was nothing obviously out of place. He did not want to go charging in finding that he had walked into some sort of a trap – at least, not without being aware that was what it was.

The minutes ticked by, and McAllister was conscious that he was frequently checking his watch. Everything was still quiet. *Too quiet?*

There didn't seem to be the hustle and bustle of a busy sheep Station. He hadn't seen his uncle out and about either, and apart from Geraint's vehicle, which was parked at the side, no one seemed to be moving. That was odd.

Or am I seeing ghosts?

McAllister heard a vehicle of some sort approaching and guessed that it was Brock. He stayed still and watched as a ute pickup arrived with one occupant – Jim Brock.

Brock got straight out of the vehicle without looking around him, and went up the steps and knocked on the door.

Ok. So he wasn't there waiting, and he didn't seem in any way suspicious or anxious. Perhaps this is a genuine meet.

The door opened and McAllister saw Geraint answer, with a smile and a handshake, welcomed Brock into the house.

Nothing wrong there then.

With that, McAllister went back to the Land Rover, threw his binoculars on the front seat next to him and drove back onto the road, appearing in front of the homestead a few moments later. He parked behind Brock's vehicle, and had a quick look inside before he went up to the house. No-one else was there or obviously hiding. So either Brock had an occupant(s) who had slipped out of the vehicle whilst McAllister was moving the Land Rover and who was now hiding in one of the outhouses, or Brock really had come alone.

This is really weird.

His mind made up, McAllister walked up the steps and knocked. His uncle again answered the door with a hug and a smile and brought him into the lounge where Brock was already ensconced in one of the comfy armchairs with a large glass of what looked suspiciously like Bourbon whiskey.

Brock looked up at him and smiled. He raised his glass, "Good to see you, McAllister. Your uncle sure has taste.

Best Kentucky Bourbon!"

McAllister walked over to him, and they shook hands.

"Well, I will leave you two to your discussions," said Geraint. "Help yourself to the Bushmills, Mike – it's over there on the shelf. If you need anything, just holler. It's just me here today: Susan and the girls have gone down to Adelaide for a couple of nights: they don't want to miss the Royal Walkabout on Wednesday. It's a big thing in these parts. Most of the women folk are going down. Once in a lifetime and all that. No doubt they will find time to go shopping as well," at which he issued a mock sigh and rolled his eyes.

And with that, he was gone.

For a few moments there was just the quietness of the homestead that enveloped the two men. It seemed to McAllister that Brock had something on his mind, and so he let the silence grow as he moved over and helped himself to a drink.

Brock cleared his throat.

Here it comes: the reason I'm here.

McAllister took a deep breath and turned to face Brock, who was staring down into the depths of his Bourbon.

"Sorry to call you out here, Mike, and thanks for coming. You must be wondering what the hell all this is about."

You can say that again.

"I really needed to speak to someone I can trust and who is outside of the Australian ring of influence - if I can put it that way. To all intents and purposes, you are a Brit and your allegiance is to the UK. I am right in that assumption, aren't I?"

Brock stopped speaking and fixed McAllister with a steely glare.

McAllister looked back and simply nodded.

"The Aussies have been infiltrated – possibly quite high up – by the Gifblaar set. We have received information suggesting that the reason we haven't been getting anywhere in real terms with the investigation is that it is being blocked from this end. There are apparently links with South Africa as well, which hasn't helped matters, although I don't yet know the extent of those links. I obviously couldn't tell you all this on an open line, or down in Adelaide, or even at Woomera: I just don't know who we can trust. However, this has all been confirmed to me at the highest level – and I mean *the* highest level – so I am afraid that there is no doubt at all in my mind that the investigation is completely compromised."

Brock stopped speaking and sat quietly, assessing McAllister's reaction.

"We knew that there were insiders, though: Lurch, for example. Are you telling me that this goes right up the hierarchy? Is that the real issue here?" said McAllister.

"Yup. All those requests that I have been putting through to South Africa? A CIA buddy of mine gave me a tip that all of them were answered – admittedly after quite a delay in some cases - but then appear to have been intercepted at this end. The question is: how? All of the material comes in Diplomatic pouches straight from the US so that it cannot be touched. And yet, it has never arrived. We are looking into that at the moment – God forbid that we have been infiltrated as well and that the Diplomatic bag is no longer sacrosanct. The good news is that we have a new machine in the field office in Canberra – state-of-the-art and only just becoming popular in the States, so the Bureau has nabbed it first to help with extended field operations such as this. It's called a fax machine, and the written word and photographs can be sent over what is essentially a phone landline quite quickly. Material is coming over from the States tomorrow, so I need to be back in Canberra then so that I can personally receive the information. It could have a bearing on where we go from here. I just needed you to know in person, Mike, which is why I flew down and did not want to speak to you at Woomera. Be careful. The stakes just got even higher than they were before, especially if they realise that we now know that there is a really serious problem at their end. I don't know who we can trust on the Australian side."

It was McAllister's turn to be sombre, and he looked out of the window of the homestead and lost himself in the distance. He thought about all of the people that he now liked to think of as friends that he had made here since arriving nine months ago. The faces of Banjo, Alison, Caryle, Kevin, Kaz and Terri – they all flashed in front of him.

Surely none of them could be bent – essentially traitors, betraying those they had worked alongside? Betraying their country?

This time, images of Zoe and Doctor Schuster, Lucy Andrews and even Lurch came back to him.

He suddenly felt very down and very alone.

"Are we any closer to knowing what all of this is actually about?" he eventually asked with a deep sigh.

"Not really," replied Brock, in equally sombre tone. "There is a very quiet whisper – and it is no more than that, so make of it what you will – that this set of comedians are up to something really big. And that the "something really big" is also going to happen real soon, so we are running out of time."

Brock went quiet again, and the two men looked at each other. McAllister broke the silence:

"I've got to be on the 0500 special flight down to town tomorrow – I have to be in Nuriootpa for the Royal Gala luncheon event, which is part of the Royal Visit, and that will take up most of the day before I go down to Adelaide for the Royal Walkabout which is the final event here in South Australia. With the end of the visit, some of the pressure should be relieved. We can perhaps then, finally, start to make some progress. Hopefully, your material will have come through from the States by that stage, and we can re-group and re-assess what we need to do from here.."

Brock nodded.

"Are you doing all that alone or are you working with Banjo as a team?" Brock asked, his face a mask.

"With Banjo," said McAllister, quietly.

The silence descended again.

I just cannot believe that Banjo would be in on all this. The trouble is, I can't believe that any of them would be.

Brock swallowed the last of his drink and stood up.

"Sorry this has been such a dismal chat," he said, looking up at McAllister. "But you had to know. I'll be in touch when I have some more news. And, of course, I hope it goes without saying that if you see me pop up somewhere you don't expect to see me, I am there because I am needed. Just watch my back for me, buddy, will ya?" Brock suddenly looked very serious, and McAllister realised that this was no off-the-cuff request.

"I take it that you are pretty certain that your back will need to be watched, then?" he asked, looking Brock dead in the eye.

Brock said nothing but nodded.

"I will, of course, keep in mind that you will be fairly tied up for the next couple of days," he replied and smiled a cheeky smile that broke the tension that had suddenly descended. "Now you know why we had a Revolution!"

They shook hands, and suddenly, McAllister found himself fervently hoping that it was not the last time that they met. He saw the American out of the house, and Brock got straight into his vehicle, promptly did a U-Turn and drove back up the track towards the main road to Andamooka.

As the dust from the track dissipated, McAllister turned back and poured himself another very large drink, thinking that it may well be the last he had for quite a while and wondering, yet again, whether this whole "thing" - as he had started to think of it - could get any more weird.

Chapter 64

Banjo was pushing the Morris Minor to its limits, and he was extremely relieved as he drove the last part of the highway towards the turn-off for Beltana Station. He was about half a mile short of the turning when a ute passed him in the other direction, going like the proverbial bat out of hell. As it passed, Banjo looked quickly into the vehicle, and had a flash view of the driver.

I'm sure that's Jim Brock.

Banjo pulled over to the side of the road.

What to do? Do I follow the ute? Do I continue on to Beltana in case McAllister is injured – or worse – and needs urgent help?

On balance, he decided that McAllister was more important and so he revved the Morris back up and continued on his journey to Beltana, ignoring the squeaks and groans as the old suspension tried to cope with the track at speed.

What was Jim Brock doing all the way out here?

Dusk was starting to fall, and Banjo had no intention of being out on the track in the dark – at least, not in the Morris. Hopefully they would be able to borrow some sort of four-wheel drive from Geraint for the morning should McAllister have "disposed" of the Land Rover in one way or another. The trip back to Woomera was going to have to be completed in the dark all the way if they were going to meet the 0500 flight. He sighed and absentmindedly slipped his hand inside his jacket just to check that Bess was still safely snuggled in.

He toyed with the idea of pulling off the track to have a quiet look at what lay ahead first, but frankly, the poor old car wasn't up to that sort of punishment. He decided to press on and hope for the best.

As he approached the homestead, he was relieved to see McAllister and Geraint sitting out in the rocking chairs on the verandah, apparently enjoying a long, cool drink together. Nothing appeared to be wrong, and just at that moment, Banjo wondered if he had over-reacted.

Was the sighting of Jim Brock just a coincidence? Or was he out here? And if he was, what was that all about?

Geraint and McAllister watched in fascination as the dust-covered Morris Minor careened carefully to a stop in front of the verandah and smiled as Banjo got out.

"Hiya. Sorry, I'm late. Did I miss anything?"

McAllister laughed and got up out of his chair, striding along the verandah to meet his friend.

"Not a thing. False alarm. Sorry to have set hares running. Want a drink?"

"Thought I saw Jim Brock hightailing it down the main highway a short time ago. Was he here?" asked Banjo.

McAllister had already decided on his story for when this question emerged - sooner or later - knowing Banjo was straight to the point, so it was sooner.

"Yes, he was. He wanted to ask me a bit of a personal favour, and was a bit reluctant to do it in the office or on the phone. Sorry to ask you to bring Bess, but I just didn't know what it was all about. I'm obviously getting jumpy in my old age!"

405

and he smiled.

For some reason, Banjo was not entirely convinced but he played along. "That's ok then as long as you are alright. Bess is happy as she has had a trip out. And thanks, yes I'll have a drink – cold beer, please."

"Just one question: what's with the car? I thought Englebert was a character piece, but this one is in another league?" said McAllister.

Banjo smiled and looked over his shoulder back at the Morris.

"Well, needless to say she was the only one left in the pool – everything else is out – so beggars can't be choosers. She got me here though, so can't complain," and he laughed.

The three men sat down together on the verandah, and enjoyed a few drinks and a bit of much-needed downtime. They accepted Geraint's offer of a blanket on the couch for a couple of hours before they left for Woomera, and with his hands behind his head, McAllister lay in the dark thinking about where they were in the investigation and worrying about what could lie ahead in the next few days. Banjo, on the other hand, had gone out like a light, and McAllister could hear his steady breathing from the other couch.

Nothing like a clear conscience to let you get off to sleep quickly.

There is something here in front of us that is so blindingly obvious we are just not seeing it. And who can I now trust? The Yanks have clearly got the wind-up, and they don't usually get jittery, so we will need to watch ourselves as if this job wasn't awkward enough.

He finally drifted off to images of Jim Brock asking him to watch his back, only to be woken three hours later by a wide-awake Banjo shoving his arm.

"Come on, sleeping beauty – time to go."

Groggily, McAllister collected his jacket and got to his feet.

"I presume we aren't taking the Morris?" said Banjo.

McAllister smiled.

"No mate, we will take the Land Rover. Leave the Morris here and we can come and collect her after the visit is over."

"Roger that," said Banjo and he promptly left the keys to the Morris on the tallboy near the door so that if Geraint needed to move her, he could.

They made good time back to Woomera and for once, the trip was completely uneventful, arriving airside at 0450. They parked the Land Rover and got straight into the aircraft, which took off on time. The flight was busy – packed with soldiers from a variety of different units together with boxes of kit – so it really was a question of finding a space to park yourself and hang on. At least the flight wasn't long, and they soon arrived at RAAF Edinburgh, where there was an orderly but fast exit from the aircraft.

Banjo and McAllister made a fast detour via the showers and changing rooms and emerged looking reasonably presentable for the day ahead. Moving out to the rear of the concourse, they were met by Terri Wilson, who – even at this time of the morning – looked immaculate in a trouser suit that shrieked expense. For some reason, the cut and quality of the cloth reminded McAllister of De Klerk's arrival at the Bank, and he frowned.

"Something wrong?" Terri asked him, holding her ear piece in place – it was being a bother this morning for some reason, and that was intensely irritating, bearing in mind today was going to be a *long* day.

"Not at all. Just thinking about De Klerk. That's all," McAllister replied.

"Right, the main – and final - briefing starts in 10 minutes and I want you to be there. Whilst you are not part of the security detail as such, I do want the guys on the ground to know what you look like – it might help if everything kicks off, so that they don't shoot you thinking you are two of the bad guys."

McAllister realised she was only half joking, and somewhat belatedly appreciated that this was probably the biggest security test the Australians had known – particularly here in South Australia. The preparations for a Royal Visit were never to be sneezed at, and somewhere like this would never have known such a high profile, demanding event. Everyone would be extremely tense, so the clearer the instructions could be, the better.

Suddenly, McAllister understood that he had not taken into account the impact this was having on the Aussies. He was so used to dealing with the Queen's Flight and ceremonial occasions back home. He had completely failed to recognise that, for his hosts and the South Australians in particular, this really was a huge and very demanding deal. In addition, the spotlight of the world was on them and they were clearly very anxious not to mess it all up.

And he really couldn't blame them for that.

"Anything we can do to help?" he asked.

Terri shook her head.

"No. I just need you two to keep your eyes and ears open, don't get into trouble and if anything should happen today – not that it will, but if it did – then help where you can, but keep out of the way if you can't. We will have a wash up after the Royal Party has gone back to Britannia, so at the moment, it looks as though the final debrief will be about 1930 tonight – final time to be confirmed in due course."

With that, she handed them both earpieces so that they could hear the progress of the day as it unfolded and gave them each a microphone so that if they needed to call in because an emergency arose, then they could. "Otherwise, you two must keep radio silence. There will be enough noise going on as it is."

McAllister and Banjo nodded; it made sense, particularly as they were really there to see what they could unearth on their own investigation and to provide backup only in the event that it was needed. Otherwise, low profile was the order of the day.

With that, they moved off to the already packed briefing room, where final orders were given by a very charismatic, imposing character dressed in black with no insignia. He did not give his name but immediately commanded attention simply by standing at the front of the room, which swiftly fell silent as if a switch had been flicked.

McAllister saw Red Leader from Waikerie in the audience, who saw him, and they nodded in recognition, but otherwise, the man in black commanded everyone's attention. Jim Brock was not there, which McAllister supposed was not surprising in itself, but somehow, that worried him, and privately, he wished that this day was over already. His mother's words to him as a boy came back to him, unbidden, at that moment and unbeknownst to him, eerily echoed those held onto by Zoe Schuster when she had been in the depths of despair during her incarceration:

Be careful what you wish for, Mikey; you might be sorry when it arrives.

Chapter 65

The meeting dispersed, and as is always the way with such events, it was as if the gathered crowd created a simultaneous bomb burst of people – each intent on going to their designated vehicle or room or destination as quickly as possible to start getting ready and preparing for their part in this huge performance. The noise level rose from near zero to deafening in a matter of seconds, as if the cork had popped out of a champagne bottle.

McAllister and Banjo found Englebert, got in, and left the base as soon as possible. They figured that if they were out of everyone's hair, then happy days.

And they wanted to sort out what they were going to do when they got to the Barossa. The Royal Party was not due to arrive at the Gala location until 1200 – which gave them a maximum of a couple of hours of relative freedom before they needed to be on the plot. How could they put that time to best use?

"Are we agreed then," said McAllister. "That we will go to Jindivik and have a look around. Hopefully they will already have left for the Gala site, so we will probably have a clear run."

"Yeah. I think that's probably the best. I'd certainly like to see what is in some of those outbuildings and any office space they have. After Waikerie, they certainly don't seem to have any hesitation in sticking a torture chamber where you wouldn't expect it." Banjo's face looked grim, and McAllister realised that his friend was also feeling the tension this morning. Thoughts of Lucy's eyeball flashed through his mind, and he roughly shoved them away. He could not afford to be distracted today of all days.

And so it was settled.

They reached the turning for the Jindivik Winery, and turned down the access track, through the vines towards the main cluster of buildings, just as they had done on their first visit here – and which now seemed such a long time ago. They found a pull in that was masked by the vines and an old outhouse, and got out of Englebert. They walked quietly along the remainder of the way, and decided to look at the buildings as they came to them.

The site was very quiet, which unnerved McAllister. He had expected there to be *someone* here – although the majority were probably invited in one way or another to the festivities of the Gala. This would be a big day for Jindivik, and if all went well, it could signal a massive boost to the business.

They crept along the side boundary and found the open garage cum car port, that had space for four or five vehicles. Only one was in situ – a champagne-coloured Mercedes Benz convertible. Both men looked at it in appreciation as it was a stunner.

"Pound to a penny, that's Anika De Klerk's," whispered McAllister, and Banjo nodded in agreement.

"Perhaps she is still here, making her final preparations for the Gala." Again, Banjo nodded.

The pair crept on, and having had a quick look into the silos and outhouse that had presented themselves but seen nothing out of the ordinary, found a partially glazed door at the rear of the main buildings.

McAllister gently tried the handle, and it turned. He opened the door and they quietly walked in, Banjo equally carefully closing the door behind them. They stood in a flag stoned entry hall – and it rather reminded McAllister of the main exhibition auditorium that they had seen on their original visit. The exposed brickwork stretched up and along, leading them to a choice of options: to the right appeared to be a kitchen and to the left was a living area. They quickly looked in both. No-one was there. Each room was tastefully furnished, and clearly, money was no object. The latest gadgets were on display, but there was very little in the way of personal items. No photographs or family memorabilia of any kind.

Very odd.

They approached the oak staircase at the end of the hall, and, looking up to check that no-one was obviously above them, quietly ascended the stairs. Each time there was a squeak from the timbers, McAllister expected to see the nozzle of a gun pointing down at them from above, but all was quiet. They arrived at the top of the stairs without interruption.

The landing again took them in two directions.

Banjo went left and found what looked to be a guest bedroom. Nothing seemed to be out of place, and there was nothing obviously of interest.

McAllister went right and found himself with another choice. There were two doors: one immediately in front of him and another further to his right along the top part of the hall. He decided to go for the one in front of him.

413

He opened the door and found himself looking into what was obviously a woman's bedroom. It was full of chintzy, patterned stuff in soft pinks and golds. There was a large dressing table in the window to the front on his left, and as he looked past the jumble of hair brushes, makeup, and fragrances that seemed to litter the surface, he looked in the mirror and stared into the wide-open and dead eyes of Anika De Klerk.

He walked further into the bedroom and looked to his right, where he saw a very large, round bed. Anika was only partly clothed and lying on her back on the bed, almost like a discarded rag doll. She was covered in blood from wounds that appeared to have been caused by a large knife or blade of some kind. There were nasty black welts around her neck, and she had clearly been beaten badly before being put out of her misery.

McAllister felt his anger rise.

Whoever did this is a real sicko. And I bet I know just who it was. You will join the list, Anika: you will join little Lucy, Zoe, and the others, and I will avenge you.

He heard a noise behind him and swung round to find an ashen-faced Banjo standing in the doorway looking at the dreadful scene in front of them.

"Don't touch anything. Did you happen to bring the little camera along?" Banjo nodded. "Then try and get a few snaps. Then we'll check through that door next to the wardrobe, and then we will check the final room on this floor. OK?" he whispered to Banjo, who nodded.

McAllister moved past the bed and went to the door he had

414

identified. He opened it cautiously and found a full bathroom – that had another door opposite this one.

I think those are being called Jack and Jill bathrooms. What will they think of next?

He beckoned to Banjo, and they moved through the bathroom, where nothing was out of place, and through the other door into a separate bedroom.

The contrast with the appalling scenes they had just left was staggering. This room was dark and sparse. Apart from the bed and a chest of drawers, there was nothing else here. The bedspread was in place, nothing had been disturbed and it was almost as if the room had been swept clean before its occupier had left for the last time. McAllister moved over towards the suite of wardrobes that covered the long wall by the door that he guessed led back to the landing, and they were completely empty.

"So it looks as if Chummy is about to do a bunk if he hasn't already," whispered McAllister. Banjo took a couple of pictures for good measure.

Together, they left the room and moved through the door back, as McAllister had correctly guessed, to the main landing. They moved quietly back down the oak staircase, through the hall, and out the same glazed door that they had entered by.

Once outside, they had a decision to make: there was nothing they could do for Anika now, so they might as well make the most of this opportunity. Silently, they moved towards the front of the main building to try and find some office space. There had to be some here somewhere.

415

They walked in through the main doors – which somewhat bizarrely to McAllister's mind had been left wide open - passed the exhibits that they had seen on their tour, and then out through one of the exits that had a twisted rope barrier with a sign across the front saying, "Winery personnel only beyond this point."

They hopped over the barrier and opened the door behind them. Sure enough, it led onto a corridor where, again, there were three doors. McAllister took the one on the left; Banjo the one on the right.

McAllister's was a non-start – it was a broom/storage cupboard of some kind and of no interest.

Banjo found his room was the secretarial hub. It contained a few desks, typewriters, telephones, paper, and cupboards, where presumably the orders were filed. Nothing doing here then, either.

Closing the doors, they moved together down the hall towards the final door. They listened at the door before opening it, but there was no noise. They turned the handle quietly and moved into the gloom of the room.

It was very sterile, with a glass desk in the centre which had a large black leather chair immediately behind it. There were only two decorative items of any kind in the room. One was a statue of a nubile, naked woman that was on the desk. The other was a large painting on the wall behind the desk, which McAllister guessed must measure about eight feet tall and four feet wide – it really was enormous and, in contrast to the rest of the room, was an abstract piece of slashing wild colours. It meant nothing to McAllister, but it seemed oddly out of place amongst such austerity. Otherwise, there were two other chairs in front of the desk and a filing cabinet. That was it.

"This has to be De Klerk's office," whispered McAllister. "Let's try the filing cabinet." It was not locked.

So this isn't it, then. Too easy.

He turned back to look at the painting.

I wonder.

He moved back towards it and started looking at the edges, but nothing seemed out of place.

Until he found the small button high up on the right-hand side.

He pushed it and heard a mechanism click into place. The painting moved about four inches off of the wall toward him, forcing McAllister to take an inadvertent step back. Gingerly, he pushed the frame to see if it moved and was rewarded as the piece slid easily and silently to the left, revealing a hidden door behind.

Bingo.

"It needs a key, and there is nothing obviously here," whispered Banjo in his ear.

McAllister reached into his pocket and pulled out a small, black cloth fold, and from which he extracted two skeleton keys. He looked at Banjo, who raised his eyebrow as if to say, "Really? Another of your talents?" and proceeded to jiggle the keys into the lock. After a very short time, there was a satisfying click as the lock shifted. Putting the skeletons back in their cloth, and away into his pocket,

McAllister then gripped the handle and again turned. The door swung open inwards, and the room was in darkness.

Banjo felt around for a light switch. The light came on and they were staring into a large room which, in some ways, reminded McAllister of what they had found in Waikerie. All of the walls were covered with large posters with names, arrows, and dates. There were some photographs there as well.

What the??????

They stood almost open-mouthed as they looked at the extent of the information on the walls, but their main attention was drawn to the main edifice that had been constructed almost like a shrine. In the centre was a huge colour photograph of HM The Queen and HRH Prince Philip. Next to it was a large silver wine bucket displaying the Nazi swastika engraved on the front, containing two upended and empty bottles of Cham-Pine. The whole display was draped with two large Nazi swastikas.

For once, both McAllister and Banjo were completely speechless.

"Have you got any film left in the camera?" McAllister asked Banjo.

"Yep. On it," and with that, Banjo started clicking away at the scenes in front of them.

Suddenly, the whole picture crashed together in his mind.

We need to get to Nuriootpa and fast.

With that, they turned to leave the room. Two large men had silently arrived in the doorway and were blocking their exit.

They were standing shoulder to shoulder, with arms crossed and grim grins on their faces as if they had been waiting for this moment.

McAllister sized them up and realised that this was probably going to be a tough fight. The usual "eyeballing" took place as each of them considered what the play was going to be and how this was going to start, but McAllister had already decided. He stepped forward and took on the slightly larger guy right in front of him. He was a firm believer in getting the first punch in if at all possible, and it was a corker. His opponent staggered under the force of the blow, then recovered, and from there on, it was each man for himself. Banjo and the other man got stuck in as well, and soon, there were flailing fists and bodies all over the room.

McAllister fell through the door on top of his protagonist, and together, they fell straight onto the glass-topped desk, which shattered under the force of the impact. Neither man was a lightweight, and together, the desk stood no chance whatever.

Banjo picked up a shard of the glass and managed to shove it in his opponent's leg, as near to the femoral artery as he could. The man let out a great howl as the blood started pouring, and Banjo wriggled free from his grip and gave him a great crashing blow to the jaw. The man slumped down in a growing pool of blood.

McAllister was still writhing around on the floor in the main office with his man, and neither was giving up. The man had McAllister in a strong headlock and was trying to crush his windpipe. McAllister groped for anything to hand and picked up a piece of the desk glass. Before he could try and strike his attacker behind him, Banjo had moved over, picked up the naked woman statuette that had been on De Klerk's desk but which had fallen to the floor after the crash, and he smashed it down on the attacker's head. That loosened the grip sufficiently to enable McAllister to swing around and get his thumb in one of the man's eyes, pushing as hard as he could whilst jabbing the shard of glass into the guy's exposed neck. The man collapsed in a heap, his face, neck and head a complete mess. There was blood and goop everywhere.

McAllister stood up, his tie and shirt smeared with blood and a cut above one of his eyes. He was going to have a real shiner there, that was for sure. Banjo also looked the worse for wear. Both were breathing heavily.

"We need to get going; we don't have time to waste on these idiots," shouted McAllister, the adrenalin pumping. They raced for the main door back out into the hallway, McAllister quickly glancing back to look at the wreckage of what had been a sterile room before. They found their way out to the main access concourse and ran back through the vines to where they had left Englebert. McAllister jumped into the driver's seat and got the engine turning even before Banjo had managed to get himself into the passenger seat. They turned the car around and left the appalling scenes behind them.

As they reached the main road, they turned left and headed towards Nuriootpa. They could not call this in over the open channels but needed to find Terri Wilson as soon as possible. McAllister floored the Freeway, which responded magnificently as if the car itself was aware of the danger that they now faced. They sat tightlipped as the magnitude of what they had found started to sink in.

Of course, Banjo was not aware that McAllister was carrying an additional worry – which was that he did not know who he could trust.

Jim Brock kept coming back to him.

"*Watch my back for me.*"

A shiver ran down McAllister's spine. He looked at the clock on the dashboard.

1225.

Christ. We are going to be too late.

Chapter 66

In Nuriootpa, the red carpet was well and truly out, and the Town Mayor, together with the President of the South Australian Wine Industry Association, were both standing on it – in full bib and tucker – awaiting the arrival of their special guests. Nuriootpa itself had also hung out the flags – literally – for such a special day, and the main road through the town was bedecked with Union Jacks interspersed with Australian flags, pictures of HM The Queen and HRH The Duke of Edinburgh and people were lining the street four or five deep in places, some of them dressed in red, white and blue.

All of the children from the local School were gathered together in a group being shooed and chaperoned by their smartly turned out teachers, with the children all neatly dressed in full school uniform, and each waving a small flag whilst excitedly chattering and waiting for the event to start.

It really was a big deal for the town and for the Barossa generally, and all of the locals were thrilled that the Royal Party had chosen to have a special engagement here.

Terri Wilson was impatiently pacing across the carpet inside the main reception area. She was extremely irritated that she had lost track of McAllister and Banjo. Neither of them was anywhere to be seen after the briefing this morning, and she had not been able to contact them over the radio. The Royal Party was due at any time, and she was growing extremely anxious that her two loose cannons were still going to be running wild after The Queen's arrival.

And goodness only knows what trouble they would cause if they got half a chance as if I don't have enough to contend with.

Just at that moment, she received a radio message to say that the surrounding roads had now been cordoned off as the Royal entourage was about to enter the main street into the Town. Sure enough, as Terri Wilson looked up from her observation post, she could see an immaculate black Rolls Royce flanked by Police motorcycle outriders and a black Land Rover with special protection detail officers making its way slowly and majestically up the main road in Nuriootpa. The crowds started cheering, the local Brass Band struck up, and flags were waved even more enthusiastically than before.

They're here. Can't worry about anything else now. Fingers crossed, this doesn't go completely wrong.

The Royal Party were greeted by the beaming local dignitaries, and, after the usual introductions and pleasantries, were ushered into the main room that was holding the Gala. The room itself had been bedecked with streamers and balloons, and a large silver banner proclaiming: "Congratulations on your Silver Jubilee Ma'am" had been erected behind the top table that was awash with flower displays.

Across the main floor of the room were a number of circular tables, each set with 12 places, to enable as many people as possible to enjoy the event. Invitations had been greatly sought after, and the organisers had faced real problems in keeping local rivalries at bay. Terri guessed that there must be over 250 guests in all, in addition to the Royal Party. For such a small town as Nuriootpa, that was quite a turnout, even if a proportion of them were not local in the true sense of the word.

No wonder they had turned the local cricket ground into an impromptu car park.

A short welcome speech was given by The President of the South Australian Wine Industry Association, and with that, the lunch started.

The food, which was all locally produced, was well received and was served to the guests by white-suited waiters who seemed to effortlessly hover around the room with simple efficiency. Terri Wilson spotted Jan De Klerk among the guests and noted that Anika was not with him. In fact, he appeared to be unaccompanied.

Now, that is strange. From the description given by McAllister, I would have thought this sort of event would have been right up her street.

Everyone appeared to be having a great time, and the wine was flowing. As a result, the noise was increasing exponentially. The time approached for Her Majesty to give her formal address, and having been introduced by The President, she rose and started speaking.

Where the hell were McAllister and Banjo?

Chapter 67

McAllister's patience was starting to wear extremely thin. Having raced from the Winery down towards the town, trying to keep their rising anxiety in check, they had met the outer cordon roadblock at the back road turning into Nuriootpa before reaching the main street, which was manned by what he could only call a "Jobs Worth" of a police officer.

McAllister and Banjo had shown their military ID and desperately tried to explain the urgency of the situation, but the officer wasn't budging. Under no circumstances *whatsoever* was anyone to be allowed through the cordon, "It's more than my job's worth."

Those were his orders and he was sticking to them. He was rude and arrogant into the bargain, and he was not going to be pushed around by any Pommie. It was bad enough that he was here looking after the Royal Party anyway, Jubilee or no Jubilee, and he knew that his Sergeant had put him out here as a punishment for his outspoken anti-Royalist views. Presumably so that he couldn't cause any trouble.

Well, this was pay back.

Whilst McAllister had tried to reason with the Police officer, Banjo was desperately trying to raise Terri Wilson on the radio. All he got was crackling and noise and he could only suppose that the equipment had been damaged during the fight in De Klerk's office.

McAllister finally lost his temper.

"Is that your last word officer: that you are not letting us through under any circumstances even though we have told you this is a matter of national security and an emergency to boot? And you won't even call it in and see if your orders are changed in the circumstances?"

"Yup. You finally got it, mister. Quite simple ain't it? You ain't goin' down there.."

The officer stood squarely in front of McAllister with his hands on his hips and a defiant look in his eye.

He never saw the blow coming; it was so fast. McAllister thumped out a huge right hook that toppled the officer from his stance, and who clumsily fell across the bonnet of his Police car and slithered dismally to the ground. He lay there groggily.

Banjo moved the wooden road blocks, whilst McAllister jumped back in the driving seat, started rolling and Banjo then jumped into the passenger seat as they drove past the still collapsed officer.

They raced through the outskirts of Nuriootpa, and met the further roadblock at the end of the high street. Realising there was no time for further arguments, they got out of the car and started running up the road towards the Gala event. There were shouts behind them as officers started to raise the alarm, and then the cheers of the crowd died away and were replaced with the rising noise of collective concern.

Some of the children started whimpering, others started crying, and adults were moving them away from the roadside. People started moving quickly away, and before long, there was a rapid exodus from the throngs that had been waiting patiently to see if there would be a Royal walkabout at the end of the Gala.

As McAllister and Banjo ran past some of the anxious children, now with other Police officers giving chase, some started wailing loudly with fear. It was contagious and a wave of panic started to grip the crowd. People started jostling whilst others watched on in horrified fascination.

Of course, McAllister and Banjo had completely forgotten that they were both heavily blood-stained and had multiple injuries to their faces. Their clothes were ripped in places and dirty from where they had been struggling with their attackers. The sight that they made was enough to frighten anyone. Without pause, they raced up the red carpet and through the main doors.

A startled Terri Wilson looked around, horrified at the sight that met her. McAllister and Banjo did not break their run but continued straight through the entrance hall and through the double doors into the main luncheon room. Her Majesty was just finishing speaking; people had risen to their feet, all holding glasses of Cham-Pine for the formal toast.

"No, don't drink it: it's poisoned," McAllister screamed out as he raced through the startled guests. He ran directly towards the Royal Party, and before her Personal Protection Officer could reach her, the Queen had frozen with the champagne glass half way to her lips. Looking at the state of the man in front of her and his obvious anxiety, she calmly placed the glass – untouched – back onto the table. The Duke of Edinburgh did likewise.

"No one drinks the Cham-Pine. It's poisoned," he shouted. "Lock the doors – no one is to leave. Jindivik Winery has

427

poisoned the champagne to try and murder The Queen and His Royal Highness."

He turned back to the table and Her Majesty was sitting quietly, watching him intently. The Personal Protection detail quickly manouevred her and The Duke of Edinburgh away from the table, and his colleague, with gun drawn, shouted at McAllister and Banjo to get to the floor and not move.

"For Christ's sake – lock the doors. Don't let anyone go. And certainly don't let Jan De Klerk from the Jindivik Winery go – he has just murdered his wife, and he is the mastermind behind this assassination attempt. He's also a Nazi – we have found a whole cache of Nazi materials at his place."

HRH, the Duke of Edinburgh, had also been standing calmly next to The Queen, watching the events unfold.

"Nazi, you say? Well, we can't have that," he said.

The rest of his comment was lost as McAllister and Banjo disappeared under a great pile of sturdy Police and protection officers who were throwing themselves at the bloodstained pair. Blows rained down on them both until McAllister heard through the distance a female voice calling for calm. He saw Terri Wilson's face through the pile of people on top of him. She was very pale, but she was shouting at him, "Are you sure, McAllister?"

"Yes – totally."

And with that, things went black as McAllister finally lost consciousness.

Pandemonium erupted in the hall. The Secret Service tried

428

to close and lock the doors, but some of the guests had already left – including Jan De Klerk – and others were suddenly extremely agitated about the turn of events.

As soon as he had seen McAllister and Banjo, and the state that they were both in, De Klerk knew that it was time to go. He had quietly excused himself from the table and had left by the side entrance. No one had seen him depart, as all eyes were on the spectacle taking place at the front of the hall. He climbed into his car and left the town by a backroad. There had been a checkpoint there, but clearly someone had got to it before him, as the Police Officer manning it was sitting against the front wheel of his Police car rubbing his head. De Klerk paid him no heed and drove past, out onto the main road and headed for the airstrip at Rowland Flat, just outside of Tanunda. His pilot was already on standby, so all he had to do was outrun the Police. And at the moment, they were too busy with other things.

He raced along the country roads, arriving at the air strip only 15 minutes after leaving the Gala. He calmly got out of the Mercedes, took the black leather bag and the suit carry from the back seat, locked the car and walked over to the waiting aircraft. It was already warmed up, and as soon as De Klerk was up the steps, they were folded away automatically as if by an unseen hand, the door secured from the cockpit and they started taxiing out on to the actual strip.

Very quickly, they were airborne, and De Klerk, looking out of the window down at the sprawling Barossa below him, finally had a chance to reflect that they had come so close to achieving their aims.

He glanced down at the shelf next to his personal chair and

saw that a bottle of his favourite malt whisky was in its usual place, with the small, purpose-made ice bucket next to it, both secured for flight but readily accessible without the need to call anyone to serve him. He took one of the crystal tumblers from the bespoke storage space next to it and helped himself to a generous splash of the drink. With a satisfying "plink," he added two ice cubes.

He settled back in his chair and took a good draw from the tumbler, feeling the warmth of the liquor start to work it's way around his body. Normally, he would only sip, but today, he needed a good strong hit.

He closed his eyes, letting his mind roam.

Well, I have finally got rid of Anika so that is definitely a positive. It is just a shame that after all of the years of planning, today was not the success that we had hoped.

He patted the leather case next to him.

Still, it's not over yet.

Luckily we have our final contingency still to play.

He smiled to himself and drifted off to sleep.

He was not aware of the danger until, still groggy from tiredness and the whiskey, he felt rather than saw an image lean over him. As his vision started to clear, he realised this was not an image but, in fact, it was a man dressed in black. Somehow he was vaguely familiar. A soft American drawl broke through his fuzziness.

"Well, it's all over now, buddy boy. Your friends can't save you. Count yourself lucky that you will be given a quick end – unlike those poor souls that you tortured and murdered.

But with any luck, the sharks might get to take some chunks out of you before you actually die. Adios, you sick bastard."

Belatedly, De Klerk realised that this man in black was, in fact, the FBI Agent that they had been keeping tabs on for so long. He struggled but realised that he had been tied down to his chair and he could not move his arms or legs.

His captor smiled, seeing his growing frustration and fear, but turned away, moving to the cabin door. Before opening it, Jim Brock turned back to De Klerk, holding up the leather case that was no longer on the seat next to him. Still smiling, the man waved one final goodbye; he swung the release hatch and then jumped through the open doorway.

De Klerk felt the cabin pressure change and the noise increase immediately. Items from inside the cabin started flying towards the gaping hole in the fuselage. He looked on in horror as anything that was not completely lashed down was sucked out of the aircraft. Suddenly, he was tipped forward as the plane started into a nose dive. He looked out of the window and saw the sprawl of what appeared to be the Great Australian Bight beneath him.

No wonder Brock had mentioned sharks: the sea here was infested.

An unusual emotion gripped him and he realised it was fear. He could not free himself from his tethers, and he finally understood that the aircraft had been rigged to crash. There was no point in struggling. He was going to die, and there was absolutely nothing he could do about it. With that realisation, he tried to relax and sent his final thoughts to his father, his Fuhrer, and Gifblaar in that order.

Jim Brock stood in his wet suit by the rail of a private fishing boat that he had rented several days previously from the port of Ceduna, looking skyward through his binoculars. He had discarded his parachute before getting out of the water, and which was presumably now languishing somewhere towards the sea bed. His previous life had come in useful on so many occasions since moving to the FBI.

Once a US Navy Seal, always a US Navy Seal.

He grinned to himself.

He watched dispassionately as a light aircraft appeared to be heading seaward but in a distinctly downward trajectory. The explosion, when it came, was very loud and very bright. Large chunks of debris started raining down on the sea. He did not take the binoculars away until he was satisfied that there was nothing of any note left of the aircraft or it's occupant.

And what the blast didn't get, the sharks sure as hell will.

He grinned to himself again, walked to the small wheelhouse and cracking open a beer from the waiting ice filled esky, turned the nose of the little boat towards the barren and sparsely populated stretch of South Australian coast line.

The US intelligence community at Pine Gap had been tracking De Klerk's flight since it had taken off from the Rowland Flat airstrip. As soon as it disappeared from the radar, the consul operator picked up the red telephone on his desk and placed a call.

Chapter 68

"Good evening and welcome to the News on 9 at 9.

Police authorities are tonight reporting that there has been a light aircraft crash approximately 60 miles south west from Ceduna, off the coast of a remote part of South Australia, with two casualties – the pilot and one passenger. South Australian Police are currently attempting to recover some of the wreckage of the aircraft to establish the cause of the crash.

Although not yet confirmed, reports suggest that the passenger was Jan De Klerk of the Jindivik Winery in the Barossa Valley, and who had only earlier this afternoon been present at the Royal Gala celebrating the South Australian Wine Industry as part of The Queen's Silver Jubilee visit to the State.

In a tragic twist, it has also been reported that his wife, Anika De Klerk, was found dead earlier this afternoon at the couple's luxury home in Nuriootpa. The cause of death has not yet been released. The couple had no children.

And in other news tonight…….."

She quietly got up from the settee and, swallowing the last of her drink, turned the television set off. She knew she had to leave as quickly as possible. That was no accident. She had known Jan since they were children, and something had obviously gone very wrong not only with the plan itself but also with Jan's get away. It should have been the ultimate strike at the British Empire – the death of The Queen at the moment of her great Jubilee celebration – that was the

433

headline news.

She lit a cigarette and paced across the lounge.

Finally making a decision, she moved to the bedroom and packed her small travelling valise. Collecting her last few remaining personal items, which she threw into her handbag together with her passport, she picked up her cashmere coat, the valise, and her car keys. Closing the door behind her, she wondered if it was the last time she would ever come to this most private – but favourite - of hideaways. She climbed into her car, gunned the engine, and waited for the electronic gates to slide apart for her exit. The gates didn't move. She sighed in frustration and leaned over to the passenger seat to rummage in the glove box for the remote control. She found it nestled at the back, under various bits and pieces that had somehow found their way there. Sitting back upright in her seat, she pressed the button.

After a very slight delay, the gates opened and she drove through. She had already decided to drive to Melbourne for the international flight. Quite a long drive, but she had time and could stop on the way. She turned the radio on and settled in for the drive.

She got as far as Murray Bridge before she realised something was wrong – very wrong. She felt sick and dizzy. She found a lay by off the main road and pulled in.

I need some fresh air. A bit of a break. My arms feel so heavy.

She was in the final throes of life before she even turned the engine off. The occupant of a black sedan that had been following her all the way from Stirling at a safe and very discreet distance watched as her driving became increasingly erratic and until she finally pulled over.

When the car had come to a halt, the sedan quietly pulled in behind, and it's occupant got out. He walked to the driver's window and observed the by-now completely unconscious woman. She had lasted longer than expected, and he was not quite sure how she had negotiated the bends of the Adelaide Hills, bearing in mind the quantity of the poison she had already ingested. He had considered a car bomb to be activated when she pressed the electronic gate's operation control. But a bomb here in Adelaide? All the fuss that followed the Rundle Mall car bomb last year – the one that had nearly killed McAllister - made that a non-option.

So poison it had been.

And to his mind, there was a certain lethal simplicity in that. His only regret was that he had not been able to administer Abrin to her.

That really would have been some kick-ass payback.

Her pale skin, dark hair spread against the cream-coloured leather interior of the car, and that streak of red lipstick that made her mouth seem as though it had been slashed into her face made his skin crawl.

He opened the driver's door and took a photograph of her before pressing a small tube of pills into her hand. For good measure, he scattered some more of the pills in the front seats of the car and left a bottle of half-drunk vodka on the passenger side seat, having made sure to liberally douse the driver. To all intents and purposes, when the Police found her, they would inevitably jump to the conclusion that she had been a drunk driver who had taken barbiturates and had killed herself: whether by accident or design was irrelevant. He would make sure that any autopsy was cursory at best. He checked her pulse with his gloved hand, and it was very weak – failing.

In fact, failing rapidly. He waited a few seconds more, and it finally fluttered out completely. Satisfied that she was indeed dead, he turned the engine off so as not to attract attention to the vehicle, quietly closed the car door, and left her where she was, probably to be found in the morning by some passing Police patrol. Not a nice start to the day for them, but that's the break.

Two down, one to go.

Chapter 69

A special security briefing had been called for 0600 the following morning. In spite of the events in Nuriootpa, it appeared that the decision had been made "at the highest levels" for the Rundle Mall Royal walkabout to still go ahead as planned the following day, and therefore the security briefing had to be early doors. News of the events in Nuriootpa was going to be completely hushed up, as no-one had any wish to publicise the close call.

McAllister and Banjo had been told to go to a Security Services safe house in Adelaide for the night, where they were given medical attention to clean up the numerous cuts they had endured over the course of the day. They shared a light supper and a few beers before gratefully dropping into bed.

McAllister lay quietly in his bunk, thinking over the events of the day. Things had got a bit hairy there for a while, and it was only because Terri Wilson had intervened when she had that had prevented them from suffering a far worse fate.

But the worrying thing from McAllister's point of view was the abject confusion that seemed to reign in all quarters. No-one seemed to really understand what was going on, who was really at the centre of the plot, or what the contingency plan actually was in the event of any terrorist attack. That worried him enormously. No plan is fool proof – it is only a plan until it goes wrong, as the saying goes – but there just seemed to be a total lack of direction or understanding of who needed to do what.

What had Head Shed been thinking when he approved the fall back plans?

Needless to say, the glasses that the Royal party had been using, together with all of the bottles of Cham-Pine, had been collected and sent for immediate forensic analysis. Hopefully the results will be available at the briefing in the morning.

And, of course, in the middle of the confusion Fuck-face De Klerk had managed to give everyone the slip.

He was particularly annoyed about that.

Unable to sleep, he turned on his transistor radio in the hope that some music would help and was just in time for the midnight news. He sat bolt upright as he heard the headlines reporting on the loss of a private air craft over the remote coast of South Australia, and that Jan De Klerk of the Jindivik Winery had been officially pronounced missing presumed dead, and that his wife had also been found dead at the couple's home in Nuriootpa.

McAllister went racing into Banjo's room and pulled him awake, telling him of the turn of events. Banjo clambered out of his bunk, and they went into the kitchen where they found a bottle of whisky and drank a toast to whoever or whatever had intervened and finally ensured that Jan De Klerk had got his just deserts and met his maker.

When McAllister finally returned to his bed, sleep came quickly this time.

I'm sorry it wasn't me who pulled the trigger, but hopefully, this is some retribution for Lucy, Zoe, Dr Schuster, and even Lurch.

It was only later in the night that his dreams turned into a nightmare, where he was being chased by a large dragon with red, fiery eyes.

So it's not quite over yet.

The following morning, Banjo and McAllister made their way to the office in King William Street and were busy downing their second coffees of the day when Terri Wilson arrived. As always, she looked trim, tailored, and in total control despite the demands the day before must have made on her. She nodded to both men before making her way to her office, where she collected some papers and, beckoning them to follow her, walked quickly down the corridor to the special security briefing room.

When they arrived, it seemed to McAllister that there was a packed house. Several of the other participants nodded to them, and they took their seats quietly, not far from Terri but not right in the front row. They found themselves in aisle seats next to Red Leader from Waikerie, and they nodded to each other.

McAllister was keen that they kept as low a profile as possible. The official de-briefing of their actions yesterday had not yet taken place, and he would bet almost a pound to a penny that there would be some criticism coming in his and Banjo's direction. The more time and distance he could put between that debrief and yesterday, the better.

A few people arrived just as the main doors were closed and locked, and from another door at the other end of the auditorium, Head Shed walked in and immediately took his place at the top of the central table.

Noisily clearing his throat, Head Shed opened proceedings.

"Good morning everyone. Thank you for attending. As you know, despite the events in the Barossa Valley yesterday, the Royal Party will still be undertaking the planned Walkabout in Rundle Mall later this morning. This meeting will, therefore, be brief, as most of you need to get to your allocated security posts. A more in-depth meeting will be held, probably tomorrow, to deal with a complete overview.."

At this point, he paused and nodded at Norman Reynolds who took the invitation and stood up so that the packed auditorium could see and hear him. He succinctly outlined the events of the previous day, including that the light aircraft that had been carrying Jan De Klerk had crashed. A land and sea search was currently underway for any survivors, but hopes were fading fast.

"As most of you know, the Bight is not the place to crash land."

Muted grins met this attempt at levity.

And so the meeting went on.

McAllister was at a bit of a loss as to the point of this, especially as some of the folks present were starting to get obviously anxious as the time started ticking away.

As if reading his mind, Head Shed interjected.

"I know you will all be anxious to leave so that we can successfully complete the South Australian leg of the Royal tour. I am keen for us to put yesterday's events behind us, and as I am sure you already realise, those events are not for public discussion. We will reconvene tomorrow – a separate note of the time and location of that briefing will come out later today."

With that, he stood up and turned to leave the room without further ado.

Before he could move, however, a figure at the back of the hall stood up and a familiar Texan drawl rang out.

"Not so fast."

As one, the entire group turned to look at who was conducting this turn of events.

Brock.

Oh God, what now?

McAllister could see that his friend was in no mood for pleasantries and immediately turned to look back at Head Shed, who was frozen at the front of the room, his thin face totally devoid of any expression, as his dark eyes stared fixedly on Jim Brock.

Brock's gaze never wavered, and his whole concentration was on the man in front of him as he carefully negotiated the steps down from the back of the auditorium towards the front. He passed McAllister and Banjo sitting at the end of their row, and walked calmly and steadily towards the front of the room.

"What the hell is the matter with you, man?" Head Shed asked tersely.

"Nothing's the matter with me," came the calm, steady reply. "I'm not the traitor. And there's only one of those left – isn't there: Gifblaar? That is what you like to be called, isn't it,

Pieter De Vries?"

There was a collective, horrified gasp from the now-silent audience watching these extraordinary events unfold.

Terri Wilson was completely ashen; Norman Reynolds was looking from Head Shed to Brock and back again with rapid movements and a look of total disbelief on his face.

Of course. The reason why none of the investigations ever seemed to get anywhere quickly; why all of the enquiries of the South African authorities seemed to take forever to reach a conclusion – if then; how it had been possible for a plan as audacious as that put into play by Jan De Klerk had come so close to fruition.

The Head of the Australian Security and Intelligence Services.

A man who would have seen all of the intelligence and information coming in and going out, and who would have been in a position of power to deflect/divert or distract as necessary and with advance warning of any threats – or opportunities, such as the Royal visit – to enable the greatest possible planning and preparation.

A clever disguise, years in the making, as he had worked his way up through the ranks of the Intelligence Service to reach his current position of power.

With a sickening sense of realisation, McAllister slowly looked at Head Shed and finally knew the truth. This was the man they had been hunting for so long, and who was responsible for so many deaths of so many good people.

Hiding in plain sight.

Out of his peripheral vision, McAllister was aware of someone two rows behind him standing up. He turned and saw the nozzle of the gun pointed at Jim Brock's back.

"Watch my back for me, buddy."

Without thinking, McAllister launched himself upward and back towards the man, forcing his arm upwards.

A single shot rang out.

Jim Brock staggered and stopped walking.

As several in the audience realised what was happening, a number of them piled on the now-fighting McAllister and the assailant. Terri Wilson and the Commissioner of Police for the State both moved at the same time, and, before Head Shed could get away, had launched themselves at him in magnificent rugby tackle style and had brought him down. It was a total free for all both on the stairs, and on the floor of the auditorium.

Banjo leaped towards Jim Brock and started calling for medical assistance, trying at the same time to find out how badly injured the American actually was. Red Leader made his way rapidly down the stairs and stood in the middle of the room and gradually re-gained control, shouting above the din.

The doors burst open, and armed officers entered the auditorium to be met with a complete melee.

Those not directly involved in this latest turn of events were immediately posted by Red Leader as per their rostered duties; the Royal Visit had to reach its conclusion without further problems. Security would have to be tight, and he briskly gave the orders to ensure the best possible coverage.

As they all trooped out to take up their appropriate posts, Terri and The Commissioner were still sitting/holding/grappling with Head Shed; Banjo was still trying to care for Brock, and McAllister was under a pile of hefty fellow officers for the second time in 36 hours, unable to release his grip on the assailant's arm but the gun having been lost in the struggle.

The fighting groups gradually unpicked themselves, and Terri Wilson herself placed handcuffs – helpfully provided by one of the security guards in the King William Street office – on Head Shed.

Well – this is going to be a career-defining moment either way.

If he is innocent, then I will be looking for another job tonight.

If he really IS Gifblaar.....she shuddered at the thought.

Chapter 70

It was a long day and night for everyone.

The good news was that the remainder of the Royal visit went off without a hitch, and looking at the news broadcasts later that evening, it was clear that the Walkabout had been a particularly successful part of the tour. The crowds had come out in their thousands, lining both sides of Rundle Mall with much cheering and flag waving. The Royal party left South Australia from RAAF Edinburgh on schedule for their next port of call, Papua New Guinea, and everyone involved in the visit on the official side of things heaved a huge sigh of relief that, somehow, what could have been the greatest Constitutional crisis to face Australia had been averted.

The problem was what to do next.

Head Shed had been removed from Adelaide under the tightest of security. He had been hooded, chained and sedated. He did not know exactly where he was, but of course, he knew where it was likely to be. He was pretty certain that he had been taken to a black site: one that officially does not exist and where the usual "rules" do not apply. If he was right in that, then he guessed he was in the desolate Northwestern area of Australia. If that was a correct guess, then he knew the layout, and he knew what the security arrangements were.

Down in his secure cell, Head Shed sat alone, chained to a chair, which in turn was bolted to the floor. He could not reach the table in front of him and there was nothing else in the room. Apart from the bottle of water, they had given him when he first arrived, and which they had used to bring him around from the sedative they had used, they had not given him anything else to eat or drink. So that was going to be part of their game plan.

He smiled inwardly.

He knew exactly how this would play out and exactly how he would handle Terri Wilson when she came to interrogate him.

And he was ready.

He smiled to himself again.

He heard the lock in the door clang as it opened from the outside.

Here she comes. This is going to be fun.

But it was not Terri Wilson who walked through the door, and the smile he had on his face vanished instantly.

This is not in the playbook.

"Not expecting us, huh?" asked Jim Brock. "Yeah, sorry to disappoint you, but I am not dead. Not even injured, thanks both to my friend here and my good old faithful bullet proof vest. But we flushed out your associate in the crowd and he *is* now dead. Just so you know. Along with your other two very special friends, by the way."

Brock looked at Head Shed with the same unwavering gaze he had in the auditorium.

Head Shed said nothing.

Pointing to McAllister, Brock went on:

"And, of course, you know McAllister. He's here because, despite his inclinations to the contrary in this particular case, as a Brit, he will ensure fair play. Ain't that right Mikey?" said the American, turning towards McAllister.

McAllister said nothing but grinned wickedly at Head Shed, who simply glowered in return.

"And just to make sure you understand your current situation - completely," Brock continued, "you may think you know where you are and be coming up with all sorts of little schemes in your head to enable you to escape and to handle your interrogation, but that ain't happenin'. You are completely outside of Australian jurisdiction, so the cavalry sure as hell ain't goin' to be ridin' over the hill to rescue you. Just so that we are clear from the beginning."

Brock watched the effect his words were having on De Vries, and despite the poker face, McAllister could tell that Brock had guessed right and that this was definitely not what the prisoner had expected.

Silence descended.

Neither McAllister nor Brock spoke, and both simply continued to look at De Vries.

Eventually, it was the prisoner who broke the silence.

"You know that I won't tell you anything, so why are you persisting in this charade?" he spat eventually.

"We don't need you to tell us anything," said McAllister.

De Vries watched him like a coiled snake.

"You see, we have picked up a lot of information along the way, and of course, De Klerk was extremely helpful in that regard."

The prisoner snorted with derision.

"Jan? He wouldn't have told you anything at all. He was used to extracting information in the most ingenious of ways: he would never give it. So you are bluffing."

McAllister and Brock looked at each other, and Brock went back to the door of the cell, knocked once and the door opened fractionally. Something was passed through the door, and Brock came back into the cell. He placed an item that was wrapped in black velvet cloth on the table in front of De Vries.

"Do you know what this is?" he asked.

"No. Should I?" responded the prisoner.

"It's both extremely informative and your death sentence," replied Brock calmly.

De Vries said nothing and continued staring at Brock.

Quietly, carefully, Brock removed the covering cloth and there on the table was De Klerk's Nazi swastika emblazoned gold casket. Despite himself, McAllister was taken aback at the size and craftsmanship of it. Looking at the prisoner's face, it was clear he had never seen the casket before.

"Oh, it's quite somethin' to look at – I'll give you that," continued Brock. "But its contents were somethin' else entirely. We have all the Bank account details – London, Switzerland, the US Virgin Islands: we've got all of that, and needless to say, those are in the process of being seized as we speak. But the really interestin' stuff were the films – particularly the one of your personal interrogation of Lucy

Andrews and your handling of Zoe Schuster. It's all there. Just like Hitler and Himmler and Goebbels, you couldn't resist filming it all, could you? Just for the record and your own sick, perverted pleasure. Well, we've got those films too and we have shown them to the British and Australian Prime Ministers, just so that there cannot be any doubt as to the level of your treachery and depravity."

Brock stopped speaking.

De Vries stayed silent but was now very pale.

McAllister felt ice touch his soul. He realised with a shock that if Brock walked out of the cell now, he would have trouble resisting the huge temptation to kill De Vries – painfully. As a loyal military man, he had always done his duty for his country, which sometimes wasn't pleasant because war is war, and war isn't pleasant. But he had never – until this moment – actually *wanted* to kill someone. Head Shed had changed all of that.

The silence that descended was heavy and oppressive.

This time, it was McAllister who spoke.

"Well, you might as well enjoy your last view of life on this earth because you have guessed correctly you are going to die. But not because I or my good friend here will put a bullet in your head. Oh no. That would be far too quick and easy. You are going to die the slow, horrible death that you committed Zoe Schuster to. You are going to die of Abrin poisoning."

De Vries laughed scornfully.

"And how are you going to do that? Force feed me?" he

449

sneered.

Brock just looked at him until the false smile faded from the prisoner's face.

McAllister realised that it was one of those moments in his life that he would never forget. He almost literally saw the penny drop on the prisoner's face as he realised that the water they had given him when he first arrived had been laced with poison. The rest of this had had been pure theatre: giving the prisoner what he expected to see and hear, but in effect, wasting time and thereby enabling the poison to get to work. It also gave them the satisfaction of letting De Vries know that they knew everything. The quantity of Abrin that had been administered had been huge, and it would not be long now before the first signs of that ingestion started to manifest themselves.

For the first time, Head Shed's mask started to falter.

"There is an antidote," he blurted out suddenly. "I can give you the details."

It was Brock's turn to laugh sardonically.

"No thanks, Gifblaar – or whatever you want to call yourself. We have already got the antidote: in that casket with the films were three vials – two contained the Abrin poison, and one contained the antidote. Our scientists are analysing it now in order to be able to produce a stockpile of it – just in case any of your mad followers have their own little supply and decide to try and administer it in order to further the Great Cause, or whatever it is you people espouse."

De Vries goggled at Brock but said nothing.

"Anything else you want to say?" asked McAllister, suddenly sick to his stomach of this man and what he had done and been prepared to do.

De Vries shook his head.

"Then we shall go and leave you to your disgusting, painful end. We won't be seeing you again. In fact, you won't be seeing anyone again as no one will be coming to help you. You will be left here alone, with no food or water, in the squalor of your own filth and vomit until you finally die, when someone will come in and take your body away. Your body will be cremated, and the ashes disposed of, so that there is no chance of any grave becoming the focus of any martyrdom pilgrimages for Neo-Nazi followers – or whatever it is you want to call them. You will simply cease to exist. So if there is anything else you want to get off your chest, then now's the time," said McAllister.

De Vries glared back and said nothing.

"No? OK then. Adios," said Brock.

As the heavy security door closed behind McAllister and Brock and they stood in the hallway breathing heavily, both relieved to be out of the cell and the presence of such evil, shouts of "Heil Hitler" could be heard from the locked room.

They turned and walked away.

Epilogue

With a beer in hand, he sat on Englebert's bonnet on Sellick's Beach, a remote but beautiful place about an hour's drive south of Adelaide, and looked at the grey, churning sea. The waves were crashing onto the beach, and rain in the wind was blowing into his face. He could taste the salt on his lips. This had become one of his favourite places since arriving here, not least because he could drive the car right onto the beach itself but also because he could walk for miles and not meet another soul – particularly on a day like today. It allowed him to clear his mind. And he had needed to do a lot of that recently.

He thought back through the long, busy days that had followed the capture and imprisonment – and death, he thought grimly – of Pieter De Vries, otherwise known as Gifblaar and as Head Shed. To the Australians, he had been Richard Mills, a man of many names as well as many faces.

So much information had been uncovered that the reach of the organisation – and of De Vries himself - had been laid bare for the first time, and it had been frightening. The US, Australian, and British authorities were busily tracing assets, seizing what they could and apprehending any of the key followers of the sect, but with the deaths of De Klerk and Cronje, and finally of De Vries himself, it seemed that the head of the snake had been well and truly cut off.

But of course, you never knew.

McAllister also knew that he had reached a huge crossroads in his own life and as with most things, opportunities were a bit like buses: they usually come in a bunch, but each with completely different destinations.

He was delighted that Terri Wilson had been appointed as the new Head Shed. She would be great and would lead a totally different sort of organisation into the brave new and very challenging world that lay ahead.

As the first woman to head up any of the Intelligence Services in the Five Eyes group, she would be a true trailblazer in every sense of the word, and she absolutely deserved it. She had offered him the chance to transfer from the RAF into the Australian Secret Intelligence Services, confirming that they would fast-track his emigration application so that he would be granted immediate Australian citizenship as well as residency, give him a pay rise, and support him in any other way that they could.

Then there was the RAAF. The Commander at RAAF Edinburgh had spoken to him and thanked him for the work he had done whilst there and how he had fitted in so well with the Australian force. He asked him to think about a transfer to the RAAF, promising to secure his existing service rights with the UK RAF but giving him better pay and accommodation, and a promotion. That definitely was not to be sneezed at, either.

And then there was Jim Brock, whom he now regarded as a good friend. He had also offered him the chance to move to the US and work with the FBI.

And finally, there was the real doozy that had come out of nowhere. The legal people had told him a couple of weeks ago that because De Vries had no Will, no children, and no siblings, the entirety of his legitimate Estate, including the mining interests in the Transvaal and Kimberley from his grandfather, the winery, and all of his businesses and assets that had been acquired through his family connections rather than his illegal activities to do with the plot, would pass to his nearest relatives under intestacy rules.

Everyone in the family tree above De Vries was long dead, but of course, there was the connection with McAllister's own family, and tracing that through his grandmother Anika meant that his uncles, Huw and Geraint, and indeed his own father, were all going to receive a share of those assets which were considerable.

So Grandma Anika had had the final laugh in the end, after all the years of being ostracised for falling in love.

Perhaps a "final laugh" wasn't how she would have viewed it, as it probably would not have made up for all the lost years with her South African family.

He had driven up to Andamooka to tell his uncles the news, and having enjoyed a fabulous meal and many beers, they had started to consider the reality of such a huge windfall.

In particular, The Jindivik Winery would be one of those assets. His Uncles had immediately suggested that he take it on to own and run his own business – lock, stock, and barrel. It would mean – as with all of the other offers – a permanent move away from the UK, and away from the military in addition. To run his own vineyard? That really was out of left field, but he loved the Barossa, and he had to admit that he was very tempted.

And then there was Banjo, who, over the months that had passed since that first day they had met at Kai Tak, had become McAllister's closest friend. Unless they were very lucky, maintaining that friendship across such a vast distance between the UK and Australia would be difficult. And, of course, the final option was to do nothing: remain with the RAF Police and carry on with his UK service.

The rain started to fall harder than before. Autumn was definitely on its way. It would soon be summer in Cornwall, and he thought back to the beginning – that hot day when he had been enjoying a lazy afternoon on the beach, listening to the radio. So much had happened since then, and he had travelled so far.

He smiled and cracked open another beer.

Time will tell, Mikey, my boy, time will tell.

The End

www.ingramcontent.com/pod-product-compliance
Lightning Source LLC
Chambersburg PA
CBHW041929260326
41914CB00009B/1229